Why I'm Not a Millionaire

Why I'm Not a Millionaire

An Autobiography

Nancy Spain

WEIDENFELD & NICOLSON

First published in Great Britain in 1956 by Hutchinson & Co
(Publishers) Ltd
This paperback edition published in 2020 by Weidenfeld & Nicolson
an imprint of The Orion Publishing Group Ltd
Carmelite House, 50 Victoria Embankment
London EC4Y 0DZ

An Hachette UK Company

1 3 5 7 9 10 8 6 4 2

ISBN (Mass Market Paperback) 978 1 4746 1845 8
ISBN (eBook) 978 1 4746 1846 5

Printed and bound in Great Britain by Clays Ltd, Elcograf S.p.A.

Typeset by Input Data Services Ltd, Somerset

MIX
Paper from
responsible sources
FSC® C104740

www.orionbooks.co.uk
www.weidenfeldandnicolson.co.uk

For
Noël Coward
With Love

COPY OF A LETTER FROM NOËL COWARD

My dear Spain,

To read somebody's autobiography in galley proof is not what I would choose as relaxation but I must say your book was worth it. I found it gay, amusing, occasionally touching and always enjoyable.

I may of course be prejudiced in this view because there are so many glowing references to me in it, as you know I am a pushover for glowing references. However, here it is, my opinion for what it is worth. I thoroughly enjoyed Why I'm Not a Millionaire *and shall enjoy it still more when I can re-read it in book form with the pages numbered. Some of your flippancy is outrageous but who am I to talk of flippancy!*

It should and will be an enormous success and I do, do congratulate you

My love, as usual
Master

Obviously you can use any part of this fascinating letter. What you can't use you might send to the British Museum, which is where I am sending your bloody galleys.

FOREWORD

It was when we were returning from a magic weekend with Cyril Lord, the textile king, that Joan Werner Laurie turned to me and said, 'Why aren't you a millionaire? Cyril is only five years older than you and he and his business are worth four millions.'

I hung my head.

What could I say? I was nearly forty. I had had the most wonderful life. I had been to New York, Jamaica, Madeira, the South of France, Corsica, and Margate. I had (at least once) been offered £47,000 by an American syndicate and had turned it down. I had written two 'best' sellers and eight detective stories. I had met and chatted with Noël Coward, Marlene Dietrich, the Duke of Windsor, Mrs. Luce, Lady Docker, Gilbert Harding, Katharine Hepburn, Humphrey Bogart, Godfrey Winn, Winifred Atwell, and half a million other people, most of whom I had liked very much. I had also met and chatted with millionaires . . .

Yet *I* was not a millionaire.

Why not?

To tell the honest truth I wrote this book to find out. For a start, the circumstances of my birth were much against me. I was born, in perfect comfort, in a maternity home called Rose Villa, just off Jesmond Road, Newcastle-on-Tyne, to two thoroughly sweet parents who were neither rich enough to be a nuisance nor poor enough to go without. More, though they didn't despise the things that money can buy (both are notable spenders) they didn't think very much *of* money, either.

They were well aware that it would be hard for their daughters to marry; and Mother particularly was always telling me that I should have to make my own life and living. But I had a supremely happy, safe childhood in a safe, warm brick attached terrace house like about nine million others. I always had enough to eat, I always had lovely toys. Apparently the money used to run short over summer holidays, but I didn't know about this and was very contented. Indeed, the only very occasional unpleasantnesses were a few skirmishing quarrels between my mother and my sister Liz. I adored them both. They both had big personalities. It was quite impossible to take sides or to know what they were quarrelling about.

Chapter One

This house was a fierce red brick job called Number Seven Tankerville Place. It was firmly attached to the neighbours on both sides. On our left was Mr. Wolf, a Jewish picture framer with two daughters called Anita and Zelna. At the bottom of the street were the Bucknells. Mr. Bucknell had rowed 'stroke' in a very fast Oxford boat in the boat race. His house was full of oars and model boats, which we found very impressive. Around the corner in Tankerville Terrace were an enormous, attractive family called the Gills. The Gills were allowed to play in Tankerville Gardens, among the rhododendron bushes, and so were we, until there was an incident – I forget what – but think it involved an air gun and shooting. 'We' were my sister Liz and me. When Liz was eighteen she fell in love with Harry, the eldest Gill, and this caused awful repercussions in the neighbourhood. But she soon got over it and learnt to play a tune on the piano called 'Ain't Misbehavin', which was considered significant by one and all.

These streets are in Jesmond, a respectable suburb of Newcastle-on-Tyne, right in the heart of the coal-burning pit country. But as there is always a terribly cold east wind blowing across from left to right there are precious few fogs on Tyneside.

George Spain, our father, bought this house after World War One, in which he served as a Colonel and was mentioned in dispatches. He is also a C.M.G. He thinks of the house chiefly as a receptacle for his books, coins, medals, and sporting prints of Northumberland. He also has a vast collection of stamps in big albums and corresponds madly with other numismatists and philatelists. He used to write very funny articles for *Punch,* very scholarly articles for the *Cornhill* about witchcraft and Roman Britain and remarkable poems and plays for broadcasting. But he seems to have got sick of it, more's the pity.

> Again is spring. The birch and pine
> Put on fresh green. The little burns
> Dance down to join the ancient Tyne.
> And all along the old Black Dyke there is a
>   stirring in the land.
> If only we could understand the dreams of old
>   Northumberland.

It is a shame that a man who could write that should write poetry no more.

He also appeared in a number of radio plays and he used to broadcast running commentaries on Newcastle United football team. He has a perfect natural radio personality. But most of the time he was land agent to Lord Northbourne, like his father before him. Lord N. is a

Liberal peer who owns housing property in Hebburn and Jarrow-on-Tyne and a shooting box with a little grouse moor round it in the valley of the River Rede where our father was born.

Quite often our father would go up to Redesdale on business and tramp across quite large pieces of Northumberland, which he did so fast that we all thought he detested the countryside. Northumberland is very beautiful, but it is also very, very cold and only people like Esther McCracken with natural red hair and strong personalities can live there and like it.

I can remember going for picnics up the North Tyne in August. I remember one heatwave at least, eating peaches pulled from a garden wall in a beautiful house called Hesleyside with a 'lime tree walk'. Once, too, on a very hot day poor Mother had an asthmatic attack and Sister Liz gallantly bicycled back to the Moorcock Inn where we were staying to fetch some remedies. Liz arrived spectacularly covered with blood, like someone bringing the good news to Aix, for she had fallen off and bitten the tyre in two. The shock of this drama cured Mother's asthma immediately. I can remember sitting afterwards in truly *pouring* heat on a river bank while Mother inhaled burning Himrod so that Lizzie shouldn't feel that her journey wasn't necessary. But, truly, heatwaves in Northumberland were few and far between.

Our father spent most of his childhood in Redesdale, which he is supposed to have enjoyed, and he used to tell how a pig went fishing with him: and how he put his arm round its neck and talked to it, calling it 'Dear pig'. Our father is a very good fisherman and a very good shot too. But we never saw him kill anything, and he was always putting the fish back. Gentle, large (he still weighs about sixteen stone), with a truly wonderful wit, he early decided that the naughty money-grubbing world was run by greed and fear. And he didn't like this, so he pretended to be deaf and disappeared into his collections. Actually, anyone who likes can carry on a conversation with him in a very low whisper about witchcraft and Roman Britain and he will hear every single word. He is a dear. He is a generous, dignified, simple darling and I love him very much.

But he is also (and this must be faced) one of the whackiest characters I have ever met. Without being destructive, he can be *naughtier* than Lord Beaverbrook and that is saying something. On the telephone, for example, in the days when it wasn't on the dial and was still one of those enchanting things rather like a daffodil with a trumpet hanging from it, he used to pounce on it and answer, praying for a wrong number. He would clasp it to his chest and his eyes would dance with joy as he called all the household to join in the baiting. On at least one occasion the dialogue went something like this:

Miserable subscriber who has failed to comply with Post Office regulations:
    '*Hullo? Hullo? Is that you, Stan?*'
Our Father with joy:

'Are you there?'

Subscriber:

'YES. I was just ringing up to see what you were wearing for the dance.'

Our Father, shortly:

'Kilts, of course.'

Subscriber, dazed:

'Kilts?'

Our Father, testily:

'Yes, yes, naturally. Haven't you got a kilt?'

Subscriber:

'I think I'd much rather speak to Stan, if you don't mind.'

Our Father:

'I'm afraid you can't. His Lordship is at present on the hunting field.'

As well as this love of fantasy our father had a horror of pretention and People who Drop In. Dinner parties where there weren't enough cutlets to go round, People who Dropped In deserved all they got. At a dinner-party he once remarked, with a sweet smile (no one has a sweeter smile than our father), 'That was a splendid ending to the football match between Hartlepool Found Drowneds and Tynemouth Graveyards United when the players battered the referee to death with his truss.'

But he was best really with people who dropped in. Once Mother had an unexpected chum to tea, a chum with a golden cocker spaniel. Sister Liz arrived a little late, a little breathless. For some reason we were all sitting round the dining-room table. And then our father leant under his end of the table, barked like a dog and pinched Liz in the fleshy part of her thigh. No one enjoyed it more than Liz. She leapt shrieking into the air, crying, 'He's bitten me! He's bitten me!' causing as much damage as possible among the buttered toast and scones. The innocent dog woke up while this fearful scene was raging and began to bark. His horrified mistress removed him, and later had him destroyed. She never Dropped In again on the Spains.

Our mother (cross though she was about this episode which alienated her chum) is also a dear. But she is also, and this, too, must be faced fearlessly, one of the great English eccentrics who has cashed in on an Irish domicile. She has for some years been getting away with every sort of electrifying outspokenness on account of her alleged Irishness. In fact, of course, there is not a drop of Irish blood in her veins. Actually she is the daughter of William Holmes Smiles, granddaughter of Samuel (Self Help) Smiles, daughter of Lucy who was a sister of Mrs. Cook Book Beeton, and the mingled blood of various go-getting Victorian tycoons whizzes through her veins. She was always keen for her children to Get On In Life, but as one half of her children was Spain (and therefore not remotely go-getting) she spent most of her life with our father in a state of violent frustration. This came to a head one day, I think, in Newcastle's most newly opened luxury cinema.

It was a time when there was much talk of The White

Slave Traffic. Old ladies, they said, or hospital nurses, would ask to be helped across the street. They would whip out a hypodermic, inject some smart soporific, and we would wake up in Buenos Aires. So watch out for old ladies and hospital nurses. I sat between Liz and Mum and all went well until a local quartet appeared and started to quaver through 'The Swan' by Saint-Saëns. Our mother was bored. And she took from her throat an extremely valuable brooch, opened it and passed it to me. I didn't like the music either, but I was at a loss as to what to do with the brooch. A hoarse whisper from our dear, gentle mother made matters clear. And I thrust it, right up to the emerald, into Liz's long-suffering thigh. The scream she gave on this occasion topped all other screams. She then turned smartly round in her seat and said to the row behind, 'Who made that disgusting noise?'

This was too much for our mother. She was led, moaning slightly, from the cinema by attendants, while we sat on, deeply enjoying Sylvia Sidney in *Street Scene*. Liz kept the brooch.

Mother was also madly loyal. 'My children right or wrong.' And once when Liz was performing a little bathing number at a children's party with a rubber hat and towel, another jealous mother said, 'I'm so glad *my* children don't show off.' To which our mother, with the speed of a fer de lance striking, replied, 'And what have they got to show off?'

Once, too, I was prancing at a children's party in lace with a blue sash.

7

'Who is the Big Girl in the blue sash?' someone asked my mother.

'That's George Spain's little girl,' said Mother.

'Oh,' was the reply, 'have you met the mother? She's quite, quite *mad*.'

Mother greatly enjoys telling this story against herself.

Our father always said it was the harsh life she had led with her ten brothers and sisters in Ireland that had made her so trigger-quick in repartee.

Her father built the Belfast Rope Works and is still repeatedly referred to in the Belfast papers as 'a Captain of Industry'. Her brother, Walter, won two D.S.O.s, was knighted for his work in India, and eventually became a Conservative Member of Parliament. On one occasion he was being heckled by a miner who asked him how he would like to spend his life 'working in the bowels of the earth'?

'So long as my bowels move at least once every day,' said Uncle Walter, 'I don't care.'

He was drowned when the *Princess Victoria* sank in the great storm of 1953: his daughter, Patsy Fisher (tallest woman in the House of Commons), duly fought and won the seat for North Down as a Unionist.

All Mother's brothers and sisters are remarkably tough. Aunt Aileen drove a baby Austin through Yugoslavia before any roads were built, and bathed in the Arctic Ocean. Her sister Lily wrote the Roedean School Song. A splendid, sprawling flamboyant family are the Smileses, all eleven of them: with red cheeks, mad enthusiasms

8

and enormous personal attraction. Our mother is the beauty of the Smileses. She had green eyes and black hair when she was young, when she and Aunt Aileen played hockey for Ulster with large red hands (the coat of arms of Ulster) on their blouses, bursting with enthusiasm. Now her hair is silver but, bless her heart, she is still enthusiastic.

Mother was born and brought up in Belfast. All 'Belfastys' have passionate loyalties to their City and themselves. For example, the Director of the BBC at Newcastle (known in those days of the blue calico-covered mike as 5NO) was a charming North of Irelander called George Marshall. Because Mother came from Belfast he was always wangling me parts in children's plays in the *Children's Hour*. And one St. Patrick's Day I appeared in a variety bill when I gave a bunch of hot, mangled shamrock to Peggy O'Neill, kissed Tommy Handley (who in those days read his jokes out of a little red notebook) and was taught a song and dance routine by Dorothy Dickson:

> We are three jolly consumptives
> (Terrible imitation of hawking and
> spitting here follows as chorus)
> Hoch-choo, hoch-choo
> We are three jolly consumptives
> (Hoch-choo hoch-choo)
> We never work and we never will
> We run up the hell of a doctor's bill

We are three jolly consumptives
(Hoch-choo hoch-choo).

Most of our strangest school holidays were spent in Belfast, too. To get there we went to Stranraer, then to Larne by the *Princess Victoria,* and were very sick indeed. Our grandmother lived in a rather ugly Edwardian villa with gables and stockbroker timbering in a part of Belfast called Strandtown. The villa itself was called Westbank and was a highly desirable residence, but I found it terrifying, what with the gardener who had fits and was often found unconscious beside his hoe: and the strange tales of 'shootings in the bad times at the bottom of the garden'. Strangers are always insisting that I *must* be Irish because my name is Spain, Sister Liz rather likes this, and like our mother she has been getting away with murder for years by pretending it is 'The Irish' in her. So she has had to start a rival genealogical theory. Father says that the Spains are descended from terribly grand Huguenots called Despaigne – he even has family trees to prove it. Liz maintains, like all other Spains in County Cork, that we were washed up in Ireland from the Spanish Armada.

Liz and I had a jolly nice childhood, so long as we weren't crossing to Ireland by Stranraer and Larne. Liz decided to be a dress designer early in life and on wet days she used to fill in books and books of fashion plates, painted in water colours. When she ran out of fashion books she used to draw her own, with appropriate fashion notes to go with them. She was very fierce about her art work and would slap down other would-be artists, calling them copy-cats. On fine days we used to go for walks in Jesmond Dene, Brandling Park, and the Bull Park where Liz would tell me what she was going to wear at her wedding. Once I pushed Billy Hardcastle (now deputy editor of the *Daily Mail)* into the lake. So it was in sheer self-defence that I became a journalist.

Our mother was determined we should get on in life. That is why (she said) we were both sent to Roedean School, to equip us for the struggle. Anyone who could survive Roedean could survive anything. But in fact, we now think, it was because she was so madly in love with the Old School that she always liked to know what was going on there in latter-day detail. She was an Old Roedeanian of Old Roedeanians. (So were Aunt Aileen and poor dead Aunt Lily, but not so aggressively, somehow.)

She also determined we must learn to ride. So at five shillings an hour, together with other little bourgeois tots, we learnt to walk, trot, and canter round the Newcastle Town Moor, under the benevolent eye of bowler-hatted Mr. Woods and his son, Johnny. Johnny was very gay and taught the pupils the Charleston on the side, capering wildly in the straw and hay. His red-faced father, *Mister* Woods, was an old artilleryman. He is dead now, more's the pity, and so are half the ponies who shared our dreams. Little Bobby, Sammy, Polly the Kicker, Tango, Jinny who-was-a-bit-of-a-one and Big Bobby the Police Horse. In spite of the fact that my sister Liz was allergic to horses (she had hay fever) this riding (which must have been a terrible expense for our parents) kept everyone very healthy indeed. Once I was run away with in a thunderstorm and the others fell off in all directions and I read a book by Nat Gould and pretended to be a jockey: but chiefly Mister Woods was concerned with seeing we rode 'like little ladies and gentlemen'. Which was jolly nice of him.

Eventually Liz went away to Roedean. Because Mum was an Old Roedeanian she had a very unfair advantage over Liz. She knew when she ought to be made a sub-prefect, she knew when she ought to get her cricket colours, she even knew when people were not catching infectious diseases fast enough.

Liz tried very hard at Roedean. 'I *know* cricket,' she told her husband the other day. 'Lift. Step. Hit.'

I was listening at the time. 'Nonsense, dear,' I said, 'that's lacrosse.' But Roedean was awe-ful. Somehow we both managed to escape being expelled. Someone threw a lacrosse ball at the Maths mistress, struck her on the bosom and was given castor oil as a punishment. Liz allegedly broke into the white marble school chapel and drank the communion wine, and then in an advanced state of intoxication is supposed to have driven the Headmistress's niece, with a broken bottle, up on to the roofs. To get there they went through various lofts and Liz said there were a terrible lot of disused chamber pots and wickerwork chairs. Later when I went to Roedean I found these as well: but don't believe this story, gay

12

though it may be. Sister Liz was only twelve when she left Roedean and went to Mayortorne Manor, a perfectly *splendid* farm school run by Roger Fry's sister.

No one ever came to grips with what went on at the Farm School, chiefly because Liz was now known as Beth. Very confusing. But she certainly sat for her School Leaving Certificate there and passed with honours – a remarkable feat for a young woman who says she still doesn't know how many feet there are in a yard. This is a singular handicap for a dress designer.

Then she went to an Art School attached in the loosest possible sense to Durham University. In spite of the gay social life of Durham University she won a scholarship to the Royal College of Art and went plunging off to the great wicked Metropolis. Eventually she became a dress designer. Almost directly, film producer Josef von Sternberg said to her, 'You turn an iceberg into a pool of leaping fish'; Sir William Rothenstein said, 'There is something daintily naughty about your work'; and Professor Joad announced, 'You have as many big guns for a woman as I have for a man.' Sister Liz can't remember her replies to any of these glamorous gentlemen. But when she was pinned up against a wall at a literary party and an author, breathing heavily down his nose, said, 'What do you want most in life?' she replied, quick as a flash, 'Brown bread and butter.' Which just goes to show that my sister Liz is A Corker.

Chapter Two

Sister Liz disappeared into the whirl of the Rag Trade almost without trace. Sometimes she would come down to Roedean and take me out to tea. By this time she was designer to Dorville, a firm of wholesale manufacturers. She talked mysteriously about 'The Collections'. She got engaged and disengaged to various young men as if it was a sport like lawn tennis, and sometimes there were fearful emotional storms. But she was always well-dressed, beautiful and very funny indeed. She once got thrown against the bathroom taps in a sisterly quarrel, and once she took my entire pocket money for the term because (she said) she was starving to death in London. But on the whole she treated me kindly and I loved her.

Roedean was a strange and pretty place. A large collection of gabled buildings, with little meaningless towers and quadrangles and cloisters, it stands among grassy swards on the cliffs at Brighton where it is referred to as 'The College'. People talk about it on the buses as they pass saying, 'All the girls have their own horses,' and, 'Whenever anyone rings a bell a mistress answers it.' No such luck. There were no bells, so far as I could see anywhere, let alone anyone answering them. Although the summer is beautiful, South Westerly Gales in February along the front at Brighton have to be felt to be believed. The wind sighed along the corridors, lifting the linoleum. Our mother, who went there, still bleeding from the assaults of her ten ravening brothers and sisters, thought it a lovely place and the girls ever so ladylike. But by 1931 when I sat my scholarship exam it was very different.

'Shut up', 'Don't chip in', 'Girls who spread butter on bread are common', were the three basic rules of life.

Anyone who caught anyone else doing anything sneaked sanctimoniously to the staff. Everyone got on everyone else's nerves. Though of course there were some good bits. I always got enough to eat on Saturday afternoons if I played in cricket matches. I always have had an appetite like a horse. In the summer the weather was often divine and the sky as blue as in the South of France. I can remember moments of rare contentment, just lying face down on the short grass, watching a cricket match in the sun, doing nothing. And various Brighton trunk murderers ran smartly through the grounds leaving little trails of clues. Oh, and suicides flung themselves off the cliffs almost daily. Roedean cliffs are almost as good for a suicide as Beachy Head. But apart from this Roedean was really sad.

Girls have to get up so early there, for one thing. Bed at 10 p.m. for the Sixth Form and then up at 7 plunging down for breakfast at 8. Young ladies who sleep through all this clanging of bells and thundering of feet can often sleep undisturbed until noon. But in theory matron crashes round, stripping beds and bundling out any lazy-bones found sleeping at Scripture time.

Scripture in those days was taught by Dame Emmeline Tanner, the late Headmistress. Dame Emmeline was a tall, powerful lady who weighed about the same as our father. She was not, however, whacky at all. Indeed, the only truly whacky character I encountered all the time I was there was Phillippa Crosby, a millionaire's daughter from Johannesburg, who grew up to marry Nicholas Monsarrat who wrote *The Cruel Sea*. Phillippa was wonderful because she had a gramophone concealed in her bedroom and used to play the records of Fred Astaire after dark, with a pin instead of a gramophone needle so Matron couldn't hear.

Girls and staff at Roedean were without exception high-minded, pure-souled conformists. Most of the time they couldn't make out what I was laughing at.

One Sunday evening, for example, a lecture was scheduled. A Lantern Lecture. This was a good thing, as it meant we could sleep a little in the dark, sitting still, which is always restful. The lecturer was announced as Mademoiselle Baguet. She was a little late. I had just dozed off when I came to with a jerk and found that the entire school was on its feet. And slowly up the middle aisle came a little lady dressed in black Hessian boots with gold tassels, white tights, a green jacket with gold froggings, a dolman, a powdered wig – The Lot. With her was another lady, also dressed as a man, but in black.

She wore lawyer's tabs, a black trailing cloak. As the entire lecture was in French I and 280 other girls have never yet discovered what it was all about. The Palace of Versailles was mentioned and the slides were of dim landscapes. But no one even smiled.

And then there was the Colour Play. Colours were awarded likes Blues for cricket, lacrosse, tennis. Half colours were awarded for dancing, gym, swimming, fencing and (of all things) acting. And people of Colour Standard were allowed to choose a play to act every year, to show the parents how jolly cultured we were all getting. One year someone chose *The Trojan Women*. Gertrude Lawrence was one of the parents (fairly obviously Top Parent). She came down and sat in the front tow and watched her daughter Pam performing as Cassandra the Prophetess. Pam was a dear, as a matter of fact, and we all loved her: but it was very unnerving to have what Miss Tanner called 'England's Greatest Actress' sitting in the middle of the front row. Perhaps ambition suddenly burned in the bosoms of those members of the Cricket First Eleven who, insecurely got up in cardboard breast-plates and little kilts and ill-fitting sandals as members of the Greek Army, were waiting round the corner of Number Three House for the three blasts on a whistle. This meant they were to storm Troy. Perhaps they saw themselves suddenly appearing with Gertrude Lawrence *and* Noël Coward in a *musical* version of C. B. Cochran's Trojan Young Ladies? Anyway, when the whistle blew the First Eleven went berserk. Heads down, chests out, they raced for Troy as though they were in the Olympics. Breast-plates burst, sandals flew and one spear caught with its top and bottom hard in the door where Cassandra was still calling down woe. And the entire Greek Army fell with a reverberating crash into the school orchestra who were hard at it grinding out a Tone Poem by an Old Roedeanian called Greta Tomlin. The resulting crash in the timpani could be heard as far away as Falmer. And no one smiled.

Pam got her colours for acting *and* dancing, I believe. When Gertie was going bankrupt Pam came to stay with us in Newcastle-on-Tyne and electrified the household by rushing out to pretend to commit suicide on the railway line. A girlish prank, which upset Mother. Nobody else minded much, least of all Pam.

It takes, I suppose, a fairly extreme sense of humour to cope with a Spain in embryo. I recollect one perfect example of this, when I was sitting for *my* school certificate. An awfully nice examiner, a man (we hadn't seen a man for some months, except through the main gates) called Mr. Rubinstein, arrived to examine our prowess in Oral French. I arrived a little early for my session and engaged Mr. Rubinstein in conversation in English.

'What an awful time you must be having,' I said. 'How many horrible little schoolgirls have you examined today?'

'Far too many,' said Mr. Rubinstein, and sighed.

At that point a very angry French Mademoiselle, like something out of Angela Brazil, burst into the room.

'Nancy!' she cried. 'What do you think you're doing?'

'She is taking her French examination,' said Mr. Rubinstein. 'And what is more, she is doing extremely well.'

I am sorry to have to record that I got a Distinction in French Oral in spite of the fact that I still do not know the past participle of *ceuiller* – to pick, pluck, or gather.

The present headmistress, Miss N. M. Horobin, a thoroughly nice woman, once tried to explain to Maurice Ambler and myself that Roedean was just like other schools.

'Last Christmas,' she said, 'when the Southdown buses were stuck in the drive on account of the severe fall of snow and all the girls were helping to dig them out, several of the girls came to me and said, "Madam, do please go in and don't catch cold." Not one thought, you see, that if they missed the last plane to Karachi they wouldn't be home before Christmas.'

There are always a large quantity of Indian princesses and things at Roedean, which is (it must be faced) extremely expensive. Even after subtracting extras like individual singing, laundry, fencing, stationery and school books, our father still had to find about £200 a year each for his two daughters, so that they might Get On in Life. Liz cost £2,000; I cost about £1,500. We both (chiefly because our mother was an Old Girl) were given bursaries of £70 a year but I don't think this helped much. Of course there were all sorts of things we could do to help. I refused to wear any but home-made djibbahs. A really swanky djibbah, and some girls had about six of them, made by Debenham and Freebody or Forma or Liberty's, could run you into ten guineas a djibbah, even in 1931. What is a djibbah? Well, the four Miss Lawrences, who founded Roedean in 1885, discovered the first djibbah on a dragoman in Arabia. It has elbow-length sleeves and it looks rather like a sack. Djibbahs were abolished in 1935, but there was a lot of fuss made by Old Roedeanians, who will do anything to hold back time. They said there could be no Public Spirit without djibbahs. And no one smiled.

The Old Roedeanians are a very rich, tremendously reactionary body. They want everything to go on just as it did when *they* were seventeen. They would like to sing the same old school songs, eat the same old rissoles and remember Jolly Old Pals, just as always. Once a year they rush down to Roedean like the lemmings (those strange Arctic rats who so often commit suicide in droves), play cricket and tennis (thus damaging their middle-aged hearts) and even (in extreme cases) change into djibbahs. There is also a Sing-Song when they get together in a great body and roar out the old songs. My favourite of these is 'The Cricket First Eleven', which goes:

> O, the Cricket First Eleven
> Is the best in all the land.
> It's the one above all others
> We admire on every hand.

May your scores be never-failing
And your bowling ever true
O, noble First Eleven
Here's our best of healths to you.

This is sung to the South African War hit song 'Tommy, Tommy Atkins' and when in 1955 I sang it to Noël Coward in the Ivy, Noël actually cried. *He* said he would put it in his cabaret and sing it in Las Vegas. Then he said he would put it in a play. This he duly did. When I went to see *South Sea Bubble* I was amazed to hear Vivien Leigh sing her version of the old song. This she did in Act II when under the influence of strong Colonial liquor; finally bonking her dusky would-be lover on the head with a bottle.

But I was very dissatisfied to find that Vivien Leigh used the *wrong tune*. I rang her up to complain.

'Leslie Bridgewater wrote the tune specially for me,' she said.

'But it's *wrong*,' I said.

'Well, then, how should it go?'

So poor Miss Leigh had to listen to me, singing it, all the way through on the telephone. I have no record of how she looked, taking it in the other end. But as she mentioned that I obviously enjoyed singing it, she, too, wept.

Joyce Grenfell also likes this song and in 1954 she sang it in duet with me in a Home Service programme. It was a big success. This song was *not* written by Aunt

Lily. I wish it had been. Aunt Lily, Mother's sister, who died at the age of eighteen from rheumatism of the heart following too much energetic piano practice, wrote 'Wimbledonia'. This was the rallying call of the school when it was still known as Wimbledon House School for Girls. Aunt Lily was one of the junior music staff.

> Cricket, tennis, swimming, drilling
> Thy dear colours, blue and white
> 'Public Spirit' is thy motto
> School of love and school of might
> Wimbledonia – fair and free
> Health and strength belong to thee
> Felix Wimbledonia

we used to sing. Perfectly splendid. Noël Coward still calls me 'Old Wimbledonia', and that is why.

Another favourite song contained a list of Heroines – 'Marjorie for Captain, Druce for Play', and had a rousing refrain:

> For all of we, whoever we be
> Fall short of those heroines old, you see
> For all of we, whoever we be
> Fall short of those heroines old, you see.

One Summer Half Term when, as usual, the school was crawling with old girls, I was running (strictly forbidden), in gym shoes (ditto), through School House (ditto), when a long arm shot out from a marble pillar where the school house-bell was tolled. A deep bass voice said in my ear, *'Har, bar, bar. You don't know who I am.'* I agreed. 'Well, *I'm* Druce for Play,' said the voice.

I don't think I have ever quite recovered from this.

But my love of celebrities was basely pandered to at Roedean. At one and the same time we had gathered there Gertrude Lawrence's daughter, Henry Hall's niece, Edgar Wallace's daughter Penelope, and Miss M. J. Mellanby. Miss Mellanby taught English. She had bright blue eyes and auburn hair and she once cracked her achilles tendon clean across doing physical fitness exercises with other members of the staff. Miss Mellanby was a very considerable character indeed, passionately loved by all her house and covertly admired by everyone else. She used to go riding on the Downs and could quite often be seen standing negligently about on the school terrace dressed in Jodhpurs, a remarkable thing in itself. Anyway, Miss Mellanby went to be head of Borstal in 1935 and Roedean made headlines in the *Daily Mirror*. She is now an Inspector of H.M. Prisons. And no one at the school could see why the rest of the world found this funny.

Chapter Three

On Leaving School and the Choice of a Career was the name of a book that our mother was always reading when we were girls. I'm sure we were a great disappointment to her. She kept expecting us to turn out to be games mistresses or hospital nurses or domestic science teachers. I can't *think* why, as ever since I can remember I have been saying I would be a journalist, while Liz has said she would be a dress designer. Nevertheless Mum dragged both of us round various domestic science colleges and me (at any rate) round Dartford Physical Training College before she relaxed and let us do our worst.

Poor Mum. Our father was much better able to deal with his embryo Spains.

Said he: 'I am not very well off and I cannot afford to give you the sort of allowances that other girls get in Newcastle. You will have fifty pounds a year and you must pay for your clothes and amusements out of that. Board and lodging we provide free.'

This has always seemed to me a generous arrangement.

To everyone's surprise I now crept furtively down the road to Durham University and enrolled myself as a member of the Art School. (I was furtive because I knew Liz would disapprove and call me a copy-cat.) I got in free because I made some drawings of people skating and showed them to Professor Maine, who was the principal. I went to Life Classes on Mondays and Anatomy Classes on Thursdays and it was a long time before anyone found out about it at home. They were surprised.

It was winter-time and I never stopped being amazed by the imperturbable half-frozen male model who stood, shivering slightly, on his throne. He was so *dignified*. Then one day someone shouted out was anyone going skating?

'Didn't even know you could skate,' replied some other rude beast.

'Of course he can, his mother was one,' said another.

This broke up the model, who laughed helplessly. For some reason this instantly made him appear indecent. The female models weren't at all shapely, but they were cosy and used to tell our fortunes in the coffee-break.

I liked the Art School very much, but I got rather sick of sitting still making drawings of the sterno-mastoid movement and the Professor of Anatomy was suspicious of me.

I was in love at this time, too, and while the other girls sat happily at their 'donkeys' (strange wooden things on which to prop a drawing-board, with a head one end and a body to sit astride) and roared out songs with swift loud melodies like 'The Music Goes Round and Around

26

and It Comes Out Here', I used to brood in a corner humming 'Serenade in the Night'.

I have never been very good at Being in Love. This time I was in love with a young man called Paddy Something or Other. Paddy 'because I had such a terrible temper when I was a baby'. He danced very well. He was very tall and very good at golf and even made *me* play golf for a little while. I found golf very boring. He took me to tea with his mother. *She* was very suspicious of me, I remember, and there was a flag-pole in the garden. He took me to dances. I remember one, particularly, in H.M.S. *Calliope*, the R.N.V.R. training-ship in the Tyne, when we stood arm-in-arm on the poop and looked at the lights wiggling in the water. It was all very innocent and rather dull.

By and by Paddy very sensibly married a very rich young woman. My heart certainly wasn't broken, for by this time I was in love with Michael.

Michael was very tall and very intelligent. He talked very well and he laughed a lot and he didn't dance anything like as well as Paddy. He once took me to a dance and got sick of it, and we went for a long walk through the snow at the back of Tankerville Place, ending up on the little wooden bridge that goes over the railway, at roughly the point where Pam, Gertie Lawrence's daughter, had decided she wouldn't commit suicide. The street lamp shone on Michael and on the snow and it was pretty, but nothing altered the fact that my feet were wet through. Next day, sure enough, I had a terrible cold, even though the tune 'I'm in the Mood for Love' kept running through my head. And shortly after, Michael married an even richer girl than Paddy had.

Mildly sickened by romance I decided at this point that I needed some exercise. (That had always been the cure for sentimentality at Roedean: 'Run like boys and you won't think about boys,' our dear old house mistress used to say.)

For example, I joined a swimming club, but when I was changing in my little cabin I heard two girls ask one another if they were staying for the water polo.

'D'ye remember the last time when Joey Latimer got his costume torn off?' they said.

Somehow, after this, I didn't go back. Instead, one day I heard there was a lacrosse club in Sunderland. I had never been very good at lacrosse at Roedean (I was in the Second XII), but the idea of fresh air and running after a ball has always appealed to me strongly. Sister Liz says it is most unnatural. Maybe she is right. Anyway, I used every means I could to get to Sunderland, where to my surprise I became a member of the Northumberland and Durham Team.

In company with eleven other muscular girls I now travelled the length and breadth of England playing matches against Lancs, Ches, Yorks, Berks, Bucks, and Oxon and (once a year) Liverpool where we all took part in the North of England Trials. Every year, monotonously, I failed to get into the team, but I made some very good friends and the sports editor of the *Newcastle*

Journal heard about these goings-on and asked me to write a report for him.

'It will give your club good publicity,' he said.

Harry Barker was my first editor. (I was eighteen.) He sat in a dim little office with the famous *Newcastle Journal* clock outside the window. The office smelt of dust, copy paper and (glory) printer's ink. Every now and then he shouted 'Boy!' and a boy called Billy stuck his head in and took away some copy.

'Ooh,' I said. 'I wish I worked here.'

'Well,' said Harry Barker, 'maybe you will one day.'

He was an absolute darling. He was short and pale-faced and I believe he had been a great footballer in his day. He taught me the basic rules of journalism.

'Write clearly,' he said, sending me away to write about lacrosse with a big thick black oily pencil and some tiny square sheets of beige copy paper. 'Write on one side of the paper only, number each page and always get your story here by two-thirty at the latest. What's the use of hanging around the pitch waiting for something better to happen if the paper goes to press without your report?'

I didn't have a typewriter in those days and I found it comparatively easy to write standing upright on a frozen pitch and very thrilling to parcel up my copy in a big red envelope over-stamped *Newcastle Journal* and then dash across country to the nearest main-line station. Someone then collected it the other end. When I graduated to more important things I would put through a reversed charge call saying, 'Meet the two-thirty from Darlington.' My excitement over the lacrosse matches was worthy of a world scoop at least . . .

Harry Barker didn't pay me anything for these inspired accounts of the Misses W. Sargeant and N. Sanderson playing 'like lambent flames along the Left Wing'. But he printed them in the paper over my initials and he gave me a taste of the power of journalism. Thinking it over, I suppose I ought to have paid *him*.

The Misses W. Sargeant and N. Sanderson were important figures in my reports. Winifred Sargeant was the height of glamour. She was known as 'Bin' to her chums and 'Girlie' to her mother. She was so good at games that it was embarrassing. Quite adult games, like Bridge. She had a streak of golden hair and blue eyes with a yellow ring round the pupil and she could run faster than any girl I have ever seen. To have seen Bin flash down the Left Wing and shoot a goal was a sporting experience on a par with Bannister's mile or Obelonsky's Ashbrook try.

But quite apart from this athleticism Bin was terribly clever and very funny. She made excellent jokes and actually kept double-entry ledgers of personal expenditure, just for the hell of it. She also had a wonderful showing-off flair. For example, she had a little green sports car with cream wings and she had two wonderful red Irish setters that sat up in the back, looking exactly like an advertisement for Sportsgirl Lipstick. Bin was an amazing girl. She drank gin and tonics in a rather lordly way and she was engaged to be married to a young man called Bill, and then to a young man called Francis, or was he Roger? It was difficult to tell them apart . . .

Nora Sanderson was Bin's best friend. She was handsome too, but plumper than the great Miss Sargeant who used to fling the ball at me crying, 'Yours, Spain!'

For years our father used to walk round the house murmuring to himself, 'Yours every time, Spain,' which used to send him into fits of silent laughter.

All the West Hartlepool girls had a lot of money. They lived in big, prosperous houses with a full quota of maids cavorting in the back premises. They drank burgundy and fizzy lemonade for lunch and I was mad about them all. I thought they were a Very Fast Set Indeed. Considering that I was all the time mooning over Paddy or Michael they were very nice to me.

Then one day I ran out of money and couldn't afford to pay for my round of gins-and-tonics. Bin pointed out in words of one kindly syllable how I mustn't allow this to happen again. I had already spent the £50 Father had given me on rushing about to Liverpool and so on. (And my share of the petrol.) What was I to do?

I remembered Dorothy Dickson and her deplorable song about the consumptives. And I went down the road to Broadcasting House, New Bridge Street in Newcastle, and said I wanted an audition.

'Was I an actress?'

Oh yes, said I with the courage of despair, I was a very good actress. And I filled up a little form with the help of a commissionaire sergeant and said I had played in *The Ghost Train* and *The Importance of Being Earnest* and *The Trojan Women*. Then I went home.

A week later I got a square buff envelope containing a letter signed L. Guildford. He was the new Director of the Newcastle Station since George Marshall had gone back to Belfast. It said I was to attend for audition at 4 p.m. sharp and be prepared to read a part. So I took *The Importance of Being Earnest* and *The Ghost Train* and a very long sheet of paper on which I had written one sentence in every known dialect in the world. (I even included an imitation of Mae West.) It took at least half an hour to read out all the sentences into a microphone with china sides: quite different from the blue calico affairs I was used to in *Children's Hour*. From time to time the terrified young producer at the control panel downstairs (his name was Cecil McGivern) tried to stop me.

'But I've several more dialects to do . . . ' I said. 'Now then. Somerset.'

In the end he came upstairs with *The Times* newspaper. 'Read that,' he said, 'for God's sake, in your normal voice.'

Years later Cecil told me, 'You gave the most appalling performance anyone has ever given at an audition. But you read a whole single column of *The Times* from top to bottom without a single mistake, and without a

single whistled sibilant. That in itself was remarkable.'*
I still can't see why. It was my mother who taught me
to read.

A week later I was asked to come in and read the
heroine's part in a dialect play called *The Lang Pack*. It
was a jolly gloomy story about a girl who lived all alone
up the North Tyne and let in a pedlar who hid in his
pack in order to commit a robbery-with-violence. The
heroine plunged a knife in the pack when she saw it
wriggle. She also said a lot of things like, 'Nowt ivor
happens oop t'valley. Nowt tae dae but watch the coos
(or was it the hills?) torn frae broon to green to white
and back ower agin.'

Radio studios in those days were just as they are
now, with a green light to give you your cue to scream
against the background of lowing cows on a gramophone record, a red light to say that if you cough you
will deafen thousands, and a white light to show that
something terrible has gone wrong and they want the
engineer on the telephone. We had a new sort of microphone again: rather like a copper wasps' nest with holes
all over it. I screamed 765 times in that production, on
a green cue light. Cecil McGivern was a producer who
liked perfection. On transmission I was covered with

---

* A good story, Nancy, but I wasn't the young producer. However, I read
the audition report a day or so later. It showed:

  (a) For an amateur actress, you had given an outstandingly good audition.

  (b) The official taking the audition had been through a most unusual
experience.

mud and so tired (I had been playing lacrosse against Lancashire that day) that I croaked like a very old lady and not at all like the fresh young girl who was supposed to be the heroine watching the hills turn colour. I got five guineas and thought it was too easy.

But then a letter appeared in the *Newcastle Journal*: that same journal in whose pages Lacrosse Notes by N.B.S. had been appearing. 'These so-called dialect plays are the worst so-called feature on the so-called region,' it said, 'and the woman was the worst. Outraged Mother of 4, Heaton.'

(There was only one woman in the cast of *The Lang Pack* – me.)★

'L. Guildford' was most kind about it however. He lent me a copy of *Aylwin* by Theodore Watts Dunton (he was the chap who kept Swinburne off the booze) and gave me another minor part in a play almost directly. I think the play was by L. Guildford, It was called *A Victorian Drawing-room* and contained such fragments of dialogue as, 'Oh ho, Mr. Ross, what a quiz you are!'

Mr. Ross was a tenor who sang, 'O that we two were Maying.' I got two guineas for this.

★ Guildford and I agreed that if we didn't give you a chance, we would be guilty of 'Stifling Regional Talent'. Hence your screams in *The Lang Pack*. You were also very good looking.

As regards the screams, I doubt the number 765. I vouch for the quality. As an amateur actress, you were a remarkably good professional screamer.

CECIL McGIVERN.

Suddenly Harry Barker, who believed in lacrosse as a good thing, asked me to go and report a badminton tournament. 'I'll pay you 1½d. a line,' he said. (This epic piece of prose was later pasted into a Press cutting book, all fifty sizzling lines, where I read it the other day.) Roughly six bob's worth. Highly excited I rushed to Sunderland. I found both Nora and Bin playing badminton, bouncing up and down on the rough wooden floor of some converted swimming baths. The fact that their activities were now worth 1½d. a line to me made their activities more desirable than ever. Then I caught the last train home and when I had 'turned in my copy' the last tram back to Jesmond had gone. It was my first taste of being a reporter. It had been snowing. And when I came out of the *Journal* offices the sad, battered old face of Newcastle was hidden under a white mask. Tram-lines had disappeared. The overhead wires gleamed silver. Everything was quiet. And *I* was a reporter. I danced home on wings.

When I got to 7 Tankerville Place it was locked, bolted and barred. I had quite forgotten to tell anyone where I was going. I tried inefficiently to climb in. I fell into a snow drift. I daren't knock. Our mother would have scalped me. So I broke a window-pane and opened the latch through the hole. I got a glazier in the morning from the builder's yard at the back. The pane of glass cost 1s. 9d. The return ticket had been 3s. So I didn't stand many rounds of drinks at the next match against Yorkshire. But I didn't care. I had a career and, later, I had a latch-key. It must have been around this time that Mother began complaining that I treated the house like an hotel.

Good old Harry Barker. Everyone was interested in hockey and badminton, he said. He would pay me 1½d. a line for them. And when the summer came, and with it lawn tennis, for some reason the price jumped up to 2d. a line. Relative prices are always fascinating. And then the *Yorkshire Post* wrote to Harry and asked him for someone to cover local tournaments for *them*, and so did *The Scotsman*. One glittering year I represented the *Yorkshire Post*, *The Scotsman*, the *Doncaster Northern Echo* the *Sunderland Echo,* the *West Hartlepool Northern Daily Mail*, the *Newcastle Journal* and the *Newcastle Evening Chronicle*. I wrote different lead-in paragraphs for all these stories and then sent off carbon copies of the strings of results. (The results were a godsend. One could fill up *lines* and *lines* at 2d. with them.) My tremendous Northern Counties-wide syndication was a deadly secret. And I remember one wonderful occasion when a local hero called W. T. Anderson said to me, with just a faint hint of patronage, 'Why, Nancy, you must be quite right about my weak service. The *Yorkshire Post* says it is weak too.'

What with all these carbon copies of results it was necessary to have a typewriter. Mother very kindly gave me hers. It was a Baby Empire. I estimated that I had written three and a half million words with it (nine books and heaven knows how many reports of one kind and another), before it collapsed and couldn't even be rebuilt. This generosity and enthusiasm of Mother's wasn't a bit spoilt by the muttering that now went on about how I lived on sandwiches and gin and ginger beer and treated the house like an hotel. I also had a little fabric second-hand Baby Austin. It cost £20 and (of all things) Bin began to be jealous of the little pile of crumpled postal orders I used to cash before I started out for a match. And I was again in love, with Dick this time. But Dick went to Germany for his summer hols and married a German girl, which was surprising, I must say.

For my part I was so jealous of the West Hartlepool girls and their superior gamesmanship that I decided I must get on to the North side for *something*. The only game I have ever been any good at is cricket, so cricket it would have to be, however much my sister Liz sniggered. It was unthinkable for Our Ace Sports Reporter not to be on a Territorial Team for something. So I dressed myself up in a pair of very tight tennis shorts and long white Tyrolean stockings and a cable-stitch sweater and my Roedean cricket cap in order to attract the selector's eye. I stood about in this strange fancy dress and all I got was a lot of black looks. So in the end I went up to one of the selectors. Nice old party, she was too, in a broad straw gent's cricketing boater.

'Oh, ma'am,' I said, sycophantically, 'I did so enjoy that innings you played against Roedean in 1935.' All the other selectors were leaning forward eagerly so I laid it on with a trowel. 'When you hit that ball into the sea,' I said.

She blushed and human nature struggled with integrity in her face, under the straw boater.

'Well,' she said, 'it is more usual for me to hit the ball along the ground.'

'But that's just it, ma'am,' I said. 'It was wonderful. It went right along the Old Flat through the netting and across the road into the sea. It was wonderful.'

It was also wonderful, wasn't it, that I got into the North side and was able to play against the Midlands at Leicester? And I wasn't jealous of Nora and Bin any more. I was awfully surprised when Bin said she was jealous of the postal orders I had earned by the sweat of my brow.

'*I* must get a job,' she said. 'That's what.'

And Bin became Northern agent to the firm of T. H. Prosser, sports manufacturers, and signed a contract to say she would sell their goods in the length and breadth of Yorkshire, Durham, and Northumberland. Fortunately Prosser made pretty well everything from hockey sticks to ladies' tennis dresses. I used to batter at various school doors with a bundle of Prosser hockey sticks under my arm. Once I encountered Miss N. M. Horobin, now headmistress of Roedean, then headmistress of the Sunderland High School for Girls, and when years later I went back to Roedean to write that famous feature article about it with Maurice Ambler, she actually remembered me dripping hockey sticks in her entrance.

Bin was very good at battering at badminton secretaries. And once she got the monopoly to supply shuttlecocks for the North Eastern Badminton League.

Bin made £75 out of that deal with the badminton league, bought a second-hand Ford 10 and invited me to go touring through the South of France with her. This was my first business coup, my first holiday. It might even have led to millionaire-dom, who knows? But as it happened we went abroad in August 1939. When we got back in September war was declared. Winifred Sargeant died in November of that year. And I couldn't even bear to go to her funeral.

No one can write happily of death, least of all a frivolous person like myself; and this book is intended only to catch the happy hours. Strangely enough I am writing these words on my thirty-eighth birthday in Cannes, within about thirty miles of that enchanted piece of coast from St. Raphael to Agay that I saw for the first time in 1939 . . . that haunted me through the war years until I saw it again.

And I now realize what a terrible shock Bin's death at the age of twenty-four must have been to me. She was so young and gay and fair. Quite often I still think I see her, laughing in a crowd; and once I am sure I saw her come into a restaurant. She sat down and ordered, of all things, a Scotch Egg. But when I leapt up to say hello she seemed to vanish, leaving a hard clear line for a second, as a piece of paper does when it burns in the fire.

I often wonder what Bin would have done if she had gone on living. She would have married, I expect, and raised tennis-playing children to the glory of County Durham.

I went back, once, to the Northumberland tennis tournament where she and all my old friends had played. There were strange gaps in the names that the referee once called to go on court. 'Dudley Hobbis, Doris Davison, Ken Marsh, Eileen Brooks, "Tommy" Wright'; these were our heroes and heroines. And now of all that bright company only 'Doris and Eileen and "Tommy"' remain to show a new generation what giants we had in those days.

But there are still many tennis courts under the spire of St. George's Church at the top of Osborne Road. The weeds that grew there through the war have been pulled up, and they have tournaments there, with the same china (pink roses on the cups) and the same band on President's Day, and the same gentle sound of tennis ball meeting gut, of umpire calling the score. If I close my eyes I can see it all still: I can even hear the bells in St. George's steeple . . .

When I was a roly-poly little girl of four those tennis courts were not yet there. That space was a cricket ground, white with daisies. There was a roller with a horse with genuine leather boots on and a dear hairy-chested man called Smith (whom I was not allowed to invite to my fourth birthday party) who looked after it all. So perhaps one day the tennis courts will go, too, to

make way for some even more modern form of exercise
. . . an ice rink . . . or a place for water carnivals. All that
memory can really rely upon is the unchanging blue of
the windy Northumbrian sky.

Chapter Four

Sometimes nowadays when Cecil McGivern, the Programme boss at Lime Grove and a very important fellow indeed, sees me, he looks at me and says wistfully, 'We really should do another *Fell Top*.'

Fell Top was a remarkable radio play. Cecil, for some reason, adores it. Written entirely in the South Durham dialect by a talented woman called Winifred E. Watson, it was all about a girl called Anne Mary. Anne Mary was raped by a farmer called Nathan Coulthard and her stepmother was beastly to her and shut her out in the snow. In revenge Anne Mary's cripple sister Jane Ellen pushed Nathan Coulthard into a waterfall so that Anne Mary could marry Roger-from-the-country. *Fell Top* was a hell of a radio play, what with the sounds of falling water and Nathan falling, screaming, into it . . .

Joyce Grenfell was radio critic of the *Observer* at this time, and she listened to it and said it was 'Excellent'.

I was Anne Mary and although the play only called for me to scream twice I actually screamed 1,756 times at rehearsal, sometimes doing other people's screams too as they lost their voices. Everyone said that Cecil was a good and meticulous producer and that he was the coming man. We (hoarsely) agreed.*

I also discovered the secret of saying impossible lines on the radio, if anyone else would like to know how to do it? The play called for me to listen to about a quarter of an hour's steady nagging from Jane Ellen to leave Nathan, marry Roger, stand up for myself, etc. etc. I then had to say (showing my warmth of nature, hatred of Nathan, love of Roger, devotion to Jane Ellen, in the South Durham dialect), 'there is times . . . in the summer . . . nights like this.' You try implying all that in one broken sentence.

Cecil took me through it 2,756 times, with various inflections. Up on 'summer', down on 'times'. Down on 'summer', up on 'times'. Eventually it had no sense at all for me and I asked for it to be rewritten.

'Certainly not,' said Cecil. 'Every bad actress there has ever been tries to rewrite her part.'

(I had a suspicion that Winifred E. Watson was down-stairs beside him, because once before I had put my foot in it with an author, saying that no girl would say anything so soppy as 'Whenever a great ship puts out to sea my heart goes aboard her for unknown lands' to her fiancé. And Cecil had said, 'Shh . . . the author's here in the control room,' and the author had been

---

* I might have been meticulous but I cannot have been good, if your figure of 1,756 screams is even representative of the truth. But we were all enjoying ourselves immensely, so what are a few numerals? – C. McGivern.

most annoyed with me and said his wife had really said it to him when they got engaged. Which just goes to show.)

Anyway, I suddenly had a brain-wave. And instead of listening to the words I just *said* them, imagining all the time a whacking great yellow harvest moon above a hay-stack with two people canoodling in the foreground. And, amazing to relate, people truly *saw* this moon as I said the line. Rather uncanny. Nowadays I even draw little pictures in the margin of radio scripts to remind me to use my imagination on them.

After *Fell Top* I became a fully-fledged member of the Rep: the Newcastle *Radio* Repertory Company. Other fully-fledged members were Gillie Fenwick, Alf Simpson, Edith Bulmer, Renee Bruce, Esther McCracken, and Sal Sturgeon.

Most of them were proper actors and actresses who had talked to George Bernard Shaw and been in *St. Joan* at the People's Theatre – a very advance guard theatre somewhere in Newcastle's West End. I felt a terrible fraud beside Sal and Esther and Co. in spite of the fact that our father's eldest sister, Katy, had rushed away to America and was a genuine 'old pro' called Katherine Stewart, who played Duchess parts and stopped the traffic leaning on an ebony cane on 5th Avenue. She also, at one point, shared a flat with Faith Compton Mackenzie, Sir Compton Mackenzie's wife – Christopher Stone's sister, who was mildly shocked by her. Auntie Katy in America was trimmed entirely in maribou and told people's fortunes all the time. Yes, a proper pro. But this didn't give *me* professional status, somehow . . .

We did plays about the Roman Wall (and I was raped by Roman Legionaries), plays about the Border Raiders (and I was raped by Picts and Scots), and eventually I was given the part of Grace Darling in a centenary play of her birth or death called *Longstone Light*. And I wasn't raped at all. I am still in two minds as to whether this was progress or not.

Fresh from some savage match against Lancashire I went up to Bamburgh to visit the Farne Islands, to learn the authentic accent. Bamburgh is a dear little grey little sea town on the Northumbrian coast, where the sea breaks restlessly against a scowling castle and where, lurking in cottages, there are any number of relations of Grace Darling. So I battered on the cottage doors. Eventually a Kindly Body looked out.

'Er,' I said, in my best Roedean accent. 'Er, I am from the . . . er . . . BBC and I am to . . . er . . . play the part of . . . er . . . Grace Darling . . . in the . . . er . . . forthcoming production about her . . . er . . . life and death.'

The Kindly Body looked me up and down and wiped her hands on her apron.

'Eeeeh,' she said. 'But Grace was a *frail* lass.'

Never mind. We even got good *local* notices for *Longstone Light*. I was interviewed, which pleased me enormously. (I was nineteen.)

'Nancy Spain, the radio star,' they said, and they went on at some length about my electric chestnut hair.

46

'Good God,' said our father, reading it, 'the girl takes you for a greyhound track.'

It was a lovely life with its dirty little collections of postal orders every month and its BBC cheques every week (five guineas flat rate per play) and its grand 10s. 6d. a week for tennis articles signed with the name of 'Atalanta' and its cheques for one guinea a week for articles signed 'Baseline'. It was a terrible thing when the war broke out and struck my little life a smart blow. It disappeared without a trace.

I couldn't bear khaki and I didn't fancy forming fours. So I pulled every string I knew to get into the W.R.N.S., eventually becoming a lorry driver at North Shields at the mouth of the River Tyne on 1 November 1939.

I wrote a book about this called *Thank you, Nelson*. I loved every minute of being a lorry driver. It was a perpetual adventure. But then, alas, I pulled every string I knew to be made an Officer. And I was drafted as a Third Officer W.R.N.S. to a Fleet Air Arm Station at Arbroath in Eastern Scotland. This served me right. Oh dear me. All I can truly remember is that I had a heavy cold when I arrived and I had a heavy cold when I left, the best part of a year later.

Royal Naval Air Station, Arbroath, at that time was in the charge of a dear, kind girl called Beatrice Jewell. We officers (there were two admin officers and two cypherers) lived in a brick hut with two Naval Sisters whose favourite gramophone records were 'The Boys in the Back Room' and 'I've Been in Love Before', both sung by Marlene Dietrich. (For the first and only time in my life I got a little bit sick of Marlene and suddenly wanted Chopin, Beethoven, and Cesar Franck.) There were about 200 dashing sub-lieutenants learning to fly Walruses, Sharks, Albecores, and Grummand Martlets, and the noise they made dive-bombing over the Wrennery had to be felt to be believed.

One of the squadron leaders turned out to be Terence Horsley, the ex-Managing Editor of that same *Newcastle Journal*, who had actually printed N.B.S.'s notes on lacrosse, tennis, badminton, and what have you. He was tall and nicely whacky and he once took me on one side and showed me his press-cutting books.

All Terence's features were very grand indeed, with by-lines. I had never had a by-line in my life except for a piece about 'gay hats at Wimbledon', so in spite of the fact that all his features began with the words 'I sat on a slag heap in County Durham' and were highly sociological, significant and (to me) as boring as old boots, I was soon jealous of Terence Horsley. Terence wrote like an angel, but when I met him at Arbroath it was his business to teach the youth of Great Britain night fighting.

Four hundred Wrens kept the machines serviced for him while he did so. My business was to administer to the Wrens who serviced the machines. And soon far too many planes seemed to me to lie about on the ground covered with tarpaulins, U/S (unserviceable). I expect I am too impatient. Although I find it funny now, I know I didn't like Arbroath.

First of all the Air Station was so big that one could only get anywhere by bicycling. Second, as it was a Training Base instead of an Ops Base we were too far from the war to feel a part of it. Then it was so overcrowded that epidemics like mumps, German measles, scarlet fever, and (once, terribly) head lice swept through us like a dose of salts. Third, it was such miles from anywhere and so little happened that everyone fell in love with everyone else and the station was always in an emotional heckle from one end to the other. I used to go to Edinburgh once a month to have my hair done to escape. Naturally I fell in love, too. I fell in love with a dear boy called Arthur. He is the only one of my loves who didn't creep off and marry an heiress while my back was turned, so, bless his heart, I love him yet. He was killed in a night raid over Germany in 1942.

A bomb wearing a parachute fell in the wood near the Wrennery one night and hung limply in a tree. Terrible announcements were made over the Tannoy. 'This is the Commander speaking . . . this is the Commander speaking. All Wrens will immediately proceed to the Main Galley. All Wrens will proceed to the Main Galley. That is all.' All Wrens were in bed. All Wrens had their faces covered with cold cream, their hair in curlers, their feet in little shaming woolly bed-socks and their shoulders swathed in little pink bed-jackets. The scene as the Wrens streamed across country to the Main Galley was a bit like the Grand National. 'I'll lay you 4 to 3 her in the Ladye Jayne slumber helmet.'

At 3 a.m. a chap in a waterproof arrived straight out of a book by Nigel Balchin, took the sting out of the bomb and went away again and all the Wrens trailed sadly back to the Wrennery with their slumber helmets much dejected, remarking as they went, 'All I want in the world is a jar of cold cream.' No one was damaged, but enough had happened for Authority to see that Personnel ought to be Dispersed.

Immediately country houses were requisitioned all round us. To my horror I was now made Officer in Charge of The Guynd, a very pretty Georgian mansion with a portico and dainty old-fashioned kitchens. I now not only had to bicycle all round the Air Station (perimeter fifteen miles) looking at the drains (which is what Admin means), but I also had to bicycle in from The Guynd in the morning to the office and out in the evening (three and a half miles). I have always been lazy and I have always hated bicycling. (I don't mind running after a hockey ball, that's different.) Beatrice Jewell went away to some even grander job and we got a new, large, attractive aristocratic officer in charge called Monica Hudson.

Monica was the Bishop of Newcastle's cousin. She was also the cousin of the Duchess of Richmond and Gordon. She had a string of polo ponies (one of them was called Apple Annie) at Rosyth and she introduced a new note into our lives. She wore a terribly swagger boat cloak and maintained her own car. We were all scared stiff of her and spent our afternoons saying sycophanti- cally: 'Monica must have her polo.' Whereas before we had crept about slowly doing the best we could to keep all the drains in order, we now rushed madly from drain to drain so that we could get Some Time Off and Away from it All. Monica said we must. Monica was all right. She had her polo. But when the cypher officers and I got our time off we had no idea what to do with it.

Once I rode a mettlesome stallion five miles across country to call on Mrs. Lindsay Carnegie. I was terrified all the way (it couldn't have been more different from Johnny Woods and his ride) and wouldn't have gone on with it, except that Monica said she despised hackin' and huntin' and only cared for polo. Mrs. Lindsay Carnegie lived in a marvellous house called Kinblethmont where she grew real old-fashioned dark red roses and Parma violets and entertained the Free French. She also made all her own butter and cream. On this occasion, when I had got rid of the stallion, I came into the house at the same time as one of Mrs. Lindsay's Free Frenchmen. The butler announced us both together as, 'Two Free French gentlemen to see you, madam.' As I was wear- ing my W.R.N.S. monkey jacket, brown Jodhpurs, and scarlet socks, I suppose I did represent a Free Frenchman dressed *pour le sport*.

Mrs. Lindsay decided to take me out to tea with her very grand in-laws who are all related to the Queen Mother. She insisted that I change first, into a *jupe* (Mrs.

Lindsay always talked very Free French), and when I had tried on several skirts the only one that would fit belonged to 'madarm' the house-guest: a Pole, who as far as I can remember designed cathedral windows in her own country.

So we set out in Mrs. Lindsay's Lanchester. She drove, wearing very smart white gloves and all the time she looked behind her and chatted merrily, waving her hands like little white doves. I was very frightened. The Southesks lived in a splendid Scottish baronial castle with a butler and a lake with cross cold swans blown backwards before the wind, and everything. When we arrived Lady Southesk was playing chess with Lady Northesk and Lady Carnegie. A strong flavour of fantasy hung around because all the ladies were deaf. Lady Northesk even had a little black box with wires tethered to her on the table. As we approached someone screeched, 'Mind the dog!' It was a little black beast, asleep in the middle of the floor. Mrs. Lindsay tripped over a wire and the dog woke up, barking and biting, and the whole caboodle came crashing to the floor.

'How do you do?' said Lady Northesk without turning a hair. 'You must speak up now, because my box is broken.'

'Talk to me,' said Lady Southesk, 'I'm the least deaf.' She had an ear-trumpet.

I loved them all at once, but I felt a little as if I were playing Mah Jongg.

Then we were introduced to Miss Eve Guthrie

who had been painting pictures of Riabouchinska and Massine. And Lady Southesk sent someone to fetch Mr. Sandy because there was 'A Wren for him to meet in the drawing-room'. This, of course, was fatal. Sandy Carnegie was then a little boy aged three who was expecting a little brown bird. Instead he found an unattractive, well-nourished young woman dressed very unbecomingly in a Wren monkey jacket and *la joupe de madame*. Naturally he flung back his head and burst into noisy sobs. I really don't blame him.

Mrs. Lindsay was a dear and everyone loved her. Her agent, whose name I have forgotten, even lent me a lovely little 22 rifle with which I used to shoot at rabbits and rooks. I worked off a lot of genuine rage in the grounds at The Guynd firing madly across the landscape and was very lucky not to hit *a single Wren*.

Once, Mrs. Lindsay asked me to meet a box of day-old chicks for her at the station and bring them up to Kinblethmont on my bicycle. Halfway up the hill the lid of the chick box was broken and about a dozen little hopping, peeping yellow bundles scrambled out and covered me from head to foot. I felt exactly like a Walt Disney Silly Symphony. One of them even sat on the top of my head.

On another occasion Mrs. Lindsay was asked to lunch in a ship under the command of one of her Free French friends in Dundee and took me with her. We had one of the most magnificent lunches of my *life* (let alone of the austerity war) and I am not likely to forget it ever.

We had Homard à L'Americaine, Tournedos of Veal, sweets and Truffle savouries. We drank gin and French, Château Neuf du Pape ('34) with the veal and champagne with the sweet (which was made of rum) and after lunch the Commandant produced some spectacular brandy. I think it was he who told me that my favourite cousin, Captain Taprell Dorling (he writes wonderful books under the pseudonym of 'Taffrail'), was in Dundee, but I forget now.

After lunch I went back to the Air Station to play in the finals of the mixed doubles of the Local Tennis Tournament. I had an awfully good partner who used to play for Cheshire. We won the first set very quickly six-love, and then lost the second set very quickly (also six-love). I have a hazy recollection that one of our opponents was Mrs. Ellis (formerly the Senorita Lizana who was Champion of South America and one of the greatest players *I* have ever seen) but as the final set went to 24-26, and the potency of the Free French wines gradually wore off, all that I can *really* remember is that we were beaten. My partner had had a perfectly normal lunch, poor dear, and I often wonder what he thought of me.

This, I may say, is the last time I have ever *seriously* played lawn tennis (i.e. putting on a pair of white sandshoes to do so).

But Mrs. Lindsay was the only glamorous thing on my horizon. There were also terrible whist drives and country dancing sessions in gym shoes with the Black

Watch (whose business it was to protect the Air Station when Hitler landed) in the vicarage. The whist drives were only mildly impeded by the Vicar counting under his breath. He had once confided in me that he got 4d. a soul, no matter of what denomination, and I always thought he was having a quick muster of souls on the sly. Actually, he was only adding up his whist points.

Arbroath is a dim grey city, surrounded by very bleak bits of the County of Angus. It was in Arbroath that the good old abbot fastened a bell to the Inchcape Rock, where Ralph the Rover tore his hair. And Barrie was born near there in Kirriemuir, which the inhabitants think quite good enough. 'What more do you want?' the good people of Arbroath would ask. Well, alas, one wanted quite a lot more. That was why some of the W.R.N.S. ratings tore their hair like poor Sir Ralph.

We did the best we could for them, keeping the boys off the booze and the girls off the boys. But even so Chief Sick Berth attendants wandered round saying darkly, 'She told me she was a chartered massewse, but I tell you, Miss Spain, she is no chartered massewse and no lady either.' We even ran a terrible little pseudo Garrison Theatre where I dressed up as Jack Warner's little gel and the chief man cook (amid roars of applause) was Jack Warner and his bike.

In the end I got pneumonia on top of my heavy chest cold and went home to Newcastle with a Naval Sister to look after me all the way and a little bottle of brandy. Mum had a row with Monica on the telephone and told her where she could put a painting called 'After Glow' (of two pine trees and a strip of sea) that I had bought to cheer up my 'cabin' and make it a home from home. This was one of the more sinister things about the W.R.N.S. If you didn't call bedrooms 'cabins', buses 'liberty boats', the dining-room 'the ward-room', and going into Arbroath 'ashore', you were called insubordinate. I once got a terrible ticking-off for not calling Victoria Street 'ashore'.

When I recovered from the pneumonia there were several Third Officers looking at the drains in Arbroath and I was able to go away to the Lake District for a holiday.

Except that Roedean had been evacuated to an hotel in Keswick it was just as though there wasn't a war on. 'Beauty' and 'view' and boats to row and hundreds of library books to read. Mother was longing to have a look at Roedean, of course, so she invited two of the staff to come over for lunch. When they told her some mildly improper stories she was shocked beyond words and said that the tone of the school had slipped a lot since her and Sister Lily's day.

When I got home to 7 Tankerville Place I found a telegram from the Director of All the Wrens, Mrs. Laughton-Mathews. It said: 'Report immediately to DWRNS London for duties as Assistant to Press Officer.'

Chapter Five

I danced all over 7 Tankerville Place when I read this telegram. It is the dream of every would-be journalist's life to get to London, at least that little bit of it that surrounds Fleet Street. And here was Mrs. Laughton-Mathews, the Director of the Wrens, apparently making it possible for me to live in London. And she was going to *pay* me (or rather the King was) for doing it.

Surprisingly enough I can distinctly remember sitting down on my arrival in London, and instead of sending a postcard home, writing a little piece to break in a new pen. It was called, of all things, 'Can-Can in Hell' and was all about Jane Avril and La Goulue and 'a drunkard, staring in his bière' (to rhyme with 'Nini Patte en I'Air') and went on about Orpheus . . .

> When Orpheus reached this Underworld
> He did not try to leave I think
> But stayed on, Acting Sybarite
> To Pluto. While the absinthe pearled
> And I knock back my thousandth drink
> Persephone, with hair all curled,

Flashed by in ramping Can-Can whirled
Under the light . . . under the light.

As at that time Huston and José Ferrer hadn't even thought of making *Moulin Rouge* (and *I* had certainly never tasted absinthe) I can't think what I hoped I was writing about. Very odd behaviour for a Wren Officer.

To make matters slightly worse I afterwards illustrated this with a poster paint drawing of extreme decadence, and exhibited it at a Services Encouragement of Art Exhibition. Eve Atcheson a nice hairdresser and wife of a very important Insurance Broker from Harrogate bought it for ten guineas. So I can't think what *she* thought *she* was doing, either.

Next day I had a short, sharp interview with a Chief Officer Osborne. She was very kind about the whole thing. She said I was going to be Assistant to Miss Eldod, who was very over-worked, and that she was sorry that living in London was so expensive and there was no room for me in W.R.N.S. Quarters halfway up Haverstock Hill. I said thank you very much, ma'am, and I would find somewhere to live for myself, and thank you very much, ma'am, all over again. I was so glad to have escaped from Arbroath I was prepared to sleep on a bench on the embankment.

'Well,' she said, 'I had better put you down for the London allowance then.'

It was in this way that I learnt I was going to be paid £19 a month plus £10 to pay my rent, food and replacements of little bits of uniform that wore out. Looking back on it it seems very small. At the time it was unheard of richness. I had managed to save ever such a lot when I was being ill in Newcastle.

'Well, then,' said Chief Officer Osborne, 'you had better meet Miss Eldod, then.' And she took me along various corridors in Great Smith Street to a pleasant office with lattice-work windows where Miss Eldod worked with two shorthand typists called Moffat and Wade.

'Have you found me two photogenic Wrens for that Yardley's ad yet, lass?' said Miss Eldod as the door swung open. 'Oh. So this is my new assistant?'

Miss Eldod, a most remarkable woman whose father was a Rabbi and whose mother was the spit and image of the Countess of Oxford and Asquith, regarded me with the firm friendly gaze of Edgar Bergen's famous doll Charlie McCarthy. I'm sorry to say I stared back. I'd never met a Press Officer before.

'Got somewhere to live?' said Miss Eldod, as the door swung to behind Chief Officer Osborne.

'Oh yes, ma'am,' I said fervently. I had, too. I was living in Penn Court, in the middle of the Cromwell Road at the rate of four and a half guineas a week and I had just realized that I would only have £5 a month left to buy new collars with. I needed a new cocked hat, too.

'Good.' Miss Eldod turned away and clasped her hands behind her back like Napoleon. She was in her shirt-sleeves and she kept her cuffs clean by a remarkable apparatus of elastic that clipped above the elbows. 'Very expensive place, London, lass. Well now. Your first job is this Wren film. Heard all about it, of course?'

I hadn't heard a word, but I could see that Miss Eldod would be mortally offended if I admitted it. So:

'Ooh, rather, yes, ma'am,' I said, nervously.

'Good. Then your business will be to introduce the very important journalists to the very important Wren Officers and tick off this list and see that everyone is happy. Agreed?'

'Agreed,' I echoed, nervously, since it seemed to be expected of me. And out I went to the film showing. It was terrifying. I had a great long list of names in my hand: the Deputy Director Welfare, the Deputy Director Manning, the Staff Officer, the Superintendent the Nore. Facing them were magic names of magazines like *Vogue* and *Picture Post* and *Illustrated* and *Harper's Bazaar*. I didn't know the Wren Officers, I didn't know the journalists. How on earth would I ever introduce them? My head reeled . . .

By now I was in the cinema and the first ugly rush of journalists was upon me. 'Who are you?' I said, firmly gripping my little list.

'Sybil Chaloner, Editor of *Modern Woman*,' said a terribly well-dressed and charming lady.

'Then you must certainly meet Miss Angela Goodenough, our Deputy Director Welfare,' said I, very firmly.

Miss Goodenough was the only V.I.P. that I knew by sight. She was round and gentle and very, very feminine and she deeply disapproved of ladies playing at sailors.

When the W.R.N.S. started just before the war Miss Goodenough, then head of all the women civil servants in the Admiralty, was sent along to help Mrs. Laughton-Mathews with Civil Service procedure. To this day I can't make out how they persuaded her to put on uniform. She was a dear. She kept a little collection of cacti on her desk. As she talked on the telephone she would stab at the cacti with a pin, over and over again. This was very unnerving, particularly if she was in a rage – which did happen occasionally because she obviously thought a great many of the things that went on supremely silly. I got the impression that as she stabbed a cactus, she disembowelled an enemy. But apart from her cacti, Miss Goodenough was calm and collected and she had a great sense of humour. When she died three years later, it was as though I had lost a relation I was particularly proud of.

She got along very well with Miss Chaloner, I am thankful to say, and by then I had recognized Lady Cholmondeley, who swept in the door with a little retinue of exciting people like Commander Tony Kimmins, who had directed the film, Noël Coward, Clemence Dane (who wrote some of the words for it), and Richard Addinsell, who wrote the music. Lady Cholmondeley is one of the most arresting characters I have ever encountered in my life. She is so beautiful that she made the reputation of several portrait painters at once. In those days she wore her hair blue to match her Wren stripes and she had cuff-links of lapis lazuli to match her hair. She was Sybil Sassoon before she married Lord Rocksavage: and by the time she was the Staff Officer attached to W.R.N.S. Headquarters, he had become the Marquess of Cholmondeley – 'A bad music-hall joke name,' she said herself about this. A great wit, she was always disconcerting me by her choice of words on great Naval occasions. '*Must* I wear my gloves, Spain?' she said to me once at a passing-out parade of W.R.N.S. Officer Cadets. 'They make my hands look like little brown fins.'

Lady Cholmondeley's light laugh and very considerable wit concealed a first-class legal mind and a frightening capacity for work. Her minutes on Admiralty dockets were very surprising. 'Head of N. is adopting his usual hedgehog attitude,' she wrote once and stunned us all. She seemed to have several teeny weeny Fiats about the size of the average portable gramophone and she drove herself to work in them, surrounded by gawping spectators. Her house in Kensington Palace Gardens was crammed with art treasures and marble halls: and once when I went there to tea I was introduced to Sir Osbert Sitwell. (He took one look at the little collection of Wrens, I may say, and fled.) Lady Cholmondeley was a tower of strength on the Press Party for showing the film. She dealt with journalists as though they were rather gauche debutantes: and they were so stunned at meeting Noël Coward and Tony Kimmins and all the rest of them that there wasn't another peep out of them about 'where was the drink?'

Then the lights mercifully went out and we all saw

the film. Miss Eldod, who had been greatly concerned in its conception, was on tenterhooks throughout. Leading Wren Gregory, who played the main part, marching from pillar to post, was photographed all over again from a hundred different angles for a new recruiting poster, and we escaped back to Miss Eldod's office where Miss Eldod's chum, Miss Nan Robinson, was waiting to give me the once-over.

Miss Nan Robinson, who is now Catering Officer for the entire BBC, was in those days Catering Officer for the grocery firm of J. Sainsbury. She lived with Miss Eldod in a bungalow in Woldingham and a small, comfortable flat in Great Smith Street. They were both very kind. Miss Eldod had been told that I had left Arbroath because I was ill and she didn't see why she should have an assistant with incipient asthma, ready to break down on her before she could even say 'Nan Robinson'. However, 'Nannybell' (as Miss Eldod called her) said I was perfectly healthy. She also said I had probably more energy than most people, and we then had a good chat about ITMA and Arthur Askey's combs. I never had a single day's illness working in the W.R.N.S. Press Office. I was far too happy.

Our business was (occasionally) to write features about W.R.N.S. activities and feed them out to the Press. More often, however, news would break about Wrens and we would then have to restrain the National Press from saying anything that would affect our dignity. The new Wren hat was a matter of vital National importance, so was Tropical Kit. And most frequently of all we had to traipse around the length and breadth of the Commands with various eager beavery journalists who wanted to write up 'Women at War at Close Quarters'. There were also advertising agencies (like the Yardley's people) who wanted to feature Wrens in advertisements and were anxious to get the details right, so that the public didn't snigger at them. Looking back through my Press cutting book, which emerged again in the Press Office where Miss Eldod called it a 'guard book', I find feature after feature about the Wrens and their activities, all written up in the same ghastly dignified language, just like advertising copy for Gracious Living: 'The words On His Majesty's Service live again as the Wren dispatch-riders roar about their business.'

In between times we were involved in various highly social functions. The Director of the W.R.N.S. played darts and table tennis against Mrs. Knox, at that time Commandant of the A.T.S. Mrs. Laughton-Mathews defeated Mrs. Knox so crushingly that Mrs. Knox said, with a wry smile, that she had never touched a dart or table tennis bat before in her life. This encounter was designed to improve inter-service relations.

I know I was fascinated by my two opposite numbers in the A.T.S. and the W.A.A.F. Barbara Beauchamp was assistant to the A.T.S. Press Officer. Barbara was a sight to behold in her khaki with militant red staff tabs and glistening Sam Browne. She had written several novels and possessed every sort of Fleet Street qualification. So did Jenny Nicholson of the W.A.A.F., who in addition to being Charles (or Robert, I never can remember which) Graves's daughter, knew everybody (*but* everybody) from Carol Reed to the late Bobby Newton. She is now a very important foreign correspondent for the *Spectator* and *Picture Post*. I felt very provincial indeed beside these two and also beside Pamela Frankau, who was (Miss Eldod confided in me) 'Just wrestling with her conscience a bit, you know, lass, before going to enlist as a private. Stout work, for someone who has held down the income in advertising she has. Agreed?' Miss Frankau was employed by the Ministry of Food.

We met Miss Frankau once a week at a hair-raising radio programme, rather like *Woman's Hour*. It ran for one hour from 8 p.m. to 9 p.m. on the Light Service and involved all three services, hundreds of film stars, Carroll Gibbons's orchestra and Janet Quigley, once Editor of *Woman's Hour* but now even more important. There was a quiz where W.R.N.S., A.T.S., and W.A.A.F. battled weekly. Everyone took this very seriously indeed, as it reflected the high intelligence quota of the average Wren rating and made the public very anxious to enlist with us. Janet Quigley is one of the really considerable brains in broadcasting. That she is still my friend is a miracle. How our friendship survived *Women at War* I simply do not know.

Miss Frankau was Ballerina Assoluta of the Programme. She had a sort of Auntie Flossie's personal problems corner when, in deep, gruff tones, she would give such smashing pieces of advice as, *'So you've fallen in love with a married man, have you? Don't worry. Everybody does at some time or another.'* From time to time Janet said that she wanted more queries about the services and Miss Eldod and Barbara Beauchamp and Jenny Nicholson and I would cook up something that didn't cause too much harm. Miss Frankau used to sit in a London flat working out the answers for these things, wearing a towel round her head.

Miss Frankau was very impressive. She had written at least four books and an autobiography called *I Find Four People*. I read them all and particularly enjoyed the autobiography which had all sorts of good jokes in it. At one of these performances of *Women at War* I met Dolly Frankau, Miss Frankau's mother. After that, whenever I wanted a giggle I went round to Dolly. She lived in Ashley Court Hotel at the top of Queen's Gate and she had some truly remarkable stories to tell.

Dolly Frankau, née Dorothea Drummond Black, was a pretty, frivolous woman whose father had been editor of the *Observer*. When I met her she was always gay and well dressed in spite of bombs and arthritis. She had married Gilbert, Julia Frankau's son (she said), because she wanted clever children. Julia Frankau's pen name was Frank Danby and she immortalized Dolly and her attitude to life in the bestselling Edwardian romance, *The Heart of a Child*. As a matter of fact, Dolly also said she married Gilbert because he had once rushed to the corner of a street in carpet slippers to fetch her a cab, crying as he went, 'A brave man can do anything.' Gilbert Frankau married twice after Dolly, and one day we were passing Harrods where the usual enormous display of 'the new book by Gilbert Frankau' was announced with streamers and posters, saying, 'There is but one Gilbert Frankau'.

'Ah,' said Dolly, without bitterness, 'but there are many *Mrs*. Gilbert Frankaus.'

Once my mother joined Dolly and Miss Frankau for dinner. Miss Frankau said, indicating me in my flashing blue stripes and gold buttons, 'I was writing novels before this little squit was born or thought of.'

'Did you say "squit" or —?" replied Mother, with an amiable smile.

Even Dolly was amazed by this. Dolly was full of good stories about Rebecca West. How they were motoring together through the South of France and Dolly, looking out of the window at the winding Route Nationale behind her, said, 'Ooh, do look, Rebecca, that's the road we've just come along . . .' and Rebecca replied, 'Promise me one thing, Dolly, never become an explorer.'

Rebecca, Dolly said, lived on the top of Orchard Court. And one day Dolly went to supper to see three fires raging, all in different parts of London.

'Why, Rebecca,' said Dolly, 'you must feel like God.'

'But such a much nicer nature, don't you think ?' said Rebecca.

Rebecca had forgotten this when I met her ten years later, but we both remembered with joy how fond we had been of Dolly.

Dolly wasn't surprised when Miss Frankau went away into the Army and became Major Frankau of the Educational Department. But I was very surprised when I asked Miss Frankau to inscribe my copy of *I Find Four People*. She was having lunch with Eldod and me at the time and she drew out her pen and poised it. What would she write? We craned eagerly forward to see . . . Would it be 'Best Wishes' or 'Cordial Good Wishes' or simply 'Yours sincerely'? She hardly paused, then she wrote:

> I from the 30s quietly observe
> The insolence and nerve
> Of one who at the age of 24
> Can say 'So what' to War
> And turn, for fun
> To the things that I have done.
> Heir to confusion's throne,
> You do not walk alone
> The Prince of these
> Light kingdoms of a legendary peace
> Was not so very different after all
> When she was young and knew
> A thing or two. Like you.

Miss Eldod and I were stunned *(a)* at the sentiment which we couldn't quite follow and *(b)* by the speed of composition, which was nothing short of miraculous. We talked it over afterwards and decided that obviously she must be a genius. Agreed.

Women at War was a formidable programme. I

remember finding myself with Clifford Mollison by the microphone. I was supposed to be interviewing him.

'Tell me, Captain,' I said. 'Do you have much to *do* with *Women at War*?'

'You *can't* say that, Nancy,' said the producer. 'It's filthy.'

So I changed my tone of voice. At rehearsal I was quite all right, but on transmission I upset everyone by saying, plummily, 'Tell me, Captain Mollison, do you come into much *contact* with *Women at War*?' Which really gave the people in Penge something to complain about.

I did a lot of unpaid broadcasting at this time. I suppose someone thought it was good propaganda. I usually represented the W.R.N.S. in two-way transatlantic telephone calls and that kind of thing. Once I disgraced a programme by saying, 'I hope to emerge from the war *big* with experience.'

In my spare time I saw a lot of Cecil McGivern, who was buzzing about collecting material for *Mulberry Harbour, Junction X,* and *Bomb Doors Open*. Whenever he saw me he said, 'We really must have another *Fell Top*.'

It was about this time I discovered that all my savings had been swallowed up and I was in an advanced stage of insolvency. I moved from cheaper digs to cheaper digs until I was living in Earl's Court, but it didn't help a bit. Most of the Wren Officers at W.R.N.S. Headquarters (by now moved to Queen Anne's Mansions and a grander thing altogether) were just managing to live on their pay. But they didn't meet the electrifying companions that the Assistant to the Press Officer met. And they weren't expected to pay for their rounds of drinks as the Assistant to the Press Officer was. It was just like being out with the West Hartlepool Lacrosse Ladies again, except that this time there was no remedy. I wasn't allowed to make money on the side as a journalist in wartime and the BBC expected one to do everything free . . . And, of course, I had fallen in love again with a young man called Steven. It didn't surprise me a bit when he married someone else.

Eventually the struggle became too much and I explained what had happened in words of two syllables to Chief Officer Osborne. She sighed. She had obviously heard all this about how expensive London was before. She was kind, but vague, and arranged for me to live in the W.R.N.S. Quarters in England's Lane. I shared a 'cabin' with Angela Sanderson, Gladys Young's niece, and we had a good grumble about everything, particularly about how they used only proper actresses on the radio nowadays. But it didn't solve the situation. Worse, for all the other Wren Officers were sneering at me (I thought) because I wasn't helping in the war effort. Actually it was Miss Frankau's clever little poem about how I was saying 'So what?' to war that rankled, but I wasn't going to tell anyone that. Miss Eldod and I had our first, last, and only row. I said I was sick and tired of tarting around with journalists and I wanted to do something that was of some *use*. Miss Eldod went as red as a turkey cock and I rushed childishly out to tell Miss Goodenough.

'Oh, what a pity,' said Miss Goodenough, stabbing at her cacti. 'Well, perhaps you had better be a recruiting officer.'

And that was that. I was. Immediately, I became solvent again.

I now worked with Lady Carter and Mrs. Woodhouse in a nice big, airy office overlooking the Green Park. Lady Carter, who now lives in the next street to mine, Clareville Grove, said, 'Call me Button,' which was alarming, until I realized it was her nickname.

To begin with this was a very happy, placid time, with a proper lunch hour when a Third Officer could walk happily in St. James's Park, furtively eating sandwiches out of paper bags on warm September days, brushing crumbs from uniform skirts before creeping back, a little late, to the office.

I love Autumn in London; that autumn was particularly good. The marvellous smell of burning leaves even stirred the nostrils in the office, where one sat all afternoon, interviewing. Bombs fell, searchlights striped the night skies, the bombardment was a perpetual firework display. But in the streets and squares and parks pink late-flowering geraniums blazed and leaves still drifted down, quite unaware that there was a war on.

And when the Spring came we knew that the London lilac at least would still be immortal.

Chapter Six

The Recruiting Department was very grand, seeing as how it was all the time in contact with the general public. Recruiting Officers were so terribly smart to look at that it hurt: some of them wore almost royal blue uniform monkey jackets and *all* of them wore black satin ties bought at Hope Brothers. I joined a circus of Third Officers whose business it was to whip around the London medical boards, making brief notes on the character and personality of candidates in the teeny weeny space provided on the interview form. People who engrave the Lord's Prayer on the head of a pin in their spare time might well take lessons from a W.R.N.S. Recruiting Officer. Contrary to general belief, however, all successful candidates for the Service were not *(a)* titled or *(b)* the Last First Sea Lord's second cousin once removed.

Writing a short, sharp personal note in a small space is one of the best exercises for a would-be journalist or novelist I have ever encountered. *You* try noting the salient points of some of *your* friends in a space one inch by three and see how you get on. You will be amazed at how few words you must use; and how important these words become.

My companions in the circus were tall, red-haired Third Officer Martha Keeling, wife of the Conservative M.P. for Twickenham, who still thought in terms of the effect everything she did had on her husband's constituents. Her husband she referred to as 'K'. She was an Old Roedeanian, but she kept it a dark secret. Then there was Third Officer Michal James, who wrote dank, savage, gloomy little short stories that often appeared in the wartime miscellanies. She was very clever. Third Officer Ross, a glamour-girl, who had once actually taught me P.T. at a school in Norfolk, and Third Officer Gamier, who knew lots of sophisticated songs and carried on long, sophisticated telephone conversations with gentlemen friends.

We were benevolently administered and kept in order by Lady 'Call Me Button' Carter and Mrs. Woodhouse, who had been there recruiting right from 3 September 1939. On the whole there were no hysterics in this department, except for the fearful day when one of the recruiting officers went quietly round the bend and left an enormous package of interview slips and medical reports (Highly Confidential) in a slow train from Victoria to Croydon.

This recruiting was really very hard physical labour. A Medical Board would be called at Acton, Whipps Cross, Ealing, or South Croydon for 10 a.m. To achieve these far-flung posts, carrying all these dangerous Confidential papers in a black dispatch-case, heavily embossed G.R. in gold (Miss Eldod had had one of these, but she only

74

used it to carry milk bottles), we had to start as early as 7.30 a.m. We had about ten interviews with potential Wrens (already unnerved by giving intimate specimens, having glands examined, telling the doctor *all* about their previous illnesses) before lunch. We had about ten interviews after. Lunch was snatched in a Cosy Café at Whipps Cross, a call in for car-men at Acton, Sally Lunne's Tea Shoppe at Croydon, and the Granville at Ealing. But if you think this was quite hard work and hard fare it was Paradise compared to the 7th circle of Hell travelled weekly by the T.R.O.

The Travelling Recruiting Officer was a first-class girl called Second Officer Vivien Akerman. She whizzed weekly round the Midlands from Manchester to Derby, sending up at least twenty-four excellent sets of papers a week. We all pitied her. I thought she was a heroine but I pitied her. So imagine my hurt astonishment when I was suddenly summoned to a terribly high-up conference indeed where all the Deputy Directors and Lady Cholmondeley turned towards me with eyes of flame. All the other recruiting officers had compassionate reasons for remaining in London (such as their constituents and so on, I thought bitterly). And the 5th Sea Lord had said we were going to do all Fleet Air Arm Maintenance by woman power. And there wasn't enough Woman Power to go round. And we had to double our quota of W.R.N.S. intake in about two months. And we had a Gentlemen's Agreement with the Ministry of Labour that we wouldn't advertise our requirements because the

W.R.N.S. was so much more popular than the A.T.S. or W.A.A.F.

'So it all depends on you, Spain,' they said, smiting me on the shoulder. 'Go out into the highways and by-ways, Spain,' they said. 'Go it, Spain. Make speeches at youth hostels and Y.W.C.A.s and Girl Guide Companies, Spain. And Roedean? Oh yes, Roedean girls make splendid Wrens. Go and make a speech at Roedean, Spain. Tell 'em we want W.R.N.S., what? And perhaps if you try really hard you will get us some jolly Good Types for W.R.N.S., Spain.'

'Yes, ma'am,' I said. 'Yes, ma'am.' And echo answered, 'Three bags full.'

With a sinking heart, but feeling for the first time for months that I was really winning the war, I caught the night train to Manchester from Euston. It was the first of a series of such interminable journeys. No wonder I started to write a book on my knee, in all these first class compartments. It was called *Thank You, Nelson* and it was all about being a lorry driver in North Shields. Ah, how desirable that carefree lorry driving life in North Shields now seemed . . .

Meanwhile the Cabinet and the Ministry of Labour, as though they were playing some infernal panel game with me, passed the National Service Acts of 1942 when women were conscripted for the first time in our history. (This fearful bit of news passed quite unnoticed in the general hurly-burly, like the licensing laws in World War One, and no one has since dared to say that woman's place is in the home.) As of this date the W.R.N.S. were only allowed to recruit those young women of Britain under the age of twenty four who had school certificate with a credit in Maths *or* were prepared to serve as cooks or stewards.

This meant that the 'interview' with its thumbnail sketch of character now became of vital importance. One had somehow to 'put it over' that a good girl who was prepared to 'cook or stew' (this was what we wittily called it, we recruiting officers) could become anything. A recruiting officer, even . . .

Medical Boards which had before contained a mere 34 bodies swelled until we saw and absorbed into the Service 80 or 120 young ladies a day. And a preliminary weeding went on at various dispersal points in Birmingham, Derby, Manchester, Leeds, Sheffield, and Bradford, I remember once entering a room at Aston Six-Ways, Birmingham, which was entirely wedged with would-be Wrens. It was only by making those who would cook or stew sit down; and by asking those with a School Certificate to make a queue against 'that wall'; that I could even get enough space to set up my little table. A touch of madness was added to my life because quite a lot of these preliminary interviews took place in football pavilions. I well remember a tricky interview with a fairly obvious local prostitute taking a turn for the worse, when a locker containing a pair of football boots burst open under my desk. We were in the Sheffield Wednesday pavilion at the time . . .

My clerk, or writer, as the Navy persists in calling it, was a magnificent girl with 'good strong legs', as my interview chits now continually said. She needed them. Wren Parker had a round, amiable face, glasses, and a marvellous calm manner. She booked me seats on trains, trotted happily from Sheffield to Derby and back, carrying two hundredweights of papers in each hand, never lost a train, and never forgot to book 'accommodation'. An extraordinarily efficient girl, Parker. I wonder where she is now?

She was splendidly co-operative and always used to tip me off about those medical sheets with 'Pediculosis plus, plus, plus' inscribed on them. This meant that the candidate was verminous: and I got very good marks from the Intake Depot if I occasionally said 'Rather grubby' on my form. This warned them against un-Wrensmanlike qualities. This reputation for sagacity and second sight was entirely due to Parker's sleight-of-hand with the (highly confidential) medical papers.

Second Officer Akerman, who also curiously enough had strong legs and glasses and a round face, received me in the Manchester Office. There was a heavy fog in Manchester and I well remember how Akerman gave the impression of instant flight.

'Right, Spain,' she said, twitchily. 'Well, I'm just off to Leeds. Best read all you can on my desk, that'll give you the form. *You've* got to go to Sheffield tomorrow. Sorry. Sheffield's hell. The approved lodgings for W.R.N.S. are in the top right-hand drawer. Parker will show you. They're best, cheapest, bye-bye . . .'

And she fled, just catching her train by the skin of her teeth.

Of course I was lucky, compared with Akerman. I had a day to find somewhere to live, a day to go to the theatre. I saw the first night of *Present Laughter*, with Noël Coward himself in the cast. This year when I was having lunch with Noël, I asked him the title, saying was it *Careless Rapture*?

'That, dear,' he said, coming the old acid on me, 'is the title of a musical comedy by a Mister Ivor Novello.'

I found digs with a lady called Leech in Stockport who told me all about my Aunt Margaret's childhood. Aunt Margaret had married Uncle Walter Smiles, the M.P. with the magnificent bowels, and we had always been terrified of her, but this cosy insight into her happy adolescence at the Golf Club at Sale was a revelation to me. Next day there I was whizzing 'over the bridge to Sheffield'. I had a big blue book of Admiralty Warrants which empowered me to issue myself with a railway ticket to any mainline station in England. Strangely enough, I often found myself quite near London on Fridays, when I would rush up to see a revue called *Rise Above It,* with Hermione Baddeley and Hermione Gingold. I saw this revue eight times.

For I found life in Manchester, Leeds, Birmingham, Derby, Bradford, a truly awful thing. Had I ever stayed in one of these splendid cities for more than a night I am sure I should have grown very, very fond of them.

But I couldn't help noticing that all the brass knockers on the doors were warped by soot and smog, and as I went round my circuit at exactly the same speed as the General Release of Bing Crosby in *White Christmas,* I couldn't even look for any escape in the cinema.

All the conversation I ever had was with the 4,556 candidates per week. So smart repartee and badinage was limited to, 'Have you got your School Certificate? With a credit in Maths?' and 'Are you a good cook?' In the evening (as the Deputy Directors had told me I must) I made public appearances in schools, youth clubs, and youth groups. To add to the nightmare the Chief Officer Administration in London changed; and in the change my application to go from 'Pay and living in the W.R.N.S. Quarters' to 'Pay plus Travelling plus hard-lying money' went through a crack in the floor. I was in Leeds in the Great Northern Hotel when my first cheque bounced with the maximum of publicity and fuss. Very fortunately for me, Christian Fenwick, Q.C., now a Northern Circuit Judge, a friend of our father's, was staying in the hotel, too. He explained how I was my father's daughter and so it couldn't possibly be my fault, which was very nice of him. But it took a month to sort out this error and, while it was being sorted out, I had to sleep in Y.W.C.A.s, in theatrical lodgings, and on park benches. (What I like best about the Admiralty is the way it never says it is sorry.) At the end of this I had a shocking cold on the chest and my voice, so valuable for making speeches in schools and for interviewing the candidates, had gone entirely.

But still there were gay times. There was the amazing old girl in charge of theatrical digs who told me all about how she had been the Earl of Egremont's mistress and how two footmen used to come around with baskets of chickens and bottles of champagne. There was North-ampton Y.W.C.A. where I shared a room with an old lady of eighty who died in the night. And there was the speech I made at Roedean (in sincere recollection of Mlle Baguet) in *English*. They roared with laughter all the way through, so I can't think what went wrong at Roedean.

I can't think what went wrong at Bradford either, where I appeared at a famous convent school where the prototype of G. K. Chesterton's Father Brown had been padre. The Mother Superior, known as Sister Mary Immaculate, introduced me by saying, 'As you can see, children, the W.R.N.S. have much in common with us Nuns. We both wear black woollen stockings.'

But all these things came to an end in Sheffield when I was billed to speak to a Youth Organization. I arrived in the black-out at a pleasant Church Hall where a fire blazed and an ancient caretaker bobbed and there was a harmonium in the corner. Now, I have always been a sucker for a harmonium. I can only play the one tune, 'Love Is the Sweetest Thing', and I started it, pedalling away with Vox Humana, Diapason and all, full out. I was just coming to the middle bit that I can't quite play, when I thought to look over my shoulder. The chairs that had been laid out for my audience were now filled up with would-be Wrens. And their heads were all bowed forward in silent prayer . . .

Chapter Seven

Sheffield was the end. After this episode I couldn't speak at all, so I telegraphed for an immediate replacement and somehow carried on interviewing by signs until the replacement arrived. This was the time at which I made the surprising discovery that the basis of all interviewing is contained in five questions:

1. Do you have any brothers and sisters?
2. Why do you want to be a Wren?
3. What do you do in your spare time?
4. Why did you leave your last job?
5. What is your greatest ambition or what are you going to do after the war?

In those days I wrote these questions on a sheet of paper and pushed it at the candidate who then replied, eagerly and at some length. I wrote down their replies. Some of my best interviews were done this way and to tell the truth, this formula also works perfectly well with Clare Luce (for Wren read Ambassador), Colette, the Duke of Windsor, Gracie Fields, and anyone else you care to mention.

After a couple of days of this highly nervous work, my

replacement arrived, took one look at Parker, staggering under the bundles of papers, remarked, 'I didn't get a commission just to do heavy manual work,' collapsed into a chair and burst into tears. I was sorry about this, but there was nothing I could do. I wrote myself one last lovely lingering warrant from Manchester to London.

I arrived in London with a heavy chest cold and the manuscript of *Thank You, Nelson* tucked under one arm. It now weighed quite a lot, but not as much as those infernal papers. As usual, there was no room in W.R.N.S. Quarters, so Second Officer Betty Gidden very kindly let me share her bed-sitting-room-cum-kitchenette in Randolph Gardens. She had two beautiful married sisters called Janice and Tommy with whom we used to go and stay at weekends. Betty was an angel. In addition to being in charge of the W.R.N.S. Recruiting London Area (which was jolly hard work) she also typed the MS. of *Thank You, Nelson* in the evenings. She also told me to take out all swear words and some bits that I had written that went too far. Then we bound it up in a smart dark blue overcoat and I staggered off with it to the various publishers. I was of the opinion that it was unlucky to take taxis to publishers, and I still am. I walked everywhere on my two flat black feet. 'Stagger' is a better word for my progress, really. For the heavy chest cold that had robbed me of my voice was really a streptococcus throat. People were dying of strep throat all round me like flies. But I didn't think I was *dying* exactly. I just couldn't walk upstairs, that was all. This was a nice quiet time emotionally, because I was far too exhausted to fall in love. I had a sentimental friendship instead with a darling man called David in The Brigade (of Guards). He had been very annoyed with me for saying, 'What Brigade? The Fire Brigade?'

I still judge publishers by their waiting-rooms and by the letters they wrote to me turning down *Thank You, Nelson*. Collins were very kind, and they shared very chic premises with Chatto and Windus because they had been bombed out. Hodder and Stoughton I never saw, because they said the book 'read like old history and their readers' reports were not enthusiastic'. The Cresset Press surprisingly said 'it should sell well'. Macmillan thought it 'unsuitable'. Robert Hale and Harrap were gayer about it. I even saw Robert Hale himself, a terribly kind gentleman with a gold ring on his tie, and *he* said if I could get him some paper from the Admiralty he would publish it. When I suggested this to Commander Kenderine of Admiralty Press Division, I thought he was going to hit me. Harrap said much the same thing; but I already knew the answer to this one, so didn't bother Commander Kenderdine again. Eventually Joe Gaute of Harrap's (and Harrap had a terribly chic waiting-room filled with educational books and fumed oak) gave me a letter to Cherry Kearton of Jarrolds. And the dynamic Walter Hutchinson, who in those days was still alive, controlling the destinies of his sixty-odd different firms, suddenly pounced on it and said he wanted it for *his* list. So I was sent for by Mrs. Webb at 47 Princes Gate, S.W.7.

I was (and still am) mad about Mrs. Webb. She is shorter than me, cosy and with a very determined jaw-line. She is also outspoken to the point of no return. But even with her plain speaking it took me five minutes gawping before I grasped the fact that she didn't want any paper, that her readers thought the book was quite good (Mrs. Webb doesn't read all the books she publishes, which gives her great strength) and that she actually wanted to *publish* it. When I had been picked up from the sodden heap into which my Wrens' great-coat had dragged me she asked what was I writing now? And I said, limply, 'A detective story. What a pity you don't publish those, too.'

'Indeed we do,' said Mrs. Webb, and as I craned over her shoulder she wrote on her pad in a firm, legible hand, '10 per cent up to 5,000' and 'Option on next two works of fiction'.

Mrs. Webb has been my *alter mater,* guide, philosopher, and friend for eleven years. She is a wonderful woman. She has paid my electric light, gas, and telephone bills without a murmur. She has paid the rent. She even turned me into an AUTHOR (that is what it said in the contract, 'hereinafter called the Author').

I arrived at 47 Princes Gate in a crumpled heap, but the effect of my conversation with Mrs. Webb was electric. I danced down to the Albert Hall and telephoned Betty Gidden and First Officer Kay Jones from the telephone-box on the corner, under the blind stone eye of Dr. Livingstone, whose effigy glares out for ever across Kensington Gardens. I also telephoned David. I have always loved that corner, ever since . . .

If it hadn't been for these two (Gidden and Jones) I should certainly have kicked the bucket around now. I must explain First Officer Jones, who is now the mother of my godchild. She was First Officer in Charge of all recruiting and applications, known collectively as 'R.A.'. She really did look after me. I think Jones and Gidden were the first people I had met since my own family who knew that I couldn't really help behaving like a sort of Mickey Mouse in uniform.

Kay Jones is still one of my dear friends. A very good organizer indeed, she is married to a man called Colin, whom she always described in those days as the most private soldier in the army. (Colin was colour-blind and very dashing. And when he saw the opportunity of buying a hotel on mortgage after the war, he took it with both fists. But even Kay's organizing ability couldn't stand up to the hex there was on the place. That and both Jones's kindness of heart. They even let me live there, at a purely nominal rent until I recovered my health . . . but that is another story.) These were still the days when First Officer Jones and Second Officer Gidden and I used to rush up to Trafalgar Square in buses to lunch at the National Gallery Canteen and listen to Myra Hess playing the piano. All the people who served food in the Gallery Canteen were famous. There was Poppy Richard and Schiaperelli's ex-London manager, and they all ladled out simply fabulous vegetarian dishes. After months and months of kippers and Welsh rarebit, I slowly felt strength returning. That and the gaiety of having *Thank You, Nelson* accepted by a real live publisher.

Betty Gidden afterwards married her cousin Noel Boyte and went to live in South Africa. But in those days when I could only speak in a whisper, the kindness of these two girls was beyond belief. They even fixed a perfectly good job for me where I had to do quite a lot of hard paper work, so didn't feel a passenger. I was actually promoted to Second Officer as I sat doing it. I had to reorganize the filing and postal system in use at W.R.N.S. Headquarters. Kay said she had got sick of being summoned by Lady Cholmondeley to her beautiful office with the fitted lapis lazuli coloured carpet and have her start, 'When I was having tea with the King yesterday, Jones, he was asking about this housemaid who is trying to join the Wrens . . . Now, surely, we can't *already* have lost her papers? You know what Royalty is, Jones, like a dog with a bone?' Kay quite agreed that Royalty was just like a dog with a bone and told me whatever ghastly system I devised in Recruiting Applications Filing (hereinafter referred to as R.A. Filing) I must never, never lose one of the housemaids from Buckingham Palace. I said I wouldn't . . .

Nor must I lose such papers as those belonging to Lady Patricia Mountbatten, Lavender Herbert (A. P. Herbert's daughter), Elvira Laughton-Mathews (the Director's daughter), Rosemary Elton (Lord Elton's daughter), and so on . . . All these glamorous people knew Lady Cholmondeley far too well and she used to pinch hit for them in no uncertain manner, inquiring into their progress almost daily. In the end I got a sort of sixth-sense as to which of her chums was passing through R.A. Filing and I used to answer Lady Cholmondeley's bell at the run, gripping all the papers of all the celebrities to my bosom as I went. I even devised a system of important little red markers, which said IF YOU LOSE THIS SET OF PAPERS BELONGING TO

ELVIRA LAUGHTON-MATHEWS OR
LADY PATRICIA MOUNTBATTEN OR
LAVENDER HERBERT

YOU WILL BE DRUMMED OUT OF THE W.R.N.S., SO I WARN *YOU*. I always nicked off these red ticklers by the time I arrived at Lady Cholmondeley's door, so I don't think she knew what system I used.

To help me in my dark design of not losing any papers I had twelve energetic Wren ratings filling up cards. I was a terribly bad administrator. And I think the only recorded case of Mutiny in the Wrennery took place under my command. I still can't remember *why* they mutinied, or what it was all about, but I can remember howls of ''Tain't fair' and 'Second Officer Spain is a meanie' and 'Won't work', and so on. My Wrens longed to set me adrift in an open boat. But even in the mutiny we still kept a grip on the papers. This was because we had a clear-eyed expert in the department called Leading Wren Hennessy.

Sheilah Hennessy was one of the junior members of that spectacular Three Star Family who have been making Cognac in Cognac for generations. Sheilah was a great friend of Beatrice Lillie and heaven knows who else. She was terribly rich. She used to make us goggle with her light-hearted tales of her brother Bobby who was on Mountbatten's staff and very grand indeed. She could play the accordion like a master and cook like a *cordon bleu*. She could speak at least five languages and had certainly been educated at St. James's, Malvern, a very swagger school. But although otherwise most magnificently unprepared for the long littleness of Life in the Wrens, she took an intense Gossiper's Interest in People and she could therefore find papers of which everybody else had despaired. Once she found a whole bundle of them stuffed behind a cupboard, where some wicked, wicked Wren had put them.

Sheilah always wore stiff rustling petticoats, large quantities of religious medals, bracelets and rings (all strictly forbidden by W.R.N.S. procedure and discipline), so she was always being kicked around by the Chief Officer Administration. Particularly was Sheilah always being tortured for her failure to attend Pay Parade. Sheilah confided in me that she had a real neurotic horror of standing about in lines in a crowd, so whenever Pay Parade loomed up I would arrange for her to be running a little message for me somewhere else. I was always getting ticked off about this. 'Your Wrens, Spain,' they said, glaring at me, 'are the most insubordinate Wrens in the whole Service, Spain.'

Once I recall I was called on to the carpet by the Chief Officer Admin for my own bad behaviour. The Chief Officer said I had been seen smoking in St. James's Park Tube Station. A Bad Thing, this. A Disgrace to the Service. How could I expect Hennessy to behave (and your other ratings too, Spain) if you do things like this in public . . .

'But, ma'am,' I said, and I was ever so upset, 'I don't smoke.'

'Don't smoke? Spain, Spain,' more in sorrow than in anger, 'I saw you with my own eyes . . .'

Now we were getting down to it.

'What did I look like?' I asked, fascinated.

It turned out that I had been holding a railway ticket in my mouth while waiting for a train with briefcases in each hand.

Yet there were all sorts of compensations to those odd and dangerous days when bombs fell, when people we knew and liked were suddenly killed, maimed, burned, buried under dust and heaps of rubble. I never knew if I left someone at Admiralty Arch, say, and walked across St. James's Park to my office, that there might not come a chuffing noise, a gliding silence: and a crash. And I might never see or speak to my friend again.

Was it this danger in the air that made me so aware of

my physical surroundings? I know I suddenly embarked upon a sort of second adolescence of composition. Having finished *Thank You, Nelson* I found myself beginning to write verse again in Buzz Bomb time. And I know lots of people who did the same sort of thing:

When they play Sousa in St. James's Park
In sunlight I can watch the blossoms fall
With white and crimson signature to mark
Dead Spring, while Summer marches up the Mall . . .
Gay Summer: red and blue, and bright with brass
Carelessly shakes the dust from everything.
Yet does not notice, beaten in the grass,
Flowers we trampled on the grave of Spring.

In spite of the glamour and the gold; the eating new rare foods (such as smoked salmon), the flood of sentimental London songs, the discovery of little pubs on summer evenings where 'the last of the German Embassy champagne' could be drunk at little tables, I must admit this was also a time of strain. Everyone's nerves were wearing thin and everyone was getting bored with the war. Under stress the nicest people began to say and do the strangest things.

One lovely Sunday morning, for example, I was leaning out of my office window listening to the Guards singing hymns in their chapel below. It was a glorious day and the noise rising to God from the chapel was an extremely jolly one:

> O, come let us sing unto the Lord
> Let us heartily rejoice in the strength of
>   His salvation . . .

sang the Coldstream Guards, and I thought, 'How beautiful,' and went back to my work.

Almost immediately one of those bloody buzz-bombs chuff-chuffed overhead, cut out and began gliding. I thought it would fall in the Park so I didn't bother to duck. But it fell on the Chapel.

I hope I, too, die singing hymns. But it was a terrible moment.

The air was filled with rubble and broken glass. The office slowly collapsed all round me. The typewriter disappeared into a heap of broken plaster. And then the stout Edwardian walls of Queen Anne's Mansions crumbled. A great crack ran slowly across the ceiling, which as slowly fell on me, together with two chairs and a table from the Small Vessels Pool upstairs. There was no door left, so I walked out through one of the holes, treading daintily on the shifting dunes of tinkling broken glass that now surrounded me like filthy, dirty snow. I was quite unhurt, but horribly shocked and very grubby indeed. As I emerged into the corridor, I saw a great rift of sunlight where a wall used to be and a big American soldier in a crash helmet darting amongst the rubble. 'Hey,' I said.

'There's girls hurt along there,' said he, pointing.

As misfortune would have it I was the only Officer on

duty. Everybody else, including Miss Goodenough, the Deputy Director, was at a church parade in Kensington. There was a terrible screaming noise (as a rabbit makes when it is wounded) coming from a department called Officers' Appointments. So I went along what was left of the corridor. The damage was considerable.

Several poor Wrens had had their faces cut to pieces with glass . . . I could actually see the white of the bone gristle in one girl's nose. We did all that we could to reassure her and stop her bleeding. But our rescue work was much impeded by the astonishing fact that we couldn't open the First Aid kits, because they were locked up and the Wren Officer with the keys was on church parade in Kensington. So I tore up the tail of my white shirt as a bandage.

An ambulance came and everything was more or less under control, except for the pools of blood, when Miss Goodenough came in from the church parade.

'Keep a stiff upper lip, Spain,' she said.

I slept for forty-eight hours after this . . . and when I arrived back at the office I was immediately summoned to the presence by Lady Cholmondeley. She waved one exquisite Persian hand at two men in waterproofs.

'These gentlemen are from Scotland Yard,' she said. 'They want you to tell them if you saw any unauthorized person in the building when the bomb fell on the chapel.'

I stood and stared. I had really only seen blood and broken glass and pressure-points and rubble. All I could remember were those men's voices singing, 'O sing unto the Lord with praise, enter into His courts with thanksgiving.' Some of my emotion must have shown in my face. Lady Cholmondeley went straight on, very quickly.

'Yes, indeed, Spain, I quite agree. But it seems that the Director has had all her silver photograph frames and cigarette-boxes and blotters stolen. And I have lost several bottles of scent that I kept in this drawer, very foolishly as I now admit, and while I don't want my Chanel Number 3 and my Molyneux Number 5, the Director *does* want her silver photograph frames . . .'

Well, I remembered the American then: but I still think that when a bomb falls on a building and a Second Officer meets a character saying, 'There's girls hurt down there,' that on the whole the Second Officer would think American G.I.s were bent rather on rescue work than looting?

After I had washed the rubble out of my hair, I didn't confide in anyone how much this had shocked me. Indeed, First Officer Jones and Second Officer Gidden were so clever at looking after me that I didn't realize it myself. But one day, to my absurd anger, I was kicked up like a partridge from my nice cosy desk. (I had taken to writing my detective story for Mrs. Webb under cover of it.) I was summoned to the usual high-up conference of Blue Blood. It was in this disrespectful manner that we spoke of our superior officers during the war. *We* said they spent their entire time saying, 'Actually . . .' which is, of course, quite untrue.

95

'Spain,' they said, slapping me on the back, 'you must go to Framewood Manor, Stoke Poges, Bucks, and take up duties there as Second Officer in charge of a section of W.R.N.S. Officer Cadets in training.'

'Ma'am?' I said, shuffling my feet in dumb insolence and rebellion.

'Now, now, Spain,' they said, brightly beginning that old-pep-talk-designed-to-make-the-girls-think-that-they-are-winning-the-war. 'Now, now, Spain. All you'll have to do is lecture, Spain, that's all. You had such wonderful results with your lectures in the Midlands, didn't you, Spain?'

Union Jacks now blinded me and I nodded. Almost, I was winning the war again, but not quite.

'Well, now, Spain. Lectures. You know the kind of thing, Spain . . .'

'But I shall miss my August Bank Holiday,' I thought rebelliously. I had planned to spend it in bed, writing my detective story. Aloud I said, 'Yes, ma'am, yes, ma'am,' and some echo somewhere replied briskly, 'Three bags full.'

Chapter Eight

I arrived at Framewood Manor, Stoke Poges, on August Bank Holiday, 1944, with a heavy chest cold. I left it three months later with the same heavy chest cold and attacks of asthma that no one understood. In a station wagon I was sent to The Hospital for Women, Vincent Square, just off the Vauxhall Bridge Road, where I found lots of people suffering from the same war weariness. Second Officer Ann Toulmin, for example, and Lady Jane Douglas and a very rebellious rating from Lime-house and Stepney called Joan Werner Laurie who had appendicitis. But I didn't meet Joan until later. First I had put in some truly astonishing work at Framewood Manor. The lectures I had to give, for example. Communications throughout the Fleet, Life in a W.R.N.S. Unit, Commands and Their Administration. The Admiralty and What it Means to Me . . .

Framewood Manor was a big red-brick mansion enlivened by sunken gardens and bulrushes and sloping lawns where cadets drilled one another, and a great big room with stained-glass windows where once a month the 'passing out' cadets did their concert. To this day I have never quite grasped how the ability to do a comic turn or sing 'I'm Going to See You Today' in a high, faint soprano should qualify one to be an officer and a gentlewoman. Still, there it is. Once a month, too, the 'passing out' cadets would take their Officer to the Bull, Gerrards Cross, on the main Oxford Road, and get mildly intoxicated.

The lectures were given in various draughty Nissen huts scattered round the grounds under dripping trees. I well remember the first lecture I gave to my thirty buttoned-up-faced cadets. It was entitled, Communications Throughout the Fleet.

As I started off towards the Nissen hut under the trees I studied the notes that my predecessor had handed me. These consisted of a half-sheet of crumpled writing-paper with the words (1) Telephone (2) Teleprinter (3) Telegraph (4) Semaphore (5) Morse (6) P/L. What could it mean? As I trotted on, looking very dangerous lashed into my khaki regulation gas-mask, I brooded about all the Communications I had seen since I was in the Navy. I knew a lot of rude stories about Bunting Tossers (as they are called). How I wished I had learnt typing. For if I had learnt to type at thirty words a minute I would have been a cypher officer and would know all about communications, instead of an Admin girl with a vast knowledge of the drainage seepage system at use in H.M. Naval Air Stations. Then I was in the hut and the young ladies were glaring up at me with their bright eyes. And to my dawning horror I saw on every navy blue arm the little bright blue crossed flags that denotes a communications rating. This meant that until they became Cypher Officers they had all been employed in some capacity as Signallers themselves.

'Good morning,' I barked, as well as my streptococcus throat would let me.

'Good morning,' said they, rising to their feet *en masse*.

'Please sit down,' I said. As well as the cadets, the hut was equipped with a blackboard, two leaky oil stoves, and two broken pieces of chalk. I seized the chalk firmly and wrote on the blackboard: 'Messages known as signals are handed on in the fleet by the following means: (1) Telephone (2) Teleprinter . . .' When I got to (6) P/L, I pointed the chalk at a Chief Petty Officer Signalling Wren in the front row (I suppose I suppose I should call her a Chief Yeoman of Signals.) She sprang to attention.

'Ma'am!' she said.

'You can tell the class what P/L means,' I said, gruffly.

'Plain Language, ma'am,' said this girl, without a quiver.

I was *not* a success as a Wren Cadet Instructor. I never could get over the basic home-truth that the cadets knew so very much more about Life in the W.R.N.S. than I did and I expect this showed clearly in my face. I was very glad indeed to escape to the peace and quiet of Vincent Square where I wrote silly clerihews about the Officers I had left behind me.

First Officer Harboard
Doesn't know port from starboard

She's old enough. She ought
To know starboard from port.

I shall never forget the first glorious moment in Vincent Square when I got into bed and lay down flat. First Officer Jones came to see me, too, bringing packets of asthma powders called Felsol. Jones saved my life as usual. For when I decided that I had had enough of Framewood Manor I simply locked all my asthma remedies in a drawer and didn't take them out. (I often wonder who found them and what they did with them.) I adore being in hospital. All that food and all that rest and everyone waiting on me hand and foot and taking such an *interest* in my chest. There were three fabulous V.A.D.s (Voluntary Aid Detachments), too, who used to sweep the floor and bully me. They were very easy to bribe. All you had to do was to tell their fortunes . . .

One day a real live fortune-teller came to see Second Officer Toulmin, who shared my 'cabin', and after she had gone I rang the bell. Eventually a V.A.D. came, very short-tempered.

'What do you want?' she said.

'Nothing,' I said. 'There's been a fortune-teller here and you've missed her.'

Oh, the excitement. The V.A.D.s swarmed like seagulls after that fortune-teller, eventually finding her telling the fortune of a Wren Officer with the measles. Afterwards they came back to apologize for not answering the bell. 'But how were we to know?' they said, plaintively. 'We thought you only wanted a bed-pan.'

Maureen was top V.A.D. Maureen was very pretty with round blue eyes and she was a great one for the boys and the easy monologue. It went something like this, with variations:

'Well, me and my friend, dear, from Hither Green, who's in the W.A.A.F.s, we got into the train the other night and we started a little flirtation with some Americans. Nothing wrong, dear, we were just smiling at them and they were saying had we seen Westminster Abbey? When a woman started in creating. She said, "You girls, you've nothing better to do than encourage them, you should be ashamed, you're nothing but a lot of tarts and those badges," (and she pointed at the Americans' chests dear, you know where the ribbons are), "they don't mean a thing. And I lost a boy this year," she said, "and I think you Yanks should go home." Well *that* was the wrong thing to say, it seems, for one of these boys had the Congressional Medal (what is like our V.C., dear) and he was ever so upset . . .

'So I turned on her and I said, "Well, madam, I'm sorry about your boy but any amount of calling names won't bring him back, madam, and if you went on like that at him before he went away, madam, nagging and creating, perhaps he isn't dead at all but only hiding." And then my friend and me were so upset we got out and it was only Praed Street for Paddington and we had forty minutes to wait for the next train.'

Yes, life in Vincent Square, apart from late night

asthmatic sessions, was easily the best bit of my war service as an officer. All day long I sat up in bed, lashed
into my pram by a very good white enamel bed-table,
typing Mrs. Webb's detective story. In the afternoons I
was sometimes allowed 'ashore'. And occasionally my
life was enlivened by visits to various London hospitals
where I was lectured on by medical students. 'What
exactly are you complaining of?' these embryo doctors
in the house would say, tapping away at my magnificently crepitating chest. I always did my best to put on a
good performance for them, wheezing and carrying on
alarmingly. I was tested for allergies. I was given nemb-
utal, soneril, luminal. I was tormented with essence of
horse, cat, dog, fish, flesh, fowl, and good red herring.
I reacted violently to everything. It only remained for
Sir Alexander (Penicillin) Fleming to open my mouth
and peer into my throat. (No one else had thought
of doing this.) He said he'd never seen such a mess in
his life.

'Get rid of that tooth,' he said. 'Clear up this strep
infection and *then* let's talk about allergies.'

I went back to Vincent Square from him full of hope.
I even had a wonderful row with the Chief Officer in
charge of Officers' Appointments and had a good sob
on First Officer Jones, who was then expecting my
god-daughter Sheilah. Then I went back to bed to
write various letters To Whom it Concerned, proving
that I had been a full-bosomed athlete in 1959, but the
Admiralty had killed me. I even wrote one of those

surprising little bits of verse about it. This one came out sonnet-shape:

> The ship's clock of serene and polished face
> Has marked a year or two of service time.
> Five years since I reported at the Base
> And found companionways were hard to climb.
> That clock avoids things not inside its powers.
> And so it only marks the happy hours.
>
> Reason assures me that there was despair,
> Bewilderment, hurt vanity and pain:
> That five years ticking unrecorded there.
> And so, in spite of reason, once again,
> Somehow I heat the bugle in my heart,
> As the sun sinks, and as the ensign dips.
> After today I shall not make a part
> Of the intolerable loveliness of ships.

I got at least 10s. 6d. for this from Tommy Woodroofe who was then editing *The Ditty Box*.

Strangely enough the Admiralty admitted that it had 'aggravated' me with war service. It then awarded me an 80 per cent disability pension of £2 a week and a gratuity of £75. So I became a Naval Pensioner. I had an advance of £50 for *Thank You, Nelson* and £50 for the detective story *Poison in Play*. On this slender capital I now determined to set up as an Author.

Chapter Nine

This has been a mad life so far, as you can see. Fortunately, too, there is little danger of it ever getting any saner. Nineteen-forty-five for the whole world came in with hope that the war in Europe might soon be over. For me it also began daintily with a Hutchinson advertisement in *The Times* announcing that a dear little book called *Thank You, Nelson* would shortly appear. It shared this column with James Agate, Alan Houghton Broderick and (a strange name to me) James Wedgwood Drawbell. I remember the parcel with the six presentation copies of the book arriving and how I opened it, crazy with excitement, in the kitchen, cutting my finger to the bone as I cut the string. For some reason I then showered the kitchen with pepper. Mother was really very nice about it considering how expensive pepper was in 1945.

When I arrived back in London, duly discharged as a Naval Pensioner from the W.R.N.S., I had the same bed-sitting room and kitchen at 4 Randolph Gardens, Kilburn, where Betty Gidden and I had so often seen the buzz-bombs blow overhead like crazy flying-fish. On King's Cross platform, on the W. H. Smith & Sons bookstall, copy upon navy blue and pale blue copy of *Thank You, Nelson* glared out in all their unsold horror. Oh dear, I thought, gripping my dispatch case and typewriter for dear life: nothing will sell that book except a miracle.

Fortunately for me the miracle was just around the corner.

I didn't know any reviewers; I didn't know any literary editors. My mind was taken up with the possibility of writing the life of Mrs. Beeton. It seemed silly to be so closely related to so noble and famous a character and not to do something about it. So I went to stay with Aunt Amy, her last surviving sister, in Colchester.

It was hellish cold in Colchester and Aunt Amy, although she was at least eighty, was a great little old walker. Through drifts and drifts of snow she marched me, round and round, her dear (but very cold) little house. She was terribly kind to me, she told me all sorts of enchanting stories about her jealousy of Isabella Beeton, her beautiful, successful sister, but the walks were too much for poor old Pensioner Spain. By the time I caught my train back to Liverpool Street (where I once again stared gloomily at unsold copies of *Thank You, Nelson*) I had the flu on top of my bronchitis and felt very ill . . . It was 27 January, twenty-two days after Hutchinson's fine, noble, expensive spate of advertising.

Even as I tottered up the steps of Randolph Gardens the telephone rang. A bored voice told me, '*Sunday Chronicle* wants you. Just a moment, I'll put you through now.'

And then a more excited voice said, 'Just a moment, Mr. Paterson wants you.' Then a pleasant Scottish Canadian voice said, 'Hullo, Nancy Spain. You've written a book, I see. Could you come into the office this afternoon? Our Mr. Drawbell wants to see you.' And I was left thinking, 'Fancy.'

I had no idea who J. W. Drawbell *was*. To me he was simply a name in an advertisement. But in spite of the flu and my reeling head I presented myself at tea-time at Kemsley House.

This is a great big building like a red brick box situated roughly in the Gray's Inn Road. Various sergeants with gold-encrusted, black patent leather bands across their chests waved me onwards and upwards. Office boys of varying degrees of height and efficiency whizzed me along corridors. I remembered the old newspaper adage, 'Don't kick the office boy in the teeth. He may offer you a job one day,' and I didn't kick the office boy in the teeth. Eventually we arrived in a large electrically lit office where a very nice man called Bob Paterson prepared me for the great Mister Drawbell. By now I was becoming used to the idea that Mr. Drawbell was something very, very special indeed. And when I reached the Presence I was ready to be *amazed*. I was. Mr. Drawbell looked exactly like the late Leslie Howard, for a start, and he conducted his interview with me by flinging a photograph at me and saying, what did I think of it? The girl in the picture had one eye much larger than the other, but apart from this she was quite pretty. So I said she was probably short-sighted in one eye and this would be difficult for her. She might not know when she was making a fool of herself in social gatherings. (I am short-sighted in one eye myself and this applies to me, too.) Whether this struck Mr. Drawbell as profound or not I couldn't say, but he then suggested I should go to Wales and interview this girl's mother.

'Certainly not,' I said. (Colchester had been quite enough for me for one week.) 'Who is she, anyway?' I very nearly said, 'And who are you?' as well. Fortunately I didn't as it was now becoming increasingly obvious that Mr. D. was the Editor of the *Sunday Chronicle*. The girl in the photograph turned out to be rather a famous murderess. So then I was quite glad I had said I didn't want to go to Wales. 'Anyway,' I said, 'what makes you think I'd be any good at that sort of thing?'

'But you've just written this book,' said Mr. Drawbell, bewildered, '*Thank You, Nelson*. Judging by this review here it's just our Monica's cup of tea.'

'And who is Monica?' I said. That really finished him.

'Why, *Monica Dickens*,' he said. Then he quickly changed the subject. 'This really is a very good review,' he said, waving a big sheet of newspaper at me. I craned eagerly forward, much preferring it to photographs of murderesses. 'Oh no,' said Mr. Drawbell, friskily, 'you buy yourself your own copy of the *Sunday Times*.' And he snatched away the sheet.

'Well, *that's* all right,' I said. 'I always buy the *Sunday Times,* anyway.' And I escaped . . . out of the Gray's Inn

Road, up the Edgware Road, all the way to my little bed-sitting-room through the snow.

The next day was Sunday and it was still snowing. Naturally no newspapers were delivered to Randolph Gardens, so I went out, down to Marble Arch to buy one. When I got off the bus the wind at Marble Arch corner was so strong and so icy that I couldn't even open the paper. Struggling, cursing, with real tears in my eyes, I eventually got round the corner and into the Cumberland where I ordered breakfast. Over the dried eggs I searched for the book reviews. The review was so big I couldn't find it at first. But there eventually I read, over and over again, the sort of review that you get once in a lifetime, that really ought to be set to music. 'A Wren's-eye view of the Proper Navy,' it said, by A. A. Milne. I promptly burst into tears.

Two huge Americans sitting at the table leant over and said, 'What's the matter, little girl?' I just sobbed. 'Must have lost someone near and dear to her,' they said, soothingly.

'No-o-ooo,' I wailed. 'I'm just so *happy,* that's all.'

I had every reason to be happy. So had Hutchinson. That review of A. A. Milne's sold out the whole of the first edition and the whole of the second. Indeed, I knew the book must be a success when the Chief Officer Administration at W.R.N.S. Headquarters said, 'The book was very disappointing after the review.'

In the odd literary existence in which I now found myself, I wrote 1,000 words a day, rain or fine. And when I wrote to A. A. Milne and thanked him for his wonderful review he wrote back and suggested we should meet.

'You will have to work up an enthusiasm for gardens first,' he wrote. 'Nothing annoys my wife (and me too) so much as seeing a visitor step heavily back on to a clump of aubretia behind her, ignore the tulips in front of her, and ask if we have been to many theatres lately.'

I wasn't at all sure what aubretia *was*, so, very frightened indeed, I set off for Cotchford Farm in the midst of Sussex in a slow green train from Victoria.

It was a glorious summer's day and the Milnes were perfectly right about their garden. All the flowers had come triumphantly into bloom at the same instant, and there was an enormous pink tree like a feather duster over the front door. It looked as though it had been worked in cross-stitch on a tea-cosy until you came closer and saw that the whole thing was real. A. A. Milne and his wife were adorable too.

She called him Blue and certainly he had the bluest eyes I have ever seen in a human being. Matching up to them were his blazer, that summer sky, his socks, his handkerchief and quite large patches of the garden. And everywhere there were relics of Winnie-the-Pooh. Daphne Milne told me that there was a first edition of *The House at Pooh Corner* under the sundial and we drank sherry poured out of a large blown glass orange reproduction of Piglet. The sherry came out of its mouth.

After lunch A. A. Milne took me to the bottom of the garden and sat, hunched up slightly on a wooden seat, biting on a pipe and gazing gravely out over a stretch of very lush landscape indeed. At the bottom of a plashy-looking meadow a string of cows meandered slowly by. I asked if they were his cows (after all, the house was called Cotchford Farm). No, they weren't, but practically everything else in sight was. Some trees, for example, had been bought with £100 given by an American for the manuscript of a fairy play called *The Ivory Door*. (I have an idea that the manuscript of *Winnie-the-Pooh* fetched £500.)

'Gosh,' I said, full of awe, thinking what wonderful handwriting he must have.

A. A. Milne was a first-class companion. He talked a lot about the importance of light verse and what an excellent thing it was for discipline to drop into it from time to time. 'Light verse writing maketh a very exact man.' He said that the important thing in writing was to keep 'oneself' out of the way of the reader. 'Otherwise the perspiration shows.' And he said that the telephone was a monstrous intrusion on privacy. At the time I was more than a little shocked by this, but now that my telephone rings frequently I know what he meant. C. S. Calverley was the chap to imitate, he said. Calverley, who wrote *Fly Leaves* and *Verses* and *Translations*.

> Butter and eggs
> And a pound of cheese

The dog said nothing
But scratched for fleas,

he said, ruminatively. And I, poor uneducated dolt, thought he had taken leave of his senses. Thank goodness I had the instinct to keep my mouth shut, and the sense to ask him for the titles of the books. When I got back to London I even went gravely to the British Museum and read them. He went on mildly talking, this enchanting blue-eyed man, all that precious summer's afternoon, distilling the wisdom of years into a casual conversation.

'Any creative writer's criticism of another is no more than a statement of the obvious truth that he would have written the book differently himself,' he told me. 'All writers write to please themselves,' he said. 'No sensible author wants anything but praise.' He even said that if I collaborated with Jane Austen I would do better. (Poor Miss Austen . . .) 'When Christopher Robin was a very small boy,' said A. A. Milne, a propos of one of the more lurid passages in *Thank You, Nelson*, 'he was talking rather wildly and not "going too well" with his nurse. And he suddenly stopped, looked up at her slightly disapproving face and said, a little apprehensively (and God knows why), "Were I too Spanish?"'

He said a lot more, that darling man, but I have forgotten the details. It has fused, shimmering into the golden light of that magic afternoon in the sun.

Yet I can remember every detail of the lunch. Hot

boiled salmon, peas, new potatoes, asparagus, straw-
berries and cream. A real cricketer's, schoolboy's or
schoolgirl's lunch. There is no better lunch in the world.
No wonder I nearly fell asleep beside him, pretending
so hard to be a better little girl and a better little writer
than I was.

Then Daphne Milne took me round the garden and
I did my level best not to walk on aubretia or fail to
admire the roses. She told me how wonderful it was for
me to have published a book like *Thank You, Nelson* at
the age of twenty-five. 'It's wonderful,' she said, 'to be
so young and have it all beginning.' I thought it was
much more wonderful for A. A. Milne to have reviewed
it and I said so. Then she told me what had happened
when the parcel arrived from the *Sunday Times*.

'Blue was livid. He took the book and he threw
it across the room. "A war book, by a girl," he said.
"Leonard Russell must be mad,"' (Leonard Russell is the
Literary Editor of the *Sunday Times*.) But then Daphne
picked it up. And, bless her heart, she couldn't put it
down. And she called out to A. A. Milne, 'Blue, you
must read this. It's all about nothing but I can't stop reading it.' And so he read it and wrote his review. 'But *Blue*
said,' she ended, accusingly, 'you were only interested
in writing and it was useless to show you the house and
garden.' (Strange, this . . . people and their houses are far
more interesting to me now than writing about them.)
And she talked a little, a very little, about Christopher
Robin, whom she called 'Moon', and she pointed at a

window that marked his room. He was still in the Army then and was expected to go to Cambridge to become a Senior Wrangler. No one thought he would one day keep the Harbour Bookshop at Dartmouth and write witty letters to the *Bookseller.*

There were certainly little hot scones and strawberry jam for tea. And then I went back to London in another long, winding, green, slow caterpillar of a train. When I went through Victoria Station with my arms full of blossom it was as though I had come from another world. And my bed-sitting-room was transformed for weeks after by the glory of the blossom.

The Milnes were nice to me. So was Esther McCracken, whom I got to know very well at this time. When Esther became a famous playwright, writing plays like *Quiet Wedding, Quiet Weekend,* and *No Medals,* she forsook the North Regional Drama Repertory Company and I inherited the heroine's parts that she had played. She it was, for example, who *should* have said, 'I never hear a great ship put out to sea but my heart does not go aboard her for unknown lands.'

Esther was born Esther Armstrong in 1902. She went to the Brown School (otherwise the Central High School) where she won the cricket-ball throwing competition in the sports every year. She is small, red-haired, and full of electricity. When she sat on the Brains Trust with Professor Joad, he said, 'Have you read Aristotle's *Poetics?*' and she retorted, 'Do I look like it?' Frankly, she doesn't. She has an attractive speaking voice with a slight crack in it. 'Got by imitating a man one wet weekend,' she explains, briskly. She married at twenty-four – a famous Northern Rugby footballer and accountant, Angus McCracken. By him she had one red-haired daughter and one mouse-coloured, Jane and Heather.

You may remember L. Guildford of Chapter 3: the man who was Station Director at the Newcastle-on-Tyne BBC Studios? Week after week he encouraged Esther to pour out plays under the titles of *The Willing Spirit, Behind the Lace Curtains, The Old Watch, The Salmon Poachers* . . . and many, many more. Then they were performed by the Newcastle Radio Rep. Some of these later burst on a delighted British Public under other titles like *Quiet Weekend, Living Room,* and *Quiet Wedding.* It was at this point that a startled Angus McCracken bought his wife a typewriter and watched her, amazed, as she pounded away with two fingers. (Hitherto she had written slowly in longhand in the backs of old school exercise books.) Esther hated typing. 'I got so sick of it that I shortened lots of speeches.' When *No Medals* was in rehearsal the producer chided many players for *adding* words to the 'divine economy' of the McCracken lines.

Then the war came. Esther went into the W.R.N.S. Angus, now a Lieutenant-Colonel, went overseas. And after a few years of heart-rending loneliness, Esther learnt that he had died of wounds in Italy. Eventually she wrote *No Medals*, probably her best, most moving, play. It was the outcome of those strange war years when

Esther, all alone in the midst of the Northumbrian moors at Rothbury, Rothley or Scotsgap, would prop a pastry board on her knees and write, write, write until two in the morning, once Heather and Jane were safely in bed.

It is pretty startling that such entertaining writing can be done as a result of extreme unhappiness.

Esther got married again. She married Mungo Campbell, a shipowner with a face like a very attractive Highland bull. And of course she was never unhappy again. *And she was unable to write a single solitary line . . .*

But she found time to be perturbed by *my* literary development. She approved whole-heartedly of *Thank You, Nelson* and, later, of the biography of Mrs. Beeton. Like A. A. Milne, who complained of them constantly, she found the detective stories (which I now wrote twice yearly in my efforts to keep the wolf away) so much waste of time. How right she was. Dear Esther. She is the only English writer who could come to terms with that formidable woman Betty (*The Egg and I*) Macdonald and beat her at her own game. Esther, like a sundial, only marks the sunny hours . . .

I remember one perfectly splendid evening in a Westminster hall when Esther represented the English Theatre along with all the rank, file, and nobility of the British Literary World. The occasion was to try to explain to Our Soviet Buddies (as they then were) what the British trends had been as a result of the war. The Literary World was represented by Louis MacNeice, John Lehmann,

Professor Ifor Evans, Arthur Bryant, and Elizabeth (or Marjorie, no one was ever sure which) Bowen.

Neither Esther, Mungo, nor myself had ever been able to find any 'trend' in anything. What was a 'trend', for a start? We looked it up in the dictionary and it said 'bend in a certain direction'. As the whole of English Literature has always seemed to me much like a field where one may roll about in the sun and scratch one's back if one wishes, I wasn't much help to Esther. I said it didn't matter to anyone very much except possibly *(a)* writers and *(b)* children taking their School Certificate. Esther said perhaps, but *she* was a writer and she had a very pretty dress to wear and nothing to say. In the end I spouted a lot of tripe about emotion recollected in tranquillity . . . and Esther sighed deeply. 'Perhaps something will come to me on the inspiration of the moment,' she said.

Well, the great day dawned. Mungo and I sat there in Row 2 while the flower of Eng. Lit. declaimed its beliefs about the growth of first-class *rapportage* since the war. They were circumspect, they paid one another little compliments. But they were very, very dull. Then Esther, her hair like scarlet flame, pounced up to represent the English Theatre. She was quite magnificent. Supported by rumbling cheers and thumping of boots from the gallery she said, 'It is the playwrights of today who are at fault! It is because *we* write so badly that nothing is happening in the English Theatre!'

I think Louis MacNeice got up to ask, sneeringly, 'If

Miss McCracken included herself in this superb gener-
alization?' and I would swear that Esther snapped back,
'Yes, and you too.'

But never mind that. In the face of this wonderful bit
of plain language the atmosphere of cant and humbug
disappeared like a snow-drift in May.

'What a fighter she is,' sighed Mungo beside me,
clasping and unclasping his hands as our Soviet chums
looked nervous, bewildered, and slightly upset.

On the morning of 8 May 1945, the war in Europe
came to an end. V.E. Day was astounding. It hit me
a blow between the eyes, like everybody else. I took
the day off from all this literary life and went to Kew
Gardens. I had never been there before and it was a most
lovely, loving May day. It was while I was wandering in
the sheltered valleys around the pagoda that I came on
a magnolia tree. I was totally unprepared for it. No one
had ever warned me about magnolia trees.

There it stood, against the piercingly, achingly blue
sky, each branch thick with wonderful white wax
blossoms. Some of the flowers were open, like hands
reaching up to heaven. Some were still buds, but thick
and spiky and beautiful like a celestial candle flame. I
nearly wept, I know, just because it was V.E. Day and
the world was safe for magnolia trees.

And when I got home that night, tired and sunburnt
and happy, and let myself into my bed-sitting-room,
all the lights went up outside and all through Kilburn's
shabby, happy streets people began fox-trotting and

Knees Up Mother Browning. On that warm and magic night they danced under the dapple of plane trees. And as I sat very quiet and listened to a radiogram blaring out 'The fundamental things apply, as time goes by', I could also hear the roar of the great crowds, like surf, like the sea, beating round Buckingham Palace to the House of Commons, calling, calling for the King and Queen.

Oh, London. What a night *that* was.

Chapter Ten

My party with the Milnes wasn't the only country excursion that summer. My cousin Mayson, Great Aunt Beeton's younger son, lived at Walton-on-Thames in a splendid Victorian mansion called Uplands or Highlands or Woodlands, or something like that. Azaleas grew everywhere in a bursting profusion. I didn't just go there for the day. I stayed the night. It was a little bit of a strain, just as it had been at Aunt Amy's, chiefly because I wanted to behave so well. But I loved Sir Mayson Beeton. Even when he addressed his letters to me 2nd Officer Spicer, W.R.N.S. or, more boldly, Miss Nancy Price, he was a wonder. (And Lady Cynthia Asquith once sent me an actual cheque payable to Nancy Price, so it is easy to get muddled.) He was in his eightieth year when we first met. For no reason at all (because there are no real blood ties) he was so absurdly like my grandmother in the face that I felt I was with *her,* as we wandered through that sunny garden, talking, talking, talking about his mother.

Mayson stooped a little when I met him, but he was still a small fine-looking man, dapper and handsome. His smile was so sweet that one couldn't find him forbidding.

With a touchingly boyish grin he showed me letters from every famous writer in the world asking if they might write a biography of Mrs. Beeton. Then he said he liked *Thank You, Nelson* and thought it 'a good young effort'. Also, he had been fond of my grandmother, 'Dearest Lucy', as he called her. So I could, with his blessing, make an attempt at the first authorized biography.

Mayson had been at Magdalen with the Northcliffe boys and he named his only son William Harmsworth Beeton because of his *Daily Mail* friends. When this son was killed in a motorcycling accident it was an awful thing. But he still had his three lovely daughters; all married. Marjorie, Audrie, and Belle. All three were at Roedean with my mother and they, too, were mad about the old School.

Mayson couldn't remember his mother. She died when Mayson was fourteen days old. But he remembered with pride his father, Sam Beeton. He was certainly most eager that a biography should be written of *him*. Mayson had collected together all the letters that his father had written his mother. He had read extensively and made notes about all sorts of aspects of Nineteenth-century Publishing. He had hoped, I think, to write his book about his mother himself in his retirement from his Empire Building, but old age and grief at the death of his wife, Lady Beeton, had caught him unawares and left him no energy. For everything was ready for a biographer, most beautifully annotated in his neat historian's hand. I still have the letter where he said he would be delighted to let me try and write the book that he had planned. To this day I don't know why he had picked me out of all the world.

He made me free of his library, with all the first editions of the Beeton Books. They glared forth at me behind glass doors, so beautifully over-bound in their coloured calf and half-calf. He opened heavy tin uniform cases filled with faded, brittle love-letters, exquisitely translated from their formal Victorian hand by his daughter Belle. 'She's the only one of my daughters who gives a damn about her grandmother,' he growled. This was wildly untrue. Both Marjorie and Audrie were fascinated by their illustrious ancestor. But Belle had been free and able to work with her father, so he *knew* of her passion. Naturally he fired me with his enthusiasm. Soon I was as pious about Auntie Beeton as everybody else in the house.

I first read Mrs. Beeton's love-letters and diaries in the dim summer sunset light of Cousin Mayson's spare room. There were linen blinds on the windows and Venetian blinds and outside the Surrey woods were ready to stifle one with sweetness. The diaries were the only things that Belle had *not* transcribed. They were mostly written in pencil, pencil that had smudged and run over the years – only the last few of which had been spent in the big japanned boxes on Mayson's billiard table. They were precious little books, describing trips to Paris and Killarney and there in that faintly lavendered and ever so slightly stuffy spare bedroom, I confirmed the decision that had begun so coldly with Aunt Amy. I would go in search of my great aunt. I couldn't sleep a wink.

It took me four years of research in the most unlikely places before I finished *Mrs. Beeton and Her Husband* to my satisfaction and sent it to the publisher. By then Cousin Mayson had died and the text had to be approved for press by Belle and Audrie and Marjorie. Then the publishers wanted the whole thing rewritten. Writing biographies is an expensive business and should not be lightly undertaken.

I researched in Bexhill where my Great Great Grandpapa Dorling had started off as a jobbing stationer. I researched on the Epsom downs, where he eventually arrived one day on a white pony having ridden over with his printing press on his saddle front. I researched in Epsom itself where Dorling later opened a stationer's shop and where his son, Henry Dorling, the King of Epsom, built the first Grandstand for the Races. This old stand was pulled down in 1926 when there was a new Grandstand declared open with a mighty family party. Mother never tired of telling me how she had driven her new motor-car to the Oaks on this occasion 'without being able to reverse'.

Only Aunt Amy remembered running about in the saloons and playing tig in the paddock. And now Aunt Amy died. Only my grandmother could have remembered everything and now she was dead, too. Soon there were no relations left of that generation either, to tell any more wonderful inaccurate family legends. But when the book came out I had fabulous family fan mail. Lots of people wrote to me and told stories. But none of them had ever seen Aunt Isabella . . . that Madame X of the Victorian Age, that music-hall joke, that poor sad, beautiful lady who died so young. And who never said 'Take 12 Eggs', or 'First Catch Your Hare', and who certainly didn't stuff Mr. Beeton like a Strasbourg goose. If you want the tragic history of Great Aunt Beeton you will find it all in another book than this, *Mrs. Beeton and Her Husband,* which retitled *The Beeton Story,* has now been republished by Ward, Lock.

To do this back-breaking job of research work really well it was necessary to have good health and at least £200. It was no use going to Foreign Parts to examine the race-track at Auteuil and then lying around in bed all day wheezing. That was why I decided to go to Bexhill where the air, if not champagne, is at least cider and where my friends the Joneses had now acquired their hotel. 'Why Bexhill?' asked A. A. Milne, as he wrote to me there, adding, 'P.S.2. Why not?' I bade a tearful farewell to David, now on leave from Germany: for Bexhill would be nothing like so convenient a place to come and have a bath when on leave: and off I went, from Victoria.

Bexhill is a wonderfully hideous seaside town, sprinkled with hydrangeas and tamarisk hedges. It lollops along the coast from Cooden Beach, where the millionaires live, to the infinitely livelier Regency façade of Hastings. There are no pawnshops in Bexhill. It is too genteel. So whenever I wanted to pawn a ring (I had three, but four years' searching for a great aunt will soon mop up all your jewellery if you don't watch out) I had to get into a big yellow trolley-bus and swirl along beside the sea to Hastings.

Kay and Colin and I at first lived on bare boards in the almost completely empty Bolebroke Hotel in Cantelupe Road. I loved it. I have a distinct penchant for living on bare boards. No one gets upset if you spill ink . . .

It was a very draughty place, though: and Kay and Colin soon began to put down carpets and spoil it all. Also, people kept telling us rumours about the place. How the last owner but one had run madly down to the esplanade one night and had dived smartly over, knocking her cranium to pieces on the shingle.

Colin started to go up to London in his demob suit and always came back with some highly complex piece of kitchen machinery. Once he pushed a big steel trolley, fit to hold fourteen steaming plates, through the length and breadth of Soho. My heart sank as I saw this wagon trundle in. Fourteen guests, I knew, would soon be upon us. I had a bed of my own by now, a typing desk made of very unfortunate orange-coloured wood, and a wastepaper basket.

Kay cooked for us, somewhat impeded by my godchild Sheilah, who was now at the age when she fell shrieking from her pram and hung dangling in her straps. Or ran blithely out into the road amongst the traffic. Between meals I slunk off to the confectioners and ate plum buns and drank glasses of milk. When I got sick of Great Aunt Beeton I used to lie on the shingle out of the wind under the breakwater. That summer I got so brown that I looked almost green. It was a very happy existence. Indeed, if Kay and Colin had never had any staff and never had any guests I should be there to this day. But it is hard to say which I disliked most, staff or guests.

Eventually I went off on my two big research trips to Paris and Killarney and I couldn't help noticing that my room was instantly let to Lady George Scott (Molly Bishop) for at least twice what I had been paying. So I felt guilty and went back to London to research in the British Museum. But I missed my dear sunny little room that had restored me to strength and sanity.

Bexhill has never failed me. I have frequently gone back there and simply fallen flat on my back. And I have always been restored, as much by the horror of the architecture as by the amazing air. Apart from Colin and Kay there was really no one to talk to in Bexhill at all, except Mrs. MacVean, a romantic novelist, and my sister's friend Geoffrey Wright, who very kindly used to come and stay at weekends.

Geoffrey is a very, very handsome musician, so like Godfrey Winn that it confuses me. Both are distinguished in their own fields. Both have the same initials – but even stranger, they have the same sort of musicianly handwriting. And they both sailed before the mast as seamen in the war. When I first met Geoffrey he was in H.M.S.

Anson, nimble and shipshape in his bell-bottomed trousers and square rig.

Geoffrey is chiefly famous because he wrote a wonderful tune called 'Transatlantic Lullaby' with nostalgic, evocative words:

> Ship to ship
> And shore to shore
> The Ocean spreads its shining floor
> To hum a sleepy Transatlantic Lullaby . . .

It made a big hit in the *Gate Revue* in the '30s. My sister Liz loved Geoffrey, too. He had taken her to a May Week Ball in Cambridge, when she had run up a little number for the night in sprigged muslin. The seams were loosely held together with safety-pins, which later burst spectacularly in a punt at midnight.

Geoffrey went on writing melodies, while he was before the mast. These were usually for a radio show called *Make and Mend:*

> Make and mend
> The sailor's playtime
> Make and mend
> Let's have a gay-time,

he sang to me, one night when he was on leave in London and the bombs were dropping. He danced happily out horn-piping into the traffic at Marble Arch. I stood, adoring, on the kerb. He has gone rather solemn now and instead of writing revue numbers he is writing a symphony and teaching music on Tuesdays, all of which he is very well qualified to do. Still I regret the dear little tunes like:

> Sweet Fanny Adams
> Your name's tattooed on my heart . . .

When Geoffrey came down to stay in the Bolebroke Hotel he had just been on tour with a revue, playing the piano and writing the music. Geoffrey was always a delightful companion, and when he told me the other day that his symphony had now been played twice by the BBC at different times on different wave lengths I was as pleased as though I'd written it myself. In spite of the fact that I'm distinctly unmusical. Geoffrey was ready to frolic even in Bexhill. We fell about laughing at such simple jokes as a lamb chasing him down a road on Pevensey Marshes, screaming at him as though he were its 'Ma-aaa'. And a witty revue number we wrote for Hermione Gingold about vampires:

> Last time I saw the Countess
> The day that the Bastille was freed
> She was walking the Champs-Elysées
> With her pedigree wolf on a lead
> Ah . . . for the Revolution
> Dear Madame Guillotine
> I founded my constitution
> On blood that was ultramarine.

(Miss Gingold afterwards said that I had gone too far.)

I remember Geoffrey was stunned by the Bolebroke Hotel. 'A *nice* way of learning the hotel business,' he said, 'from the bottom *up*.' But he played the piano in a most extroverted fashion, thumping his way with energy and brio through the 'Peer Gynt Suite' while the guests sat open-mouthed.

I found a diary about this Bexhill summer the other day. It was one of those locked affairs and I had to break it open with a cold chisel. Geoffrey's name occurs again and again. He seems to have been a great little walker, as well as a gay companion. I can't think of anyone else (except possibly Godfrey Winn) who would make me walk seven and a half miles.

'Got kittens. Tea with Geoffrey who played me witty revue number about Mrs. Tracy who always takes a double Scotch to bed. I said two Highlanders and we both fell about laughing.' Which obviously meant a lot to me at the time, but whose kittens these were I can't say.

'Took a bus up to Battle with Geoffrey, walked the remainder of the way, laughing about Holiday Camp.'

This was a title for a musical play he was possibly going to write with Mabel Constanduros, which was afterwards used by Godfrey Winn (you see?) for a film for J. Arthur Rank.

'Saw a splendid little house and talked quite seriously about living in it together. "Perhaps I should disturb you with my *music?*" said Geoffrey. I suppose he would as I really only like common music and Sousa Marches and I can see by the look in G's eye he is all set for symphonies any minute now . . .'

I have often meant to have a dinner-party so that G.W. could meet G.W. to see if they *are* so very much alike. Perhaps it is only my emotional confusion over these two delightful companions that makes me think they are.

My other great chum in Bexhill was white-haired, fiftyish, handsome, stoutish, pink-and-white complexioned Mrs. MacVean. She wrote so many novels under so many pseudonyms that it was hard to tell which novelist one was talking to. There was witty Phillipa Vane, for example, who wrote stylish detective stories; there was sentimental Phyllis Hambledon who wrote jolly good romances; there was Rita Something or Other who wrote for the American market, and Morag Something Else who wrote for Scotland. Morag seldom spoke. Mrs. MacVean was in hospital when I first met her. We shared a doctor, who said as we were both writers it would cheer us both up to meet. So I went along to the Bexhill Cottage Hospital at visiting time. The doctor was right; I liked Mrs. MacVean very much.

I well remember her sitting up in bed, with rather good hands picking restlessly at the eiderdown, wearing a pink bedjacket and saying, 'But *you* must be Maimie Spain's niece. Maimie Spain read my first novel. *I* am Tommy Allden's niece.'

Tommy Allden. This name rang an inefficient electric bell in my subconscious. When I got back to the hotel

I wrote to Mother (I still wrote letters in those days) and asked who Tommy Allden was. 'He was a friend of your father's who upset a pan of boiling water over your father's foot your father says on purpose of course this is rot,' was the reply. As for Aunt Maimie, she was the last of the English gentlewomen. Our father's second sister, she always dressed in black with neat touches of peacock blue. In the Summer she carried a parasol like Queen Mary and all the year round she did the crossword puzzles in the *Sunday Times*.

She knew all James Agate's reviews by heart and used to vex mother by quoting them. Mother would often point out, acidly, that she read the *Sunday Times*, too. It seemed strange in that year of peace, so long after Maimie's death, so long after Maimie's head had bobbed eagerly round our nursery door at home (somewhere below the level of the latch) saying, 'May I come in?' that I should meet someone upon whom Maimie had apparently had a profound literary influence.

I learnt all sorts of things from Mrs. MacVean about Auntie Maimie and Auntie Katie, our father's sisters. One of them had been friends with Aubrey Beardsley's sister and had reviewed books in *The Saturday Review*.

'No?' I said, aghast. 'Then what became of the review copies?'

(Weeks later, after a prolonged hunt about, I found some in 7 Tankerville Place with slips tucked into them: 'The Editor presents his compliments to Miss Mabel Beardsley and asks her for 500 words on this novel.'

They were first editions of *Elizabeth and Her German Garden* and *The Enchanted April*.)

Marvellous. Quite apart from her interest in and knowledge of the dashing Spain girls, Mrs. MacVean had led a stirring life. She had married a doctor who had died and left her with four children to support. Her various pen-names had fed and clothed them until they grew up. At this point, I gather, they began to educate themselves and get Government Grants. They were frighteningly intelligent, the MacVean children, and would talk about Dostoevsky and whether decadent art could possibly be good art. Mrs. MacVean would counter as a rule, 'You young people are so uninhibited, but why do you always find it necessary to be psycho-analysed?' which is more or less unanswerable. I can remember one story her daughter told about a horsy little man in a bow tie at a Foreign Office party saying to another little man, '*Vous etes Frongcais?*' To which the other chap had mildly replied, '*Nong, je suis Australian.*'

Mrs. MacV. was more than kind although she once alarmed me by saying that she thought I was probably a reincarnation of Emily Brontë. Later on, when I was in need of Bexhill air and she was in need of seeing a few editors, she would change flats with me for a week or two. She had a flat overlooking the gasometers, which was much more beautiful than it sounds, as a great field of clover lay between De La Warr Road and the gas-works, where larks sang like steam kettles all day long. In the evening when the sun set the whole twilight would become a strange shade of blue, like blue-black ink. I once lived on this view and nothing but kippers for a fortnight when I was trying to finish a book. I have only to taste a kipper nowadays and 15c De La Warr Road swims back with its view of the meadow and the sea and various winking light-buoys flashing along the inky horizon.

Then, of course, there was Hermione Gingold. One day in London, possessed by some mad instinct, I went into a telephone-box and dialled SLO 5921.

'Hullo,' said the inimitable voice.

I said who I was and how I had lately read her book, *The World Is Square*, and how I would like to write a piece about her.

'What sort of piece?' said Miss G., in deep purple tones, and cautiously.

Then, as I nervously suggested that I hoped to do something like those profiles in the *New Yorker,* Miss G. said what else had I written? 'I am afraid I am a little behind with literature myself at the moment,' said Miss G., 'as I have only just begun to read *Magnolia Street* by Mr. Louis Golding.'

I hadn't read *Magnolia Street* either. We met for lunch (in spite of the fact that Miss G. never really gets out of bed before tea-time) and I see now it must all have been a terrible strain for her. 'Actors always get furious when Channel swimmers and things try to go on the stage, so I wonder writers aren't furious when actors write books,' was one of her remarks at lunch, I remember. Soon I was enthralled by her. I went to rehearsals of the new show *Sweeter and Lower* (or was it *Sweetest and Lowest*?) and she electrified me by taking me out to tea at 'the Poor Man's Ivy' (her phrase, not mine) and wiping the cups out with the hem of her skirt. She was carrying a box of twenty-four fresh eggs and she had the man behind the counter boil us four, two each. Then Brian Desmond Hurst walked in accompanied by the entire Gate Theatre company from Dublin, and Miss G. remarked, 'The O'Hurst and his nine leprechauns.'

Altogether, Life with Miss Gingold was wonderful. I got into her house eventually (and it is a strange but fascinating fact that everywhere that Miss G. lives all over the earth always looks exactly the same, gay, pretty, airy and glowing with her uncanny charm) when I used to stay far too long, simply because she made me laugh so much. With the possible exception of Noël Coward, I know nobody who has seemed to me down the years so consistently *funny*.

She will tell you she was born of 'good peasant stock' in St. John's Wood. Her Aunt Helena Gingold wrote some stirring tales in Edwardian days, and had her picture taken peeping through a lyre. Hermione became a child actress and went on tour in *Pinkie and the Fairies*. When I was in New York last year, she suddenly stirred around with her foot in a cardboard box and produced a sepia theatre programme that showed her as Pinkie: an exquisitely pretty, solemn child of two with a bow on the top of her head. She waited in silence for my reaction.

I gulped a bit and handed it back. For Hermione has grown to be the most beautifully ugly woman in the world. She can actually radiate beauty for five minutes at a time and then ruin the whole thing with some fearful grimace, worthy of the gargoyles of Notre-Dame.

When she grew up she married Michael Joseph, the publisher, and had two sons. Then this marriage was dissolved and Hermione married again: Eric Machswitz, a light-hearted genius who invented such dissimilar things as *In Town Tonight,* the nightingale that sang in Berkeley Square, and 'These Foolish Things'. I once accused Miss G. of inspiring this last number and she looked dreamily out of the window and said, 'A cigarette that bears a lipstick's traces. Hmmm. But I don't smoke, except cigars.' Once, too, I complained that her house was full of cut flowers instead of the artificial ones covered in dust that I had been led to expect. 'I'm sorry,' she said, with tears brimming in her enormous pale blue eyes, 'but you must admit they are *dead.*'

Hermione lived the sort of centrally heated life that seemed to me highly desirable. She stopped in bed until tea-time, and she was always surrounded by highly decorative young men, who all adored her. She chatted endlessly, wittily on the telephone. But most important, she had a heart of gold. Her kindness and generosity are even remarkable in Show Business; that little world where gold hearts grow on trees and kindness and generosity are thick along the paths like an herbaceous border.

For example, when I arrived trembling in New York for the first time and Hermione was the only person I knew, she took me under her wing. She fed me. She lent me her kitchen. She sat up with me eating lemon meringue pie from Hamburger Heaven till way after midnight. Then she led me out to show me Times Square after dark.

'What is that steam coming up from the man-holes?' I asked her.

'It is the Red Indians, dear. They are smoking down there in their reservation,' she said. (The taxi-driver laughed so much at this that he refused payment, a record in itself.)

Then we arrived in Times Square, where signs flashed and cinemas were still open at two in the morning, SCENES OF DEBAUCHERY AND VICE they promised, THE LAST DAYS OF HITLER said the signs. 'Aha,' said Miss G. 'Debauchery. Vice. This is nice. That's for me.' And in we went.

Well, it was a perfectly ordinary film with a highly talented man giving a fulsome imitation of Hitler, but there was no debauchery and no vice. Miss G. got a little upset. She began to move in her seat restlessly, to attempt a slow hand-clap and to complain fretfully. 'No debauchery,' she said, 'No vice. Money back.'

The two American boys who accompanied us were upset too.

'What is it?' they said harshly, and, 'Pipe down, will-yat. And anyhow, what kinda vice *do* you want?'

'Anything *de-ar,*' replied Miss G. in tones that rang through the cinema. 'So long as it isn't Vanilla.'

Imagine then my consternation when one day in her dressing-room this legendary figure leant towards me and said (that purple voice husky with emotion), 'Put me in a book, Nancy. Oh, please put me in a book. I've always wanted to be in a book. Send me up as far as you like, but I do so want to be in a book . . .'

She then made a little chant out of this, wandering around her dressing-room, lugubriously putting her tongue out at herself in the mirror as she passed it. 'Ooh,' she said, 'I am old . . . and I am ugly . . . whoever would want to put me in a book?' In the end, going too far as usual, I put her in six books. (This makes the seventh.)

Hermione's fascinating rococo features, her wildly chic ideas on interior decoration, her impetuous demands, 'What's *new?*' (which she always said as though it were Welsh), were a breath of warm, dank, exotic air, straight from a conservatory drawn by Charles Addams. Infinitely preferable to the fresh air of Bexhill. I well remember at one Gingold tea-party scoring a hideous social success in reply to the usual taunt, 'Come on, old girl, what's new?' by saying, 'Miss XYZ,' (a famous writer) 'has just been locked *up.*'

In those days there was always an edition of *Sweet and Low* to see at the Ambassadors, just as in the war there had always been *Rise Above It*. There was always Miss G.'s dressing-room to linger in, a buzzing hive of gossip (usually with a smashing chocolate cake baked by Prudence Hyman handed round) and endless absorbing, fascinating discussions about Love. Miss G. never talked about Money. Her face would become exactly like the Durham Cathedral door-knocker at the merest mention of it. And she once worked for me for six whole months for six little bunches of flowers. But I am rushing ahead of myself . . .

Whenever I came up to London I would race through all my business in the morning to go to tea with Hermione in the afternoon. Once I nearly got her to come to Bexhill, but she went to Birchington instead and stayed with Walter (*Look Down in Mercy* and *The Image and the Search*) Baxter. 'What can I wear?' I remember her moaning in, of all places, Woollands. 'Do you think my blue satin would be *suitable* for *shrimping* at Birchington?' And again, 'The eagles are flying very low this summer. Do you think that means rain?'

I flew to Dublin in the middle of this summer and when I came back I was accompanied (in the loosest possible sense) by the Captain. The Captain was a nice man with a thick black moustache who had been at Eton and fought in the Spanish Civil War. I have always felt he somehow got into my luggage at Collinstown Air Port in error. He was 6 feet 4½ inches and could appear very elegant indeed when he was trying. 'You're a lucky, lucky girl,' said Miss G., looking him up and down in the corridor outside her dressing-room. Then she signed his copy of *The World Is Square* 'To the other

Old Etonianonianonian'. For one of the nicest things about Miss G. is that she cannot even spell 'Gingold'.

The Captain liked Bexhill. He thought nothing of sitting in Forte's Ice Cream Parlours swigging ice cream sundaes and talking to retired colonels. Much to my alarm he once insisted on coming to Roedean where an Old Girls' Reunion was raging, with my mother in the midst of it. He said he *liked* girls' schools. As the Captain was so tall, it was impossible to conceal him behind the Sanatorium, so I sent him into Brighton to wait in The Old Ship.

'Who is that?' said my mother as he went trotting off. 'Does he want to marry you?'

'I shouldn't think so,' I replied. 'And anyway, he's married already.'

Chapter Eleven

The Captain was an exotic and rather jolly character, what with his reminiscences about Eton and the Brigade of Guards and General Franco's daughter and fightin' for the Fascists in Spain. He was *not* unreliable. Far from it. One could always rely on him to spread the maximum amount of chaos and confusion in any situation. Emotional or social, it was all the same to him. Once he arrived unexpectedly in the middle of a working day, would *not* go away and finally turned up at a performance of *The Rape of Lucrece* shouting, 'Am I in time for the rape?'

Our friendship came to its lunatic conclusion one sad evening when he rang me up and (hiccuping slightly) asked to be taken home. He had drunk six bottles of gin, he said, with a lady and now could not walk, so he repeated would I please take him home? With a series of co-operative, disbelieving, overlapping taxi-drivers and oyster men, I eventually filled him up with brown bread and butter and got him to the Turkish Baths in Russell Square. He agreed to lie down in a cubicle and sleep it off. The last time I saw him he was a courier attached to a continental char-á-banc tour, slightly vexed because the

ladies thought him too grand to tip. I can't help being
fond of the Captain.

The biography of *Mrs. Beeton and Her Husband* had
now reached a most irritating stage. It needed completely rewriting and I was sick to death of Great Aunt
and feeling far from pious about her. Even without the
Captain, Bexhill had lost its charm. Moreover, a medical
board in Tunbridge Wells had told me that I should try
to winter abroad, but was well enough to forgo my £2 a
week pension. So I decided I would go back to London
and find a flat and a job.

I got the job entirely through my own stupidity.
When I went to Paris and walked around the race-
course at Auteuil where Mrs. Beeton had somewhat
strangely acted as a racing correspondent for *The Sporting
Life,* I had sat down in a café and written a number of
little sketches of Post War Life. Just how Black can the
Market get? That sort of thing. Then I posted them off
to Terence Horsley, who I thought was back at his old
job, Managing Editor of the *Newcastle Journal.* But not at
all; when he returned them regretting that they weren't
quite his cup of tea, I couldn't help noticing that he was
now Editor of a paper called *The Sunday Empire News.*

And Terence offered me a job, at £12 12s. a week,
as Assistant to the Features Editor. I couldn't have been
more surprised. By the time I had accepted and got my
first pay packet and the P.A.Y.E. had been removed,
I had at least £7. With equal stupidity I had also got
myself a furnished flat on the ground floor of a block

in South Kilburn. It was called Chesney Court and it cost £7 7s.; so you will observe that each week I now had a deficit of 7s. Added to which I have never been able to fill up and get passed that important part of a reporter's paraphernalia known as the 'swindle sheet' or expenses claim. So one didn't need a crystal ball to see that I would soon have no money at all . . . Let alone be a millionaire.

However, innocent of my doom, I went serenely on, thinking I was very grand. I had a job and a flat . . . and sister Liz wrote and said the flat sounded like a popular comedian.

I was never, to be honest, fond of that flat. It was very small and every door that opened simply shut one off into another box, as it were. A lot of fairly repellent furniture went with the flat, including a little pink china ash-tray guarded by a grey china dog.

It was very hot that summer, so I left all the doors and windows open, hoping for a through draught. But one night at 2 a.m. I was woken by a terrible thumping on the door. When I opened up, six enormous policemen filed through and into the sitting-room. They complete- ly filled it. One of them carried a napkin, in a biblical manner, folded over. He opened it and there lay the horrible little china dog in two pieces.

'Is this your little ash-tray?' said the policeman, accusingly.

The ash-tray was *not* the sort of *objet d'art* I would own voluntarily, so I answered cautiously, 'It forms a part of the furnishings of the flat.' Which for some reason sent all the policemen into paroxysms of rage. One by one they told me that by leaving it as I had on the window-sill of the kitchen I was inciting all the youth of the neighbour-hood to crime. To quieten them down I agreed to bring a charge against a young man who was dangling in the background, and they all filed out. The flat felt much emptier and I went back to sleep.

For the next three weeks my life was punctuated by a rather attractive, sandy, young C.I.D. sergeant with a pussy cat moustache. He would call around at all hours to ask me to sign statements and to sneer at me for writing detective novels. In the end he promised that he would take me round the pubs near the Elephant where he would show me *real* criminal types at play. But meanwhile I was a witness for the Crown and mustn't forget it.

The first hearing was comparatively painless, in the magistrate's court. But the second was months and months later and cost everyone a lot of money. So far as I remember I had to be fetched from Newcastle-on-Tyne and Bexhill and was paid 30s. a day to compensate me for loss of income. The case was dismissed on insufficient evidence, but not before I had several times gone through the shaming process of identifying the ashtray as my property.

'And how much,' smiled counsel for the defence, 'would you say the ash-tray was worth?'

'I think the police say 2s. 6d., but I think 9d. is nearer

the truth,' I replied. Which obviously didn't get poor Sergeant Pussycat any promotion.

Meanwhile, of course, for the first time in my life I was 'on the staff' of a newspaper. I was very excited about it. For weeks I went around with the uncomfortable feeling that we were all giving a performance. Certainly the conversation was larded over with terrible words, words that still seem to me to have precious little meaning. 'Flong Box', 'Matrix', 'Flam', 'Cheese Cake', 'Beef Cake'. These were some of the words constantly on the lips of my colleagues. I used to slip them into my own conversation, much to the horror of my chums. They (and I) hadn't the foggiest idea what they meant.

When I arrived at Kemsley House it was as red and brick as ever, I had to work for a nice man called Ned Barton. A little bit smaller than me, he always wore bow ties and had a very sweet tenor singing voice. When there was nothing else to do, I would bribe him to sing me:

> The moon has raised her lamp above
> To light my way to thee, my love

which happens to come out of 'The Lily of Killarney', by Sir Julius Benedict. Sir Julius Benedict was Auntie Beeton's music master, but even Ned's singing didn't reconcile me to rewriting that biography.

Ned was a good features editor, I am sure. He reminded me a little of Miss Eldod. But try as we might, Ned and I could never produce anything that got actually printed in the paper. Ned sent me to do such unlikely things as interview a clergyman who believed that spinsters should have babies if they wanted, to find a man and wife and two children who lived on £5 a week in budget week, and to congratulate Sir Laurence Olivier on becoming a stage Knight. Sir Laurence had just dyed his hair cream colour and consequently looked rather like Hermione Gingold. All these things I dutifully did. But Terence said they weren't News in Manchester. In Manchester, of course, they were confusingly busy doing the things that London would be doing the day after tomorrow.

For the *Empire News* was printed in Manchester. Terence and another set of staff crouched up there like eagles, killing all our poor little stories stone dead. I was particularly upset about the Sir Laurence Olivier story, for I knew quite well it was a very surprising thing for anyone to be allowed on the set of *Hamlet* while it was being filmed, let alone actually watching the whole of the 'incestuous bed' scene shot with Eileen Herlie. 'He has as much news sense as a cat,' I muttered bitterly.

Then Ned suddenly said, 'Terence says you are to write about the films.'

'Well,' I said. 'That is nice.'

'Hm,' said Ned, turning away.

To understand what happened next you must understand *(a)* writing about films in a newspaper is a plum job and one widely sought after, *(b)* film critics are therefore, very properly, formed into a neat tight cabal for self-protection, *(c)* Elspeth Grant, a very good film critic indeed, was already writing about them for the *Empire News* under the pseudonym of Kay Quinlan.

I asked how I should know what films I ought to be writing about. Some innocent bystander suggested I should approach the Critics' Circle and get tickets sent to me from there. This I did. I forget the name of the man who kindly dealt with me. He seemed ever so charming and was obviously very powerful. Anyway, he agreed to send me tickets for the Press shows of film previews. He then (apparently) told Elspeth Grant that somebody else called Nancy Spain was going to do her job on the *Empire News*. Miss Grant and I then had a telephone conversation, every burning word of which is still inscribed on my heart. 'Unprofessional behaviour' are the two lightest of these words.

Naturally, Miss Grant went on writing about the movies and getting what she said about them printed in the paper. I did at least have the sense, after I had swallowed the basic truth that nothing I wrote was *ever* going to get into the paper, to read Miss Grant and study why she was so much better than me.

After a month or two of this kind of thing, I began to think with more pleasure of Auntie Beeton. Indeed, I even began to rewrite her under cover of the table. I finished her before Ned Barton went away to be features editor of one of the Graphics while Terence called conference after conference. I remember he once appeared with a parachute cord round his trousers, which I thought very strange. It is only now after all these years that it strikes me that Terence may have been as new to being an editor as I was new to being on the staff of a newspaper.

After one of these conferences I meanly button-holed him in the corridor and asked why had he hired me. Would he like to fire me?

Terence looked wildly round him and said he was sending me to cover the Wimbledon Tennis Championships. He had remembered, poor darling, that I used to write the tennis notes for the *Newcastle Journal*.

The *Empire News* sports pages were magnificent. They were very well edited by a very dear soul called Harold Mayes, with a sweet gentle face and a pipe clenched between the teeth. Harold knew all about football and cricket: he even had Denis Compton writing for him at the time and I think he, too, was horrified at the idea that I should write about tennis.

'*Tennis?*' said Harold. 'But we haven't written about tennis, except possibly agency reports, for *years*. Nobody really cares about tennis, particularly in Birmingham, Manchester, Leeds, and Bradford,' said Harold.

By 1947 I wasn't so crazy about tennis either. As you know, I had gone all literary. And by July, any year you care to mention, there aren't any centre court seats to be had except for spivs at about £12 a seat.

So I had to cover the Championships from the free standing room on the Centre Court. This involved pushing, shoving and bounding like a mountain goat on inoffensive people, in order to send off the five separate messages that the *Empire News* required for the Irish, Scottish, Northern, Midland, Southern, and Late London editions. (The first one had to be through by 3 p.m. I *do* remember.)

Worse than the lack of seat was the lack of telephone connecting me with Kemsley House.

I really do think this is one of the taskiest tasks I have ever undertaken for any organization. Because Kemsley newspapers on the whole are uninterested in Lawn Tennis, thus showing their sense (as Kemsley papers are mostly sold in Birmingham, Manchester, Leeds, and Bradford) no Kemsley House private line connected me with Terminus 1234; with the exception of the *Sunday Times*, of course, where the tennis notes are brilliantly handled by Susan Noel. Fortunately for me, I was still on nodding terms with some tennis people, notably Stanley Doust in those days of the *Daily Mail*, who was darling to me and let me use his telephone when he wasn't using it. This was O.K. until Finals Day when Stanley was glued to his telephone all the afternoon. *Then* I had to run a quarter of a mile to a telephone kiosk outside the grounds and phone through my five editions, losing my five foot by two inches cattle-pen space in the concrete standing room whenever I did so.

In the end I rang up Harold and asked if he could take in the Agency stuff.

'Just what we should have done in the first place,' said Harold, sulkily.

That vexed me. So I went wandering off, peeking and peering into that Holy of Holies, the Centre Court, looking for an exclusive story for dear Harold. I got there just as Margaret Osborne and Louise Brough had lost to Doris Hart and Pat Todd in the doubles and Queen Mary was coming downstairs, ready to go to tea. It was a lovely hot day, sunlight lay on the floor and one could hear the crowds cheering.

'Out of the way,' said a policeman, digging an elbow into my stomach.

'Hey,' I said. 'Who are you shoving?'

'Don't you know better than to hang around when *Royalty* is coming down?' said the policeman. And he *threw* me down the steps. I landed on my right ear on the tarmac. This was my second taste of the power of the police, and in spite of Sergeant Pussycat of the C.I.D., who was still hanging about Chesney Court trying to tell me that women detective novelists knew nothing about crime, I found I wasn't too keen on being on the receiving end.

The summer went on being terribly hot and instead of enjoying my performance as an eager cub reporter, I found myself longing to get away from the highly hygienic oven of Kemsley House, into the countryside. This is nonsense, as I infinitely prefer hot grey streets to cold green fields.

The *Empire News* occupied about five rooms on the second floor of the oven. One of these rooms was very, very grand indeed. It had a carpet for impressing the customers, a book-case and a view of endless glass-fronted offices. When the sun shone down on these, they didn't half heat up. Next door there was a secretary's room with two charming girls and next door there was a smaller room with a big desk. This was the Features Editor's Room. In the corner there was a smaller desk where I was supposed to sit, but I didn't really care for it.

When Ned Barton went away to one of the Graphics I shared this room with Jack Thomas, a Welshman with white hair and a black moustache. I remember Jack writing a terrifying series about Glands, which was a big 'circulation puller', and singing, 'Now for the Gonads, the Jolly, Jolly Gonads, now for the Gonads, one, two, three.'

Across the corridor from Jack Thomas and me was the News Room. There was some sense in the News Room. The stuff they wrote in there really *did* get in the paper. There was only one empty desk in the News Room and that belonged to Gerry Byrne, an Irish Cockney crime reporter. Gerry had a big bull terrier whom he used to bring into the office and it seemed to me they were both always spoiling for a fight. Gerry was a great Trade Unionist. He was the Father of our Chapel.

Working round the room from left to right I met Vic Hudson, gentle and appealing, rather like a leprechaun with a bass voice, who looked after Royal Gossip; Dyke Pierce, also gentle and very hot on stories from Government departments; Ralph Cooper, of the light touch, who always had several copies of *La Vie Parisienne* in his desk: and Jack Fishman, the News Editor. All these boys lived on the philosophy of the Little Book.

The Little Book is the journalist's vade mecum. In it are all the telephone numbers, all the names of all the Contact men and women that there have ever been, all the ex-directory numbers, the chaps who knew, the chaps who know chaps, and the never failingly wonderful people like Hermione Gingold and Lady Docker who will give you a good quote at the drop of a hat.

In control of all this was Jack Fishman, the News Editor. Jack is a fabulous character, the Cockney boy who would have made good no matter what the odds; he has one of those light, alive, impossible faces that aren't strictly anything but 'interested', rather like a good-looking coconut. He has a loud braying laugh and is very quick indeed. Jack was born in Stepney. Sometimes when there was nothing doing he would tell what happened in Whitechapel when he was a kid; and once he told how Hitler had patted him on the top of the head. 'That's why I'm a little bit thin on top.' Jack is still one of my dearest friends, in spite of the fact that in his spare time he has written such song hits as 'The Queen of Tonga', 'I Told the Valley of Echoes that I Love You', and 'Sing Gypsy'.

When I had quite despaired of my unprintable existence I went to Jack and asked him to give me a job 'on the news'.

'All right,' said Jack. 'You can help Ralph Cooper do John Gay's Show-Down.'

WHY I'M NOT A MILLIONAIRE

John Gay's Show-Down was one of those unlikely columns that carry smart, wise-cracking paragraphs about film stars, film directors, playwrights, actors and actresses. Every paper and magazine has one. It is probably the most widely read part of the paper. Yet as the stars live entirely on publicity it is not very high-class journalism. It was in John Gay's Show-Down that I learnt to use such phrases as 'I bumped into Cary Grant (Mae West, Ingrid Bergman, Glynis Johns) at a party', 'My spies tell me', and 'It is not generally known'. I also learnt to cherish the people who would allow themselves to have their names put to a wisecrack (set in bold type with a little star against it, called Crack of the Week), the people who would not write in the next week and complain, and say *they* would do the job better than me; the people who would give free luncheons, cocktail parties, dinners, where one would meet people who would go yackerty, yackerty yack, dropping great big luscious Names all the time. I also learnt to go round film studios, how to live for fifteen hours on nothing but a double Scotch, and how everybody really despises the newspapers. This gave me a terrible shock. After this I gave up reading newspapers for ever. (They put me off so.)

One day Jack Fishman sent me to a cocktail party at the Savoy that was being held in aid of the publicity of Mae West. He said that it would be tough, but I must get an exclusive paragraph. The whole of Fleet Stret would be there, he said . . .

Popey (W. MacQueen Pope), the wonderful theatrical

historian and publicist, had arranged this party. Popey doesn't drink, so he stood apart, his arms folded, leaning against a pillar in the middle of the room. From time to time someone would ask him where was Mae West. And he would reply, 'All in good time.' Against one wall of the room was a long white-covered table, groaning with more food and drink than one would believe possible. The ladies and gentlemen of the Press fell on this rich, free fare with little yelping noises. I remember noticing that all the ladies wore little black suits with diamond clips . . .

After about an hour the door opened and Mae West walked in. She stood there, vibrating ever so slightly, against the pillar where Popey had been. There was a noise like bees swarming as the journalists rose in a cloud and settled on her. Mae West is quite small and I could only just see the top of her head as she dealt with her interviewers. Four lugubrious-looking young men, each one taller, darker, handsomer than the last, stood beside me by the bar. 'And who are you?' I said to them. 'We are her leading men,' they replied.

After a while I cautiously joined the swarm and after much manoeuvring I arrived under Mae West's left elbow. Then I very, very cautiously prodded the upper part of her famous torso. It was as hard as iron.

Another time, together with Lisa Moynihan of the *News Chronicle*, I went to interview Vivien Leigh at Shepperton where she was making *Anna Karenina*. I infinitely preferred Sir Carol Reed, who was angelic to me while he was making *A Fallen Idol,* and Warren Chetham Strode who told me that his wife had been secretary to James Hadley Chase, author of *No Orchids for Miss Blandish.*

'Lor,' I said, 'what was he like?'

'Very nice and quiet,' said Warren Chetham Strode, 'although one day he did say his *wife* was awfully good at all-in wrestling.'

All my friends now looked at me askance and Hermione Gingold said I was a 'Nark'. So I was really quite relieved, I think, when I arrived at the office one day and found there was a letter for me from Manchester. It had arrived 'Per Flong Box' and was signed Terence Horsley. It said, 'While I am sorry that things didn't work out, I am sure you will admit you have gained some useful experience,' and it gave me a month's notice. As luck would have it, this particular sacking coincided with a general axe-ing of the Kemsley staff. Before I knew where I was I got involved in a great big N.U.J. row.

I am afraid Gerry Byrne found me a very uncooperative Union Member, except that I always paid my dues. He even got a Banker's Order out of me before I scraped the dust of Kemsley House off my feet and went back into the big, wide world, where I only wrote to please myself. 'I will,' I said foolishly to myself, 'never go back until they send for me.'

Jobless, with my ridiculously expensive flat now eating its head off, I made a small, pathetic attempt to join the Women's Police. I was egged into it by Sergeant

Pussycat, who had already taken me to the pubs round the Elephant where lurk the muddy-eyed characters, who are prepared to commit grievous bodily harm at the drop of a hat. They were all spotlessly clean, but without exception, when introduced, they looked twitchily over my right shoulder. No one, thank God, dropped a hat.

'They can't help it,' said Sergeant Pussycat, 'they don't like women.'

Pussycat said that for a crime novelist to go on writing about murders without knowing about them at close quarters was plain silly. So he persuaded me to fill up a set of forms. Because I had a school certificate I was exempted from an exam, which rather disappointed me. I sailed through the medical (good old Bexhill) and then attended for a viva voce and eye-sight test at Beak Street or Bow Street or Vine Street, I forget which.

The viva was a big success, but I failed the eye-sight test with such flying colours that a burly sergeant who stood in the corridor gripped me *hard* above the elbow.

'What d'ya mean by wasting the surgeon's time?' he said.

'I *beg* your pardon?' I remarked, in my Roedeaniest voice.

'Sorry, miss,' said he. '*I thought you were a police force candidate.*'

Still, things were becoming a little bit desperate. Mrs. Beeton wasn't due out for another six months and even if she were a big success, I would still have to wait another six months before I got any money. I had to make a weekly pay packet somehow, or starve to death. Then Kitty Elliston, who had been in the W.R.N.S. with me, found me a job with Bart's Hospital. I was to go around the pubs and factories in the City of London and empty the collecting boxes. I got £1 a week for *not* stealing the contents. I have never been mad keen on handling copper coins, even in small quantities, and by the time I had finished with the Bart's collecting boxes I smelt, tasted, and looked like a penny. I was also sick and tired of going out to work to keep a flat that I didn't awfully like. David had turned up again, too, looking sweet in a cheese cutter hat and telling an awfully good story about how he had told the Army psychiatrist, 'It's a straight case of mother fixation and you can carry on from there.' David pointed out how uneconomic my existence was. So I tried to find two sub-sub-tenants to whom I could sub-sub-let at a profit.

But not at all. Nobody wanted the flat.

I had a great big sell-out and sold all my books, staggering to Foyles with some of them in a suitcase and inviting Miss Eldod and Miss Robinson round to dinner to buy and carry away my collection of cookery books. (I had amassed these while writing Mrs. Beeton and very bulky and unhandy they were.) I remember Miss Robinson's astonishment because, instead of cold *consommé*, we ate Brand's Meat Essence out of the pot with teaspoons. 'Well,' I said, 'I could have turned it out of the pots, but I would have lost some if I had . . .'

With difficulty I found two sub-sub-tenants prepared

to pay £4 4s. for the flat and hastily moved out, at a big loss, bed, desk and all. I finished Mrs. B. to the satisfaction of the publisher and started to write some more detective stories. I found a postcard outside a stationer's on the way to the British Museum, offering a room in an architect's flat at £2 a week, so I went round to see the architect . . . Her name was Barbara Cole and she was really a Russian, being descended from Gorki and Catherine the Great. *She* lived in a flat in New Cavendish Street, which I think belonged to the mother of Lana Morris, the film star who married Ronnie Waldman. So she explained I couldn't really be a proper tenant. I could only be a chum of Barbara's living there, who sometimes paid for things. This worked very well, as I quickly became a chum. I liked Barbara very much. I would often come back from the British Museum and find her eating tea with two or three assorted Countesses and Princesses and the man who had come to cut the telephone off. The telephone, the gas, the electric light were (we now decided) all *my* responsibility as Barbara was so often in the South of France or her little cottage at Wheeler End near High Wycombe. So every now and then we would have a terrible financial reckoning and I would have to ring up Mrs. Webb and ask for £25 more. (Then the sub-sub-tenants failed to pay the rent in my flat, too, so I might just as well have stayed there.) But as a matter of fact I liked it much better in New Cavendish Street. I lived mostly on eggs, butter, and newly baked croissants from a lovely Jewish bread shop opposite. The scents, sights, and glimmer of Soho seeped up towards New Cavendish Street via Percy Street. And I threw off for ever the last rags of conventional dress and behaviour. For when I had trotted about representing Kemsley Newspapers and sucking up to my relations writing Mrs. Beeton, I had always worn great heavy hairy tweeds and thick brogues, which was *my* idea of the way ladies dressed in Northumberland. And I was sick of it . . .

With Barbara I wore dungarees and never went to the hairdresser. I cut my hair myself with a pair of curly nail scissors and washed it every day in the bath. I never spoke to anyone, least of all celebrities. I decided then and there that I could never have another job that would demand little black suits and diamond clips. I decided that I didn't want to meet *anyone* who would make me put on a skirt. I was sure that it was those awful clothes that had made me fail to pay the rent. David and the Captain, who had now got to know one another and to like each other very much, encouraged me in this. Indeed the only *man* I have ever known complain of it is Noël Coward, who says I look like '*A degringolée* farm hand'.

Almost immediately darling Sister Liz, whose *entire life* at that time was devoted to making beautiful clothes for beautiful conventional women and celebrities, wired and asked if I would like to go and live with her in Ireland where she had a dress factory. My departure was delayed by a very unfortunate incident at Wheeler End when I fell off a motor-car outside Barbara's cottage and sprained my ankle very badly. But eventually I arrived at Collinstown Air Port, leaning on a thick walking-stick, dressed in a duffle coat and a pair of brown corduroy trousers.

It was when I was in Ireland that I heard that Terence Horsley had been killed in a gliding crash.

Chapter Twelve

My life with Sister Liz from this time on was punctuated by little screams of, 'Darling, must you?' and, 'You look so *odd*,' and, 'They will think you *very* peculiar if you don't wear a dress.'

Sister Liz lived in 8 South Mall, Cork, a tall Georgian house with a red door. It contained a fairly satisfactory penthouse flat and a very flourishing dress business.

Most of the floors, being so genuinely Georgian, were uneven. The ground floor was the store-room, where large bolts of cloth and tweed lay about waiting to be made up into bestselling models. Once, the River Lee flooded and cloth was floating all about the place, while the young ladies who worked in the factory leapt and praised God. This was a great little drama and much enjoyed by one and all. On the next floor there was the factory itself where the young ladies sat and stitched, singing like thrushes. And then there were the cutting rooms where Mr. Tallboy the eighty-year-old tailor, who had actually learnt the trick of cutting real coach-man's capes from his father, cut. Above this was Sister Liz's penthouse.

When I arrived this was very simply furnished indeed

with one bed, one chair, a sofa and a kitchen table. It is too difficult to explain why.

To begin with I slept on the sofa, but I soon proved allergic to this, and preferred to sleep on the floor of Sister Liz's clothes room, among her clothes. I liked it there very well,

I did all the housekeeping and cooking. I spent about 30s. a week on this, which we shared out between us. Mrs. Webb, I may say, was greatly relieved. We both like milk chocolate and bananas and we both agreed we had never eaten better.

I am not a good cook, but I can roast a chicken and make chicken fricassée from the fragments, and as Liz really dislikes meat, this was just as well. So we mostly lived on potatoes and cabbages, boiled eggs and chicken and bananas and cream. I was delighted to have cream again, and butter too, though some of the butter was very strange with wool and actual *fur* in it. From time to time Sister Liz remembered to praise me for the food. At one point, I must admit, we both came up in strange green circular spots, but a course of sun-ray treatment removed them.

Sister Liz breakfasted about 9 a.m. on toast and black coffee. There were no newspapers taken at all, which was a big relief. I was always repulsively brisk at breakfast and would slink upstairs to the kitchen, where I furtively cooked myself pork sausages and bacon and eggs. (No kippers.)

The kitchen was easily the best room in the house,

I thought, and we ate all our meals there. It had a red floor and two saucepans and a kettle. It got all the morning and afternoon sun and it had a beautiful view of the Cathedral where 'those Shandon bells' used to chime like anything. There were also roofs: mauve, green and grey, stretching away in wonderful shapes until they came to the open water of the River Lee, winding about through the town like precious metal. It always rained in Cork for two hours every day. After rain the sun would come out with peculiar brilliance and make the roofs like paradise.

Cork is still a beautiful city; swan-haunted, bell-pounded, seagull-spattered. Twice a week the English packet, the *Innisfallen*, sails home up the glassy stream, sending the wake rippling in a wide arrow-head. And English visitors and homing Irish pour down the gangways, through the Customs. On the quays all is chaos. Muck lies in gutters, men curse, little donkeys bray, railway horses pulling great trucks slip with clattering feet, sending sparks up. Beggars and lunatics stroll in the streets, saints pass, people kneel in the gutters and pray, books are banned. Ireland is another world. It is a world of a Hogarth print, teeming crazy, falsely beautiful, grandly alive.

I walked through Cork in a dream, shopping. The people in the shops lilted at me. When I told them I was a writer (they were quite sure I was Irish, I looked so rum, and you will remember Spain *is* an Irish name) they tried to please me by reciting poetry they had written.

The butter woman in the market said she had *two* poems, 'One very strange and sad about something very sad happened a long time ago. The other about the birds, 'tis very beautiful. Both are marvellous,' she said happily, slapping the butter with her wooden butter hands.

Sister Liz had many friends in the district, notably the Mahonys of Blarney, who live in a house called Leemount and make cloth out of wool. When the flood entered the ground floor of Sister Liz's house, it swept away several of the Mahonys' mills and overtook a lady walking on the road. 'Ah God, I had to put the dog on me head and continue walking. The river was up to me shoulders,' said this lady, unperturbed.

Liz and I used to go and dine with the Mahonys, whom I loved. There was Reets (Mother Mahony), E. T. (the chairman of the mill), and Gretta (who was Liz's friend and once golf champion of Ireland and in the Irish hockey team). On one occasion I well remember driving in a closed car into the yard, met by barking dogs. There was the usual heavy downpour and a gutter had become stuck above the back door. The side of Leemount looked something like Niagara. Just inside it stood E. T. Mahony, charming, smiling, with outstretched hands.

'Welcome to Leemount,' said he, taking the deluge for granted. 'My, how wet you are,' he added, patting me on the shoulder.

'I was *dry* until a second ago,' I replied, but E. T. didn't hear me.

Irish people think you extremely odd if you say you mind getting wet to the skin.

I well remember the day my sister persuaded me to write to Elizabeth Bowen, the novelist and book critic of the *Tatler*. To my amazement Miss B. wrote back and we were invited to tea.

Bowen's Court is a big, white, square house surrounded by hay-fields. The gutters seemed in excellent shape when we drove up and we were shown into the library without mishap. Alan Cameron, gentle, short-sighted, welcomed us. Miss B., also very short-sighted, joined us. Sister Liz, rather vain about her appearance, took *her* glasses off: and we had a very gay tea. Silver tea-pots and thin bread and butter. But I couldn't help noticing out of the corner of my eye that one of those large blue-black Irish clouds was sweeping up towards Bowen's Court. It tilted itself up and a cloud-burst hissed down the windows.

Miss Bowen rose to her feet. 'I expect you would like to see the garden?' she said, very politely.

Lizzie and I were halfway *round* the garden before anyone dared to say that we were soaked right through.

But Ireland is a wonderful place to write in. Even although the atmosphere was so Faith-laden that I was often worried that I was *not* writing a book to the Glory of God, I had to admit that words flowed from my pen like all-get-out. To be honest, there is *nothing to do in Ireland but write*.

On the north side of the house, facing down into

the Mall, never getting any sun and only interrupted by the twittering of the sparrows, as they got up and went to bed in the eaves, was what had been my sister Liz's dining-room. Painted a soothing chocolate brown, it had grotesque carved cherubs, a marble fire-place, and a long mirror. Eventually, too, it had a cutting table from the factory and the kitchen table.

There was also, rather fortunately, a plug for an electric fire.

From 8 a.m. till noon, when I had a bath and darted out and bought and cooked the lunch, from 2.30 until 6 p.m., when Liz and I would meet again and quarrel, I used to sit in that dining-room and write. I wore trousers over my pyjamas and a big thick sweater and a big thick woollen dressing gown.

Sister Liz's day was very different. After her breakfast she would bath, make-up and dress to the teeth. Then she would plunge downstairs into her factory and design, cut and cause to be sewn up at least six collections of models a year. This was very fascinating stuff and I was particularly pleased when she used to let me help choose names for the little numbers.

By that time she was so vexed with the pretentious nonsense talked all over the rest of the Fashion World by couturières, and the pretentious names (like Dawn Dream) given to gowns by couturièrers that she preferred to call *her* numbers names like 'Tom', 'Bob', and 'Kit'.

To inspire her, Liz had an elegant office with a long mirror and lots of carefully sharpened pencils. There was a side-table made of marble with cherubs for legs and on this lay heaps and heaps of *Vogues, Harper's Bazaars,* and a lovely American paper called *Woman's Wear Daily*. It was in this last that I found the advertisement for a brassière with the slogan, 'Hi-yah tits'.

She would yearly produce a Spring, two Summer, an Autumn, and two Winter collections of thirty models each. Sister Liz would dart up to Dublin with the collection and there 'take the orders' with the help of a model girl called Anne Murphy, whom she had trained.

In scenes of indescribable confusion and lack of glamour these delicious garments were paraded in front of various Buyers.

They would sit pondering deeply as they decided how many of which particular garment they would sell to their clients. Then Sister Liz would write it all down in a little book, pressing hard with her pencil because she would have to go through several carbon copies.

There were splendid people among the buyers: Mrs. Fitzsimons, Mrs. Hague of the Mansfield Sisters, and there were some terribly nice people from the deepest bogs of County Mayo, who really only wanted tweed coats with straight skirts, as they are worn in County Mayo.

As a matter of fact, the buyers were more fascinated by Sister Liz's private life than they were by the numbers themselves; and it may well have been true that they ordered *more* if they were listening to some terrible instalment of murder and rapine. For example, Sister Liz at that time had an acquaintance in Mountjoy Prison (he had run over two cyclists with a motor-car) and she would visit him and give him packets of ham under the warder's eyes. This was, of course, very saintly of her. 'Ah, for heavens' sake now,' was what the buyers usually said, as they listened.

I used to come up with Sister Liz to Dublin, driving her very slowly in the little Ford 10 that she had bought from the local undertaker. It was garaged among the coffins and had been very well run in, as it had travelled at fifteen miles an hour for so long behind the mourners. The dresses usually went ahead with Anne Murphy, by train, in laundry baskets. Much as I should have enjoyed talking to the buyers, or writing down their orders, or egging them on to buy several models in different colours, Sister Liz usually told me that I mustn't. So on one of these occasions I was standing gloomily in Grafton Street, trying to persuade the head buyer of Brown and Nolan to buy more copies of *Mrs. Beeton and her Husband,* just about to be published, when I went bump into Janet Quigley. I was very relieved, for I was finding it hard to keep up my end in a conversation about James Joyce.

This encounter set off a strange chain reaction of thought.

Although, since I had last seen Janet Quigley in the radio programme *Women at War,* I had travelled a long way and encountered strange worlds, like one of those diving birds who disappear for whole moments together under the surface of a lake, it had never struck me that people all round me were diving, too. What had Janet been doing? What right had she to be idling here in Grafton Street when she should have been away running *Woman's Hour*?

Janet explained briskly that she had married a terribly nice Irishman called Kevin Fitzgerald, who wrote detective stories and climbed mountains, and she was having a very nice time in Dublin doing no broadcasting at all, thank you. But she would shortly be back in London because Kevin was getting another job in I.C.I., when she would probably be mopped up by *Woman's Hour* again.

This forced me to recognize the fact that I hadn't broadcast for about four years. And as a direct result of this encounter I wrote off to the Director of the North Regional and did two gramophone programmes (based on *Thank You, Nelson* and *Mrs. Beeton),* several talks (one was about Collingwood and Nelson, the other about Sir John Vanbrugh), and three ghost stories. But every time I did them I had to travel, at vast expense, to the Corporation, to either Newcastle or Belfast, which struck me as a bit silly. I began to think it was about time I stayed in London.

It must also have occurred to me, around this time, that the only way back to Fleet Street was by making my name at something else. It was no good writing detective stories; at that time I obviously wasn't good at it and I was too old for the rough and tumble of the

Centre Court and the hockey pitch, so I decided that I had better become an expert at something else. *What,* I didn't know, as I had never been any good at anything except People (whom I like enormously) and Books (which I cannot do without).

Brooding away like this I can't have been much of a companion for dear Sister Liz, who, as usual, had troubles of her own. *Mrs. Beeton and Her Husband* came out in August. There were three enchantingly bad reviews, by Margaret Wiley, C. E. Vulliamy, and Rosamund Harcourt-Smith. But, as a result of the kindness of the other critics the publishers were sold out and had to reprint, which was very satisfactory. For a little time I didn't feel hunted by creditors and actually starving to death. Auntie Katie, too (she who had told fortunes wrapped in maribou), died suddenly in New York and left Sister Liz and me £400 each. So we decided we would go on a jolly good holiday and blow the lot.

As a last long sisterly fling we went to Madeira and Tenerife, dipping through the tropics in the good ship *Venus.*

I remember with much joy the strange movement of the ship on the way out, rhythmic as a waltz; the beautiful wine-dark sea sliding past, with beaded bubbles winking in the wake; and I remember my first sight of Madeira at dawn with cocks crowing across the bay at Funchal, the green, cool, deep water in the harbour and splashes of bougainvillaea on the shore.

Funchal is beautiful in any light. The pink and burnt

umber and golden houses with their red, mad hats; strange flower markets and Portugese peasants stitching lace at street corners; and fussing bullock-cart men, dressed in Edwardian tennis kit, eager to propel us downhill in wooden bullock-drawn toboggans.

But it was difficult for Sister Liz and me to enjoy all this. Due to over-work and a distinctly Russian streak in her temperament my darling sister had decided at this time that Life was very, very sad. She would sit and brood about it. Quite often she would weep.

And this went on all through our holiday in Madeira. Liz contemplated the tragedy of life and wept. Assurances that she was probably the greatest dress designer in the world did nothing to cheer her.

But Sister Liz had only to sit on the poop in a very becoming series of costume changes and weep, for people to come from near and far to comfort and protect and sympathize. I marvelled. I can do all sorts of things (like cook a chicken fricassée), but I have never been able to weep becomingly.

When we got to Funchal, Madeira, life continued much the same. The sun blazed merrily out of a baby blue sky and every now and then Sister Liz would feel the Tragedy of Life. And the big round tears would gather in her eyes. And she would immediately be swept up into a whirl of comforters.

But wonderful things happened. The bathing attendant took a great fancy to me (I was terrified of being left alone in the cliff-lift with him) and used to leave bunches of freesias daintily in my wet bathing dress. We bathed and swam and got exceedingly brown and spent Auntie Katie's legacy exactly like water.

And when we got back to Waterloo we parted: each to our own new life.

It was with the greatest regret I set out to find myself a new flat in London. I must have had at least £200 left out of Auntie Katie's money.

Chapter Thirteen

The flat I found in Baker Street is the first home I have really loved. Until the mice and rats got in near the end and made their strange smell about the place, it was very nearly perfect. When I called there the other day and found that the whole place had come down to make way for a block of modern flats, I was sad.

My flat was very near Portman Square. If you dangled from the window or stood on tiptoe on the roof, you could just see the tops of the green trees. The traffic that went by most of the night was downright soothing. And when I walked through Manchester Square to the baker and the laundry, there was a glorious jangle of pianos in mad counterpoint all playing different melodies in the Conservatoire of Music.

My flat was on the top floor. On the ground floor was Miss Locking, my landlady. She dealt in pretty things like antique china and lace. She quite often surprised people by refusing to sell something because it was *too* pretty. The only thing I have ever sold at a profit in my life was a beautiful bull, with Europa mounted on it that I bought from Miss Locking for £12, which a bull-crazy collector bought for £20. (This proves nothing except that lots of people like bulls.) My flat had a sitting-room and a bedroom and a dear little staircase and a ladder that mounted up to the roof, through the tiles. I could sit out there in complete and smutty security when the sun shone and I often did so. The only snag about this flat was that it was so pretty I was always wanting to give parties to show it off.

Elizabeth Bowen, when she wasn't living at Bowen's Court, lived at the top of Baker Street in Number Two Clarence Terrace. She was very kind indeed to writers and would often invite them to meet there for a drink. Her house was elegant, and hundreds of drawings that looked as if they were by Holbein hung upon the walls. The drawing-room seemed (to a clumsy young writer with clumsy, slipping, insecure feet) to consist entirely of parquet flooring. An electric fire glowed, dimly reflected in it. There were certainly red glass candlesticks on the mantelpiece. Outside the window, Regent's Park, with shouting crowds and boys with kites and vulgar children eating ice cream, was so much of another world as to be non-existent. The only Regent's Park that existed inside 2 Clarence Terrace was the Regent's Park in Miss Bowen's books.

All sorts of writers would be there, standing round and sipping gin. Miss Bowen, splendidly stuttering, her heavy hair piled in a beige bun, would pass among them carrying a bottle and enjoying conversation with such marvellous people as Eudora Welty, Alan Pryce-Jones, Henry Green, Philip Toynbee, Francis Wyndham, and so on. I remember hearing Miss Bowen say, 'I think it is so mean of Cyril to say that the only one of us whose work will live is *Ivy*.' It took me ages to work out that she meant Ivy Compton-Burnett. Trembling, I expected them to turn and ask me what I thought of Dostoevsky.

As I grow older the more dismayed I am by this intellectual pawn, which people are always introducing into the conversation. 'Well,' they say to me truculently, 'since you think so little of *me* as a writer, what do you think of Dostoevsky?' It is the literary equivalent of, 'Nice weather we're having for the time of year.'

But in those days I thought all writers were marvellous anyway, and I was particularly impressed by the writers that I met in Miss Bowen's house.

Eudora Welty, for example. Eudora Welty still takes high marks as a Remarkable Author. She is very tall, pale, and slender, and she comes from Jackson, Mississippi, in the deep, deep South of North America. She has hands like graceful fish. Her books are always exclusively about those deep, deep parts and I cannot understand one single solitary word of them. In those days that pleased and impressed me very much. I longed to write a book that no one could understand. (Alas, when people read my books they understand me only too well.)

I first met Eudora when she was actually staying with Miss Bowen in Bowen's Court in Ireland. Eudora had enjoyed her stay very much, and to show her gratitude she determined to bake Miss Bowen a Mississippi Witch

Pie, which had to be eaten on the stroke of midnight. Miss Bowen tried hard to stop her.

'We have no onions,' she said, gently.

'That is all right,' said Eudora. 'I have bought some of my own.'

'But I have no oven,' said Miss Bowen.

'That's all right,' said Eudora. 'I will make one.'

And, my word, Eudora *did* make an oven, using an old biscuit tin and a frying-pan.

When the pie was baked one end was all runny and sticky and uncooked. The other was charred to a cinder. We bolted it manfully.

'Creative genius takes us the strangest ways,' murmured Miss Bowen mildly, on the stroke of midnight.

Later, in the Bowen's Court drawing-room, a fine, tall, dark, handsome room without electric light where, surely, a bat flittered in the tapestry curtains, there was a piano, covered loosely in review copies, and a spinet that didn't work. I sat at the piano and played 'Love Is the Sweetest Thing'. And instantly Eudora came to life. She pushed me off the piano stool. She played the 'Blues', she played 'Tiger Rag'. She played and she sang and she sang and she played (and very well, too) until about 2 a.m., when Miss Bowen began to worry about the maids and whether they would be disturbed in their sleep.

'Can *no one* play God Save the Queen?' asked Miss Bowen. Throughout this splendid scene she had sat bolt upright on the edge of a sofa . . .

In efforts to return such hospitality I would sometimes give a party myself in 6 Baker Street. I can recall Mark Bonham-Carter and Ngaio Marsh sitting on the floor, arguing about the Theatre. I can remember Monty Mackenzie playing spillikins with matchsticks and Angus Wilson talking very earnestly indeed to Miss Bowen about Dickens.

Angus Wilson is one of my friends. He was brought up in South Africa and when I first met him he was the Supervisor of the Reading Room at the British Museum. I became very fond of *all* the people who worked in the British Museum when I was researching about Mrs. Beeton, and we often used to have lunch together in the Museum Tavern right opposite. Angus was very little older than me, but his hair was already quite, quite grey. I deeply admired this and I loved his stories about Oxford, where he used to wear a big woollen muffler and suck peppermints that he carried about in a big bag. Angus said this was necessary to identify him in those days, which I can hardly believe. But as in those days Marghanita Laski was called 'Pearl' I have begun to think that *anything* can happen at a university.

I forget exactly *why* Angus wrote *The Wrong Set* and sent it to Secker and Warburg, but I do remember reading the stories in manuscript and being shattered by them. Perhaps Angus didn't like the museum and really wanted to be a writer all the time . . . Either way, there was very little of the sweet, kind Angus whom we all knew and loved in those malicious, brilliant, angry little stories. Angus is one of the kindest people I know. And he takes endless trouble over people.

I am also very fond of Margery Allingham, whom I met about this time. I wanted to write a piece about all the lady detective story writers, so I rang them all up and went along to see them. Marge was the only one who invited me to stay. She is a perfect darling, who lives in a big Georgian house in the middle of Essex and is married to Philip Youngman Carter, the editor of the *Tatler*. Marge has never been to one of *my* parties, more's the pity, but I have been to several of hers and gigantic things they are.

Indeed, Marge sees everything in gigantic terms. Life, parties, dinner, conversation, literature. That is why she, too, is on such a grand scale, mentally and physically. When I first met her I was knocked down by the weight of her thoughts, the living profusion of her ideas, the glory of her language. When I asked her if she had a message she said, 'Only old ones . . . Like God is Love and Mind the Step.' Usually, though, when she makes a remark like this she carries a bottle of champagne in one hand and a glass in the other and she fills the glass and hands it to you, so you can find a reply. Other simple ideas of hers that have stunned me are, 'Mock bathrooms to impress visitors, all done with mirrors in country houses,' and, 'You must get yourself a doctor with the garage-hand instinct, Nancy. Good doctors get a mechanic's pleasure in making you tick over.'

Marge once told me that she listened to a little old

lady dictating in her mind and wrote down everything she said. This little old lady has even shown Margery how to write a *Saturday Evening Post* serial (imagine that). Margery Allingham is easily the most impressive professional writer I have ever met. She could write anything from a sonnet to a 100,000-word Book Society Choice. And, bless her heart, she has never asked me what I think of Dostoevsky, whom she deeply admires.

My life in Baker Street continued to be highly literary, but as you can see it was not conducive to *work*. Or to becoming a millionaire. If your telephone rings all day long, you will find it easier to write a piece (say) 800 words long than a book 80,000 words long with a beginning, a middle, and an end. A telephone conversation is complete death, too, to the imagination, killing stone dead anything you might have had inside your mind at the time. So by and by, while I was having such a high old time listening to the clever ladies and gentlemen talking about writing, I failed to write a single word of the detective story that Mrs. Webb was wanting. Worse still, I failed to pay the rent. And as I got friendlier and friendlier and began to know more and more people, the circle became positively vicious.

Looking back, I am sure all my misfortunes at that time arose from having been black-balled from the Detection Club.

This splendid body of men and women meet once a year to praise each other in a vault near Westminster. They carry skulls about on cushions, they light candles and they intone a terrible oath which conjures the members on pain of diminishing sales and returns to stick to the rules of clues and foot-prints. Christianna Brand, a witty doctor's wife, author of *Heads You Lose* and other noble works, who is a member of the actual Committee of the Detection Club, delights in teasing me about this, calling me 'Little Spoil Sport' and 'Little Nothing Sacred' simply because in those days I was so bad at working out plots. I am sure that terrible oath of the Detection Club was the reason for all my financial insecurity.

Every now and then Veronica Wedgwood sent me a lot of novels to review for *Time and Tide*. Michael Foot was very kind and allowed me to do detective stories for *Tribune,* but the cheques from these two august weeklies were not enough to keep Miss Locking happy. So I took to answering advertisements in the *New Statesman* and meanwhile lulled Miss Locking to a sense of false security by giving more and noisier parties. No one seemed eager to employ me, though T. Werner Laurie, whom I had approached in an effort to become their publicity manager, were kind enough to interview me.

All this time was lived on borrowed money (from the bank, or from Mrs. Webb on the advance of the book I never delivered) so it seemed very gay indeed. I remember one splendid lunch when Faith Compton Mackenzie came and we ate game pie and drank champagne; and Faith went home to Denchworth Manor where she then lived, and very nearly died.

And as a result of the book reviews that I wrote I

made new friends: Mrs. Robert Henrey, for example, and Noel Langley. And of course I lost old ones, like Pamela Frankau, who was very cross indeed about the things I said about her novel *The Willow Cabin*.

Mrs. Henrey and Noel Langley were grateful, though, and when I met them I liked them both very much. Strangely enough, they lived within about fifty yards of one another in Mayfair.

Noel is South African. He is very tall and very amiable and somewhat like Orson Welles to look at. I can truthfully say that he has never spoken a cross word to me. Yet this talented author of *Cage Me a Peacock* and *A Porpoise Close Behind Me* is always supposed to be in a state of hardly-suppressed fury about Hollywood or the English Film Industry. Once Noel struck a very bad patch and had to lie in the dark with his eyes bandaged, but even then he used to roar with laughter and egg me on to tell him worse and worse stories of my life. I never got so far as inventing any, but if necessary I would have done so. Noel had about five children, handsome tow-heads, who didn't really care for father's friends. Only once he asked me round for a cosy chat, and I was horrified to find the room filled with movie tycoons and film actresses on their way to a film première. 'Don't mind *her*,' said Noel. 'She's a good scout.' But that didn't alter the fact that Mr. George Minier was wearing his black tie and a red carnation and Miss Kathleen Byron was wearing a low-bosomed evening dress with orchids at the *décolletage*. They all talked about Sir Carol Reed's movie, *The Third Man,* I can remember, and Noel said he was expecting the lady in the picture to leave the screen and hit him over the head with the zither. I was rather shocked by this, for to me *The Third Man* is a sacred thing.

Madeleine Henrey is very different. Small, fair-haired, very pretty, she lives a life in the heart of Mayfair that approximates to that of the Paris housewife. She has her sewing-machine and a large bag of knitting. She hates going out. I'm sure she makes all her own clothes and she cooks nearly all the meals. She usually makes an excuse if you try to take her to a restaurant and says, 'Is the food clean?' She has knitted for me two glowing scarves (one turquoise blue, one shocking pink) and everyone always envies me *(a)* for having the scarves, and *(b)* for having had Madeleine Henrey knit them.

Madeleine works in bed every morning, wrapped up in woollen shawls. Every now and then she flies to Normandy where she has a famous farm. Bobby, her son, is one of my favourite people.

I remember going to the movies with Mr. and Mrs. Robert Henrey *and* Bobby to see *The Prisoner of Zenda.* Bobby and I adored it, clutching one another and squeaking as the duels came on the screen. But Madeleine and her husband Robert behaved very badly indeed, and evidently thought Anthony Hope's immortal story a terrible bore. But perhaps Bobby will read this book of mine one day and then we can sneak off together to the movies and see some marvellous Technicolor epic *without* chaperones who can't appreciate a good sword fight.

The Henreys are a wonderfully talented family. Bobby is also a marvellous confectioner and can make madeleines and croissants and brioches as well as any pastrycook in France.

I was lucky to have been able to give Madeleine Henrey what *she* considers to be help at this point, because she has proved to be one of the most intelligently grateful people I know: unfailing in her efforts to be constructive. (Margery Allingham is another. So is Esther McCracken.) Should you ask Madeleine's advice she always says exactly what she thinks and feels. So even if I disagree with her, I have still gained a valuable point of view that is different from my own. Naturally, amongst other things, we talked about writing. But Madeleine never asked me what I thought of Dostoevsky.

I went to far too many literary parties at this time, given by publishers to help launch books by authors. Usually I hadn't read these books, sometimes (worse still) I had read the book and not enjoyed it. But I found that all that was necessary to get through was to say 'Marvellous', 'Wonderful', and 'Jolly Good' from time to time. Authors only want praise (just as A. A. Milne told me) and they certainly don't care for ladies who seize on them at an unguarded moment when their mouths are full of gin and smoked salmon sandwiches and attempt an analysis of their work. Good reviews, that is what authors like. Pity we can't all write our own reviews, the same way we write our own blurbs.

I well remember meeting Elizabeth Taylor for the first time. This author had just had a terrible pasting for one of her books, particularly in the *Sunday Times* where she had been accused of being deeply under the influence of Elizabeth Bowen. Miss Taylor was very pretty indeed. She had very blue eyes and she gave the impression of a Siamese cat, curled up in melancholy pride in one of Miss Bowen's arm-chairs. All round her Miss Bowen's polished drawing-room reflected her sadness. It was a dripping wet evening, I remember, and this, of course, added to the gloom.

'I remember the last time I had a book published,' she said, with gentle sadness. 'My school magazine said Elizabeth Taylor had written a book that had been praised in the *Sunday Times*. At least they can't say *that* about me now, can they?'

'What nonsense, dear,' said Miss Bowen, briskly. 'That's nothing *like* as bad as the things *my* school magazine, the *Dome House Magazine,* says about *me*. Last time, in among all the notes of which old girls were keeping rabbits and who had become midwives, it said, "Betha Bowen (which is what they used to call me, you know) Betha Bowen has become a writer."'

I seldom allowed myself to peer into my penurious state at this time because that depressed me, too. So I seldom opened my letters, in case they concealed some terrible disguised note from the manager of the

National Provincial Bank. I never, never opened the horrible little square buff envelopes from the Income Tax boys. (As all these came from different places, as I had moved so often, I thought this was fair enough.) Sometimes I would turn them over and over, like the hero of *The Light That Failed,* wondering what was inside.

How I ever got the message to go and meet Thayer Hobson at the Dorchester Hotel, I can't think. Perhaps he telephoned?

Thayer Hobson is the president of a firm of American publishers: William Morrow and Company Inc., and he said I couldn't write detective stories for toffee. Americans liked their detective stories one particular way, he said, just as they liked Westerns. Indeed he, Thayer, had never succeeded in making any radical change in Western Literature. The readers even objected if the hero had two horses instead of one. Thayer Hobson was a fascinating man. He had just bought darling Angus Wilson's book for vast sums of dollars, so I was not only vexed that he thought I couldn't write detective stories for toffee, but I was jealous of Angus. This put me in a highly receptive mood.

As Thayer paced up and down the room, saying what he thought about me and Literature, his wife limped in wearing one stout shoe and one mule with feathers on. The reading-lamp, she said, had fallen on her toe and smashed it.

'I think you are wasting your talents on mystery

stories,' said Thayer. 'I would like to advance you 250 dollars to write me a straight novel.'

'How much is that?' I said, surprised.

'About £100,' said Mrs. Hobson, who was fresh from the Casino at Cannes, and knew all about gambling and the dollar exchange.

'Lor',' I said. 'For that I would rewrite *King Lear* as a modern comedy.'

Now the awful thing about this remark is that it was meant as a joke. But Thayer Hobson picked up a dictaphone that was concealed in the woodwork and he dictated a letter to me about how he would give me 250 dollars and I must write him a novel 'the theme to be a twentieth-century Lear'. My jaw dropped. When I got home I even tried to do it once or twice, but it didn't work out, somehow.

This £100 didn't actually save me from starvation. My life was too badly organized. Other visiting firemen appeared in the shape of further American publishers visiting London to see what they could buy for sale in New York. This was how I found out that Thayer Hobson meant what he said and that he had bought an option on my first work of straight fiction. Thayer Hobson has a great reputation as a gambler.

So life continued to be mad and gay and *totally* unproductive.

At one point during this year I collected a little pile of about forty unopened letters from maniacs. Most of these, when I *did* open them, turned out to be from people who had read *Mrs. Beeton and Her Husband*. They always had a very old copy of *Household Management* and wanted to sell it to me.

Then to my amazement, the firm of T. Werner Laurie offered me £500 a year if I would come and edit a magazine for them called *Books of Today*.

It was as though a man had rushed up to the scaffold on a horse, waving a parchment, crying, 'Reprieve! Reprieve!'

Chapter Fourteen

Books of Today was a dear little moribund magazine originally published by the firm of Hatchards in Piccadilly as a sort of library list. It was sent out by Hatchards, monthly, to all Duchesses, Marchionesses, Countesses, and other good customers of this famous bookshop. When I became Editor, it had a terrible shock. It burst out into nasty, crude, primary colours on the cover, and it contained some pretty pungent stuff in the shape of book reviews. So all the Duchesses and Marchionesses wrote in and cancelled their subscriptions.

T. Werner Laurie, as I afterwards found out, was a firm built on the genius of one man. When he died, his widow, no less brilliant in her own right, but not wishing in the midst of war to continue with such a business, sold the firm. All but her own life directorship. Walter Hutchinson *and* Clarence Hatry made offers for this rich little firm. Clarence Hatry was the lucky man who bought it.

When Mr. Clarence Hatry became interested in the book trade he also bought a number of bookshops and some printing firms. In this way he had the beginnings of a little book trade monopoly.

T. Werner Laurie was Hatry's publishing firm and Hatchards was one of his bookshops: so we all lived together in a big building in the heart of Piccadilly, and I had a very grand office with a carpet and red velvet drapes. George Greenfield, then Managing Director of T. Werner Laurie, hired me. He was a plumpish man, almost exactly my age, with a little dark moustache and a Hawks tie. (This claret and gold tie apparently denotes enormous Cambridge cricket prowess.) On my first day I was hauled up to Mr. Greenfield's office to meet Mr. Wilson, one of Mr. Hatry's advisers.

'How do you do?' said Mr. Wilson. 'And how many words a day can you write?'

This struck me as an amazing question: I usually write 1,000 (*a la* Trollope), but if necessary I could write two, five, or even ten thousand. They wouldn't necessarily be *good* words, though. In a series of such strange conversations, I now discovered that I was to produce a review sheet of thirty-two pages, which would pay its bills on its advertising revenue. (This was £12 a page.) So I would pay the contributors nothing whatsoever.

'Nothing at *all?*' I said, staring.

'Nothing at all,' said Mr. Greenfield.

I had already planned a very expensive first number with G. B. Stern reviewing Rose Macaulay's new novel, *The World My Wilderness*, so my face must have fallen by a good mile.

'Unless, of course,' he said, 'you need Big Established

Names for your first issue to attract sales. Such as Wilfred Pickles,' he concluded.

Wilfred Pickles, I now discovered, was a Werner Laurie Author.

'Will *Books of Today* be a house organ for T. Werner Laurie?' I asked, cautiously.

'By no means,' said Mr. Greenfield, swiftly.

'Oh,' I said.

So a truly astonishing magazine was born, in which *all* the characters you have already met in this book, who were my fast friends, rallied round me and wrote reviews *for no money at all*. Particularly my father who wrote about shooting and fishing and archaeology over the initials G.R.B.S. Imagine a magazine, if you please, with a list of contributors like Mrs. Robert Henrey, Angus Wilson, Margery Allingham, Hermione Gingold, Christianna Brand, Noel Streatfeild, Compton Mackenzie, Faith Compton Mackenzie, Gilbert Frankau and Esther McCracken. (A formidable gallery of expensive talent.) *Then* imagine that you are going to pay them nothing at all, except to allow them to keep the review copies of the books they are reviewing. Then you will have some idea of how great a debt the Editor owed to her friends.

Hermione Gingold was, while she lasted, the reviewer who attracted the most attention.

Once a month I would creep along to 85 Kinnerton Street with my portable typewriter, whirl in some paper and take down whatever Hermione said. I would send her a pile of specially selected books first and she would read them aloud to her friends. Usually, she found this a social asset. She intended at first to call this feature 'Worst Book of the Month', but in spite of the fact that this was a personal opinion about a matter of public interest, somebody breathed the word 'Libel' and the title was changed to 'This I Have Loathed'.

The bright sequins of memory dance round her review of Netta Muskett's *Cast the Spear*. In this romance Lady Veronica 'raked Europe during her long and entrancing honeymoon, till she found the material she wanted for curtains'. 'Lor',' said Hermione, wistfully reading this out to a roomful of cronies, '*I've* never had a honeymoon like *that*.' Then she passed on to the villain, Randy de Marney who 'drank neat whisky in a way . . . that made him purse his small womanish mouth, which was belied by the diamond brightness of his eyes. Randy knew his job, too, which was that of a parasite.' 'Who am I,' said Hermione, 'to sneer? After all, a job is a job in these hard days.'

'If you want to laugh,' concluded Miss Gingold, 'I should put your tongue in your cheek and pick up that Muskett.'

Some time later I met Netta Muskett and she was very gracious about all this. 'I expect I could be quite funny about a name like Gingold,' she said.

Once Hermione had discovered that Nothing Sordid Like Money would change hands, she was amiability itself. Every month, as she continued to loathe books, *Books of Today* sent her a bunch of flowers. But then one day she sailed for U.S.A. and *Books of Today* lost its most mentioned column.

The established writers, who gave me their names and talents free, make a formidable list. But even more to be commended are the young, the unknown, the unheard-of who used to queue up at 187 Piccadilly with hope in their eyes. Starving poets were picked up regularly on Thursdays. I have always been a particular sucker for a poet.

Amongst the hitherto unknown but not necessarily starving were Audrey Erskine Lindop, who in those days had not yet written *The Singer Not the Song,* Elizabeth Jane Howard who was yet to sell 60,000 copies of *The Long View,* John Raymond (who left us to become assistant Literary Editor of the *New Statesman*), and a young man called Wolf Mankowitz.

Wolf was about twenty-four, a rather overweight young man with a slipped disc and a strong line in criticism. He limped along from the Piccadilly Arcade where he had a big shop full of repulsive objects made of Wedgwood china and he said he would write about *anything.* He really wanted to write a 'column' he said, and that was all right, no one need *pay* as long as they *printed* him. 'I've got more money than *you* have,' he said, looking at me shrewdly. 'I made seventy nicker this morning.' Wolf wrote and wrote and wrote. He wrote about Criticism under the smart title of 'Eng. Literate'. He wrote about Canasta and Ronald Duncan and Pleasure from Pictures with a wit that obviously concealed a sentimental heart.

I pointed this out to him, for otherwise why was he, a successful Wedgwood dealer who had made seventy nicker that morning, mucking about writing for nothing? And worse, writing about things he knew nothing about? And he took the huff and rushed away and wrote *Make Me an Offer* and *A Kid for Two Farthings*. And I venture to say that he has never looked back.

Wolf was introduced to the magazine by Joan Werner Laurie, the daughter of the firm.

Miss Laurie, hereinafter referred to as Jonnie, lurked upstairs in a bigger room than mine surrounded by very modern art work (but without velvet drapes) that overlooked Piccadilly. She was the Production Manager of the firm, which meant that she bought all the paper, read all the manuscripts and marked them up for press, ordered all the art work and paid for it and quite often told authors how to write their books. It was easy for her to do all this because her father, *Tom* Werner Laurie, had been a genius and he had discovered such authors in *his* day as Upton Sinclair, George Moore, and Norman Lindsay. Jonnie had the makings of a genius, too.

From time to time, since my strange conversation with George Greenfield and Mr. Wilson, I had been advised by George to 'go and talk to Miss Laurie'.

'Miss Laurie is very clever,' he said. 'And she will tell you how to save, money. Miss Laurie knows all about printing and she will help cut down the costs. Miss Laurie . . . Miss Laurie . . .' until I was sick of the sound of her name.

I envisaged (and I would like to know who wouldn't) the daughter of the great Tom Laurie as an elderly spinster, grown etiolated and dry in the service of the firm, possibly wearing pince-nez and certainly in a high-boned blouse with Edwardian fixings and a cameo of Beethoven. You could have knocked me down with a little statue by Henry Moore with a hole in its stomach when I walked into her office and found a girl four years younger than me, very good looking with rather a long nose and a very small waist. She was married, she had a little boy called Nicky. All of which gives no idea of Jonnie's excellence. Her friendliness and generosity are such that she is always surrounded by lame ducks and doting boyfriends. And very rapidly I was a lame duck too, living in her house, rent-free. 'If you save up what you earn,' she said, 'you will eventually be able to pay back Miss Locking.'

She had a very small red M.G. J2 model with brakes that seldom worked. Using this splendid vehicle, which was built in 1932, we moved my belongings to 35 Carlyle Square, Chelsea, where Jonnie lived. My belongings still consisted of a bed, a yellow wooden typing desk and a typewriter. And there they stayed and so did we, until dry rot crawled like a monstrous flower along the ceiling of Nicky's nursery and the ceiling slowly fell in on him. He was very good about this, hardly complained at all.

I loved living in 35 Carlyle Square. It had been the town house of the Earl of Carlisle before the Chelsea Council took it over. It had a garden and many, many families were able to hang their washing there to dry. Mr. and Miss Goggin, I remember, and their little white dog, Cheeky; but there were a lot of people on the top floor whose names I never discovered and a Mrs. Crampton on the ground floor. Her ceiling fell in, too. Then, more sadly, her husband died one night. Life, real life, quite different from all that stuff at literary parties, surged all about us in Carlyle Square. Across the square lived the Sitwells and Anthony Devas, the portrait painter. One could occasionally see Sir Osbert crossing the road, walking very slowly with great dignity. Jonnie paid a certain sum (was it 30s. a year?) to help with the upkeep of the square, so Jonnie, too, had a lawn to walk on, surrounded with cheerful trees and prams. I can't say I ever saw the Sitwells sitting around there, and I got awfully cross when poor Nicky wouldn't play cricket with me.

Possibly the best bit of 35 Carlyle Square was Lady Carolyn Howard's bathroom, a vast affair with a parquet floor, fiercely labelled Heavy Rescue Squad. The A.R.P. had used this house during the war. There was an enormously grand black marble bath and a wide window that looked down on the back garden; not that one could get anywhere near the window to look out, because of a dressing-table, built from orange boxes during the war by Paul Seyler. Paul Seyler was Jonnie's husband. He had obviously been a darling and 6 feet 8 inches tall into the bargain. After Paul died Jonnie didn't like to be called by her married name because it caused too much confusion at work. 'Miss Laurie' was a name to be reckoned with, a name that struck terror into printers. But Mrs. Seyler was a dear little thing, rather naughty, who wanted to sit in the bath and eat bacon and eggs . . .

What a difficult thing to write objectively of a relationship in which I have been happily bound up for five years, and which is still going on! Jonnie is, I think, one of the most remarkable people I have ever met: remarkable in her potential greatness and past achievement, but even more remarkable in being the only person I have ever met (except Lord Beaverbrook) who has never bored me. She is certainly the only person who has ever let me be myself . . . therefore the only person with whom I can cheerfully live in close disharmony.

I say disharmony because Jonnie is better educated than I. In spite of (or should I say because of?) the fact that she has never been to Roedean, she has read everything like *War and Peace* and *Moby Dick* and *Rosmersholm*. And she likes really good music and really feeds upon it, loving Beethoven and Bach and Sibelius and César Franck in the way that I love Sousa and Ivor Novello. And she can read books on comparative religion for pleasure . . . in the same way that I might read a modern novel. But here any possible sources of disharmony end.

We both like cities and we both love books. *(Any* books: it doesn't matter which kind.) We both dislike authors and authors' chat, we both like looking at television and we both love Lord Beaverbrook. And where Jonnie likes getting wet to the skin driving traction engines in the rain, I am perfectly happy admiring her from the warmth of a closed saloon car. Jonnie has an absurd hankering for grand vintage cars like M.G.s and Aston Martins and Rolls-Royce drop-head coupés, whereas I would be perfectly happy driving a Ford Anglia. She really loves machines and factories and great big statements of accounts. And she is always glad (thank heavens) to hand on her total knowledge in this direction, which means that I have an almost perfect complementary brain, available for consultation. In many respects it makes me even lazier mentally than I am already. For I don't care to make any decision without consulting Jonnie.

Lord Beaverbook, in his book about Success, has made it plain that young people of judgment, industry, and health can succeed in life. I have lots and lots of health and physical energy. Jonnie is rather weak in health but she has lots of mental energy. I have no judgment at all. Jonnie has enough for twelve. But when we work together, we are equal to most things.

You must have noticed that, although I have only written about the funny bits, until I met Jonnie I was a miserable sort of creature, a failure, hating everybody, living in a sort of ivory tower of work, refusing to allow Real Life in the shape of Family Life to intrude on me at all. I had become a terrible cynic, chiefly because all my boyfriends had darted off and married someone else.

On the day that I began to make judgments with Jonnie's hot beautifully controlled mind assisting me, the whole pattern of my behaviour changed. I began to make a little sense. Instead of doing and saying something from blind instinct and then discovering some weeks later what an ass I had made of myself, I quite often proceeded upon a basis of Jonnie's sound common sense. The result was spectacular. Pieces that I wrote for magazines succeeded. Things that I said to Editors began to make sense. Instead of leaning forward dramatically and asking, 'Where is your heart?' (as one Editor once did to me) they actually began to think I had a heart already.

In fact, of course, I had the beginnings of one. Jonnie and Nicky awakened my fondness for humanity, which had lain hidden for so long; hidden away under a sort of barrage of smart attempts at wit and brisk repartee and clever little detective books.

Of course, Jonnie wasn't always there, alas, available for consultation. She was quite often hidden behind a wall of printers, typefaces, book jackets, and so on, but it was always well worth waiting, or making an appointment, to see what she said.

It is a matter of simple fact that I have never yet known her wrong in a matter of judgment. You may find this word 'judgment' a cool one. Don't you believe it. Think of the judgment and nerve control it needs to drive a racing car, control your temper, navigate a raft in a river of rapids: then you will see why I think Jonnie so remarkable. Her mind is not cold. It is full of red-hot enthusiasm and impulse, just as mine is. But she can control it with nervous determination far beyond her years. I am always forgetting how *young* Jonnie is.

It is easy enough to talk or write about casual acquaintances, friends even. But it is impossible for me to take a step without consulting Jonnie, it is inevitable that she will shape my behaviour, read everything I write, tell me what other people will think of it, and I cannot write lightly of her, for she saved my life. She brought me back from the angry little garret when I sat, writing angry little books, lonely and bitter, despising the world and the good people in it who were bringing up families. By her example and her faith in me she has taught me things I could never have learnt in books. Her faith in the fact that I am doing my best is worth a hundred paragraphs of praise from other people. Oh, how difficult it is to write of gratitude. Of real goodness of heart. My pen dries and my heart spills over and cannot express itself when I think of everything that Jonnie and Nicky have done for me.

Jonnie, who uses her nervous energy in so many other directions, dislikes the unnecessary wear and tear of emotional scenes. But perhaps she will forgive this written demonstration, so sincerely meant.

Why, she has even taught me, by precept, how to love little children and animals. Quite *beastly* little children with dirty faces.

More immediately, however, Jonnie was a terrific asset to *Books of Today*. She could write on anything at all, just like Wolf Mankowitz. It is no accident that she is now Editor of *She*, the fabulous 1s. monthly magazine that has made journalistic history. But, as usual, I am rushing ahead of myself. We are still back in our mad beginnings with *Books of Today*.

First of all, Jonnie said we had to go and see various printers. So we stumbled round all sorts of clanging, clanking, chugging works in Soho and elsewhere, where it seemed to me all the foremen had terribly smelly breaths. As I bent with them over the dummy of the first issue, I would reel back, horrified, while Jonnie told me to be brave. Eventually she relented and told me we could have the printing done by Odhams (Watford) Ltd., where everything was as sweet and efficient as a nut.

But Jonnie was determined that I should see what I was asking the printers to *do* when I sent back a marked up proof. So she led me down into the basement of 35 Carlyle Square and there amongst all the ancient dangling bells that had once connected up with the Lady Carolyn's bathroom and Lord Morpeth's bedroom and His Lordship's dining-room and library she introduced me to a little devil-machine called the Adana. She also introduced me to several enormous, very heavy boxes of type. 'Distinguish,' said Jonnie, cruelly handing me a 'b' and a 'p' and a 'q' and a 'd', 'between these.' They were quite indistinguishable as well as upside down and backwards. 'Now put them into their proper compartments,' she said, laughing heartily. This took hours and hours and hours and my eyesight has never really been the same since.

So I was delighted after this experience to leave everything to our dear friend Maurice Collins, the

London Representative of Odhams (Watford) Ltd. Maurice was a big man, very good at amateur theatricals, with a splendid taste for beer and whisky chasers. On press days when the Paste Up was due he would come round to 187 Piccadilly crying, 'Pastey uppy! Pastey uppy!' On occasions he even held the paste-pot and scissors for me and grasped the 32-page dummy in his great big hands. Sometimes the velvet drapes would become hopelessly pasted up into a dainty little essay on Tennessee Williams and Ernest Hemingway: sometimes we would work far into the night. But never, never did we quite overlap beyond closing time when Mr. Maurice Collins and I (and Jonnie) would lurch downstairs into the bright lights of Piccadilly and revive ourselves with double Scotches at the Yorkshire Grey. Several times Pastey Uppy day extended beyond midnight, once even finishing (to the strains of a rumba band) in the Caribbean Club, where Jonnie and I took turns with Mr. Collins round the ball-room floor.

Jonnie, well aware of my lack of cash, would suggest all sorts of subtle spare-time activities. Indexing cricket books, under the pseudonym of W. C. Earl, at £5 an index . . . making up the Werner Laurie picture books (or did we do this for nothing?) . . . Jonnie was a great little midnight-oil burner. I have often nearly starved to death, I have often wondered where the rent or my next meal was coming from; but never in the months when Jonnie first started me on my long, uphill struggle to solvency have I felt so *tired*.

Normally I creep to bed at 10 p.m., delighted to get there. But midnight would strike (and one and two) and we would still be hard at it, indexing the cricket books. Once I even got up at five in the morning during a whole sopping wet winter week and worked in the kitchen with the oven turned on, to write a short story for the *Evening Standard*.

But, crazy though it now seems, I look back on those days with joy and grateful laughter. The other day I passed by the Yorkshire Grey – and it has been renamed The Yorker and I could have wept. But I suppose it is a good thing that nothing remains still and stagnant.

Goodness knows at what point I suddenly became aware that out of the 3,000 happy subscribers with which I had started I now only had about 2,999. (At the point, I suspect, at which the last Duchess wrote to Hatchards.)

Originally the idea was that the Werner Laurie travellers would plunge in and out of bookshops, saying, 'This is the latest literary magazine . . . this is designed to put all other literary magazines out of business,' and then the bookshops would order twenty-five copies each. The Werner Laurie travellers were jolly good at selling Werner Laurie books, of course, but in order to do this they went into *bookshops* and bookshops don't stock magazines.

It was only when the bundles of twenty-five arrived back with the string uncut, the parcel undisturbed, and all the delicious little essays by Spain, Mankowitz, Henrey, McCracken, and Allingham *unread*, and I began to be unable to get into my office among the velvet drapes, that I began to realize that booksellers really don't care. I began to realize that we needed to reach, not bookshops but bookstalls; and that needed a completely different set-up.

I remember one Werner Laurie traveller well. He wrote Westerns under eight different pseudonyms and he used a dictaphone. I always think of him as Hank McCoy and, indeed, the name suits him, so bustling and bronzed and fit is he, just in from the Last Round-up wearing a ten-gallon hat slightly on one side. Well, Hank used to ring me from some far country place (like Stowe-on-the-Wold or Penge) and reverse the charges and say, 'You're on to a winner here, Nancy . . . we're all on to a good thing.' He had the vibrant tones of a man with a six gun in each hand who has just headed them off at Eagle Pass. To begin with I *reacted* to these moods of Hank's and would rush upstairs and tell Jonnie and then rush down again.

But soon I had no time to react to such tidings. I was advertising manager as well as Editor, and now no publisher in London was safe from me and my salesmanship.

Every day I rang round very grand firms like Chatto, Constable, Collins, Hutchinson, Harrap, and Hamish Hamilton and demanded that they take a column, a half-column, a half page, a page. At £12 a page that was not much, I thought, for publishers who frequently expended a whole £150 on an author's book. But no. After an early spurt of enthusiasm, most publishers continued to be impervious to *Books of Today* and yet bought space at £10 an inch in the *Sunday Times*. That is why there are certain publishers for whom I now have a deep, deep affection. You will find that they once bought A Whole Page in *Books of Today*.

In order to sell space, I now discovered, you have to have something to sell alongside it. So I adapted a character, peering over a prison wall. He was called Mr. Chad: and the idea was that he was Looking in on Crime.

Fortunately too, Jonnie was a detective-story addict.

I was a detective novelist myself, wasn't I? And I had suffered for years from not being reviewed. And, the vanity of detective novelists and the appetite of readers of detective fiction addicts being what it is, I still think this was the most valuable bit in the whole magazine. John Betjeman said that the magazine was the Literary Editor's bible, but he was just being sweet. Month after month we read more and more detective novels and stuffed in more and more pages for Chad and sold more and more space alongside it while Turgenev and Tennessee Williams and Graham Greene languished unsupported in the front of the book. Once I even rang the great Olive Bird, advertising manager of *Good House-keeping* magazine, to sell her some space, and she gave me lunch. And she told me how 'You Editors are always so divorced from advertising.' Blimey, I thought, I wish she'd heard me this morning talking myself into doing three more pages of crime reviews to get three more columns of advertising . . . After this, strangely enough, the book department of the National Magazine Co. actually advertised some cookery books. But what was infinitely more important, Olive gave a copy of *Books of Today* to Oliver Robinson, *her* editor.

I remember the day that letter from *Good Housekeeping* arrived. It was pouring wet outside and the little gas-fire was hissing away: and it really seemed a very dismal thing to be writing hundreds of paragraphs under different pseudonyms. Some time before this, too, I had seen some production figures (Jonnie had kindly kept me in ignorance hitherto) and was going quite wild with frustration. I had talked excitedly about buying the magazine myself, had even tried to involve various businessmen who might have had £1,000 tucked away, and they had all been alarmed by my naïve attitude towards life, arithmetic, and running a magazine. Now here was a man offering me a job as book reviewer in *Good Housekeeping*, a very rich magazine indeed. Maybe the money they paid me might even pay for a circulation manager.

In spite of the wet and the work I was still madly in love with that fickle jade *Books of Today*. Anyone who has edited a magazine will tell you it is like a marriage or a love-affair. The adored object reflects, for a little while at all events, the nicest parts of the Editor. But oh, with what eagerness and insincerity will a magazine begin to reflect her new editor and the nicer parts of *him*.

I went to lunch with Oliver Robinson eager to talk about the fickleness of magazines, which I had only just discovered. I think Oliver thought I was nuts. I found a gentle, shy, fubsy man, rather plump, wearing a black, blue and old-gold tie (it was a Savage tie and denoted tremendous clubmanship) and a navy blue suit, with a soft, brown moustache and pretty, wavy brown hair and nice blue eyes. He seemed worried by me and he frequently patted his finger-tips together. But he was prepared to pay me twenty guineas a month for a book feature. Not quite enough to pay a circulating manager, I thought. 'And of course we would be only too glad to consider feature articles about other subjects, you know. We are always short of feature articles.'

'And how much would you pay for feature articles?' said I, quickly.

'Oh, about twenty, I expect.' Now forty guineas a month *would* be enough to pay a circulating manager. (It was also enough, though it hadn't occurred to me, for me.)

'Of course,' Oliver explained, 'monthly magazines are strange. I mean, we are now working in February on the June issue.'

'That should be quite easy,' I said, delighted. 'I shall ring round my friends the publishers and ask them for page-proof copies of books that are coming out in three months' time.' At the back of my mind I immediately thought this would make an excellent talking-point. There might even be a possibility of selling space . . .

And when I got back to the office I wrote to Mrs. Robert Henrey.

'Obviously,' I said, 'you have written a book which will be published in about three months' time.'

Twenty four hours later I had her reply. Yes, she was just about to have a book published called *The Little Madeleine*. Yes, she would love to have some publicity for it. Yes, she thought it had all the best of her in it. She hoped, moreover, that it might be the Book Society Choice. (It was.)

I well remember reading the galley-proofs in Carlyle Square, hunched up over the coal fire: for the central heating at Carlyle Square had ceased to exist at some point during the war. There was a massive great boiler in the garden, in its own little cottage, so to speak: so big that it would have used five families' coal ration. And every frost one radiator would burst with a spectacular clanking and slowly flood the room that it used to heat in the grand old days when the Earl lived there. Indeed, this was the only difficult thing about Carlyle Square. It was very cold and very draughty, in spite of the marvellous relaxation there, the fact that Jonnie really let me do as I pleased and be myself.

But that night, as I read I was warmed by talent. That this has happened to me more than once is one of the compensations for all the ghastly, dull, boring books I have to read as a book critic. *The Little Madeleine*, in galleys that wound themselves around my feet, was one of the most exciting pieces of prose I have ever encountered.

When I wrote my piece about *Madeleine*, Oliver

Robinson said it was too good for a book column, so it appeared under the pen-name of 'Jane Dorling' in the front of the book. 'Jane Dorling', Oliver saw as a rather middle-aged cosy body with a round felt hat with a brooch in it, a heart of gold and big brogue shoes. From time to time down the years, whenever a subject seemed too soppy for Nancy Spain, Jane Dorling would pull on her metaphorical fur felt and her big thick shoes and rush into the breach. She wrote about 'A Girl versus London', she wrote about an Italian sculptress who had come up the hard way called Fiore Henriques; and she was downright lyrical about 'High Street, London'.

About this time, much to Jonnie's dismay, for she knew I was doing too much work for too little money, I acquired another column: a weekly one this time. And under my own name. I couldn't see it very often, because it was published in Paris, but when I did see it I was gratified to see it had my name very big indeed and a little picture of Miss Spain, peering out amongst the typescript. This, alas, is one of my greatest faults. I like to see my name in print *very big indeed*.

The column was called 'Piccadilly' and it appeared in the *Continental Daily Mail,* at that time flourishing and edited by a fabulous, young middle-aged man rather like Jean Gabin. He was called Noel Barber.

Noel Barber wrote a column for *me* in *Books of Today* called 'The Pulse of Paris'. We intended fair exchange and no robbery, but as his could only appear every month and mine appeared each week, by and by there was a handsome little balance of francs waiting for me in the coffers of M. Malherbe, the Manager of the *C.D.M.* By Easter 1951 I had my heavy chest cold again and it didn't need Jonnie to tell me how wrong I was to take on all this work. A weekly column for the *C.D.M.*, a monthly column and a monthly 'soppy' piece for *Good Housekeeping*: and all these little bits *and* selling the advertising for *Books of Today*. Yes, it was too much.

Jonnie sent me to Brighton and told me not to come back until I had made up my mind what to do about my various commitments. *Books of Today* (she decided) must go, as far as I was concerned. But to compensate for my disappointment over this (after all, I had deeply enjoyed being a real live Editor) Jonnie said she would come to Paris with me and spend my francs.

Oh, we did have a good time. It was Easter-time and we shot with rifles and won silly dolls in the fair-grounds round Montmartre and there was a bus strike and we travelled triumphantly in lorries. And we met Nancy Mitford and Colette and Christian Dior. In between whiles we lay exhausted in our beds at our hotel, reading French and American women's magazines. I can see now how the inspiration for *She* stemmed from that staggering forty-eight hours so long ago.

While Jonnie was picking away at the glossies, explaining to me the basic differences between English, French, and American magazines, I was talking to Nancy Mitford.

Nancy is still one of the most Remarkable Authors I

have ever met. She lives in Number Seven, Rue Monsieur, in a flat spasmodically heated by a big patent stove with a cover like a crusader's helmet. Whenever I arrive there the stove belches out clouds of wood smoke and Nancy always kicks it vaguely and says she's so sorry, can't think what's wrong.

Nancy is tall (5 feet 10 inches), shy, and vague. She is perfectly capable of looking dreamily out of the window and not speaking at all, unless something interests her. She had just been to Chantilly, I remember, staying with the Duff Coopers. It is in Chantilly that the museum harbours a wonderful Book of Hours, *Les Tres Riches Heures du Due de Berry*, and she came blazingly awake to talk about it. She was quite a different person immediately. As a matter of fact, the very first thing I ever asked Nancy Mitford (after I felt cosy with her) was 'In God's name what is wrong with saying *mantelpiece*?'

Nancy, you see, has a curiously scholarly outlook (which isn't surprising really, as she has two scholarly Grandfathers). She early adopted a somewhat donnish outlook towards the English Upper Class, which she adorns. Such words as *handbag, perfume* and *fishknife* form no part of her vocabulary, and when she started (in 1945) to give away such linguistic secrets the whole English Middle Class was ruffled. *Perfume* we understood. We had always said *scent,* anyway. But *fishknife* and *mantelpiece*. What could be wrong with these?

Nancy was kindness itself as she explained.

'A mantelpiece is a ghastly Victorian thing made of

mahogany,' she said. 'Proper Upper Class houses have stone things built into the walls above the fire. So they are called chimneypieces. And the same thing applies to silver. Upper Class families have silver that goes back for years: and as people ate fish with two silver forks, it was considered awfully vulgar when in Queen Victoria's day someone thought of fishknives. The mantelpiece came in with Queen Victoria, too: and very nasty it is, I must say.'

Nancy discovered a scholar with the same outlook as herself in Alan Ross of Birmingham University. His nickname for the cult of Upper Class Usage: U and Non U became a National Game in 1956. So much so, that Nancy and I were invited to debate against one another on the floor of the Cambridge Union. The subject before the House was 'That this House would like to be U'. I decided to oppose it, considering that the Upper Class women have always had a poor time of it: what with no education and such a small vocabulary. And worrying all the time about whether or not to say lavatory or toilet, writing or notepaper. But, alas, Nancy couldn't face it, and so the motion was lost by 78 votes to 43. 'My poor old nerves won't let me appear in public,' said the High Priestess of U. And I remember thinking, so poor nerves are U while poor feet are Non U.

Anyway, I had a good time at Cambridge. And when it was all over and I had had my little triumph, I telephoned the other Nancy in Paris to tell her all about it.

'One young man,' I said, 'wore one brown shoe and one black and grey trousers and a yellow pansy in his buttonhole.'

'Goodness,' said Nancy. 'How very English. Do you know, in London, when rationing came in, all the women sighed with relief? You see, they never need try again about clothes. On the very first day I counted *two* women in one brown shoe and one black.'

So then I told Nancy what happened when I got up to speak.

'I bowed to the house and said "Gentlemen" and they bowed back. So then I asked, "Do I say Ladies?" "No" they shouted in unison "you say *women*".'

'Quite right, too,' said Nancy. 'Lady is a terribly Non U word.'

I have often wondered, after all this, whether Nancy is a rather U Christian name. For since all this U and Non U business people have got the other Nancy and myself muddled up (almost) to a point of no return. Apparently someone was saying the other day: 'It's Lord Redesdale's daughter, isn't it, who is carrying on with Gilbert Harding?'

Then she discovered that I was George Spain's little daughter and she perked up even more. Lord Redesdale, her father, had known of my father well before the First World War: and my mother is able to tell a good story about Nancy when she had a fine collection of frogs behind wire at Redesdale Cottage. My father's mother . . . Georgiana Louisa Spain . . . was a real person to

Nancy Mitford. She spoke with awe of my grandmother's garden on the moors, which was magnificent.

My father's mother had lived in Netherhouses, a little house that faced towards Redesdale Cottage across the valley of the Rede in Northumberland where my father went fishing with his Pig Friend. Nancy said lovely stories were told about her: how she ran up the white ensign when people died and dropped it to half-mast in salute. When people died she also 'told the bees'. My great grandfather had been a Captain, R.N., called Thomas Dilnot Stewart, who had discovered the mutineers of the *Bounty* living on Pitcairn Island and *that* was why my Auntie Katie had called herself Katherine Stewart when she went away to America. When Sister Liz wanted to be romantic she always said we were descended from Bonnie Prince Charlie and the girls at school would goggle. All this Nancy Mitford and I were able to laugh at in our first meeting.

I thought Nancy Mitford a dear. She has five fabulous sisters herself: Pamela, Jessica, Deborah, Diana, and Unity Valkyrie. Pamela married Wing Commander Jackson, R.A.F.V.R.; Deborah is now the Duchess of Devonshire; Jess married, first, Esmond Romilly and tore the curtains down in a country house where she was staying, in revolt, and then married, second, a nice American, Robert Treuhaft; Diana married Sir Oswald Mosley and spoke of Hitler, Himmler, Hess, and Streicher as 'those poppets'. Unity Valkyrie's story will no doubt some day be written by someone better qualified than me. She is supposed to have had a mad craving for sweets before she died so tragically young, the most golden, the most anarchistic of the Redesdale daughters.

The Mitfords are really the Freeman-Mitfords, which name was added in the nineteenth century when they took over the arms and lands of the Freemans of Batsford in Gloucestershire. They were originally Earls of Redesdale. The present Barony was created in 1902. Their motto, 'God Careth For Us', has always seemed to me singularly apt. If ever a family could be described as God's Children they would all be handsome, blue-eyed and rebellious as fallen angels, like the Mitfords.

Take Nancy, for example, the only dark-haired Mitford.

She wrote three novels, *Highland Fling* and *Christmas Pudding* and *Wigs on the Green,* and I gather they didn't sell very well, though all her friends loved them and laughed at the jokes.

'That was just the *point*,' says Nancy, who emphasizes the strangest words in her sentences, which are always full of vogue words and phrases like 'Blissikins' and 'Do *admit*'. 'They were just strings of jokes and no plot at all. Pity.'

Then the war came and Nancy went into Heywood Hill's bookshop in Curzon Street. She was a brilliant manager, so frequently spotting and ordering large quantities of bestsellers that it was almost embarrassing. 'Sweet of you to say so,' Nancy murmurs in her best social manner, 'but really you know anyone could have done it. There was a paper shortage, you see. Blissikins.'

But it was while she was thus brooding over the bliss-ful ingredients of a bestseller that Nancy determined to write a book about her strange family. Yet it must not be *too* obviously about her family; it must be a novel full of love and prettiness and beauty and romantic melancholy. In short, she wrote *The Pursuit of Love,* which in its wit and its mild malice about the crumbling upper crust will never be beaten. Evelyn Waugh attempted a story much the same with *Brideshead Revisited,* but here his theme was religion as well as snobbery, so the fabric of the aris-tocrats didn't crumble with so bright a grace.

But Nancy enjoys and has had no compunction about betraying her class. And furthermore she looks at Evelyn Waugh with awe. 'Oh, he's wonderful,' she says, with a little cry. 'I don't know how you could say that I am in the same street with him.' And one of her books, *The Blessings* is dedicated to him.

The Blessing has a fascinating story of its own. Sir Alexander Korda wanted a script for Mrs. Robert Henrey's son, Bobby, then under contract to him and getting leggier every minute. So he scribbled a sentence, 'A child is torn between France and England, Mother and Father,' on a sheet of paper and handed it to Nancy. Fresh from her triumphs with *The Little Hut*, Nancy plunged in eagerly, producing a film script that for some reason Korda didn't want to use.

'Very well then,' said Nancy. 'May I have it to write as a novel?'

'Of course,' said Korda. 'But remember the film rights are mine.'

Time went by and Nancy produced *The Blessings*, a book that was Book Society Choice, American Book of the Month and of such fearful shock value that her publisher very sensibly refused to allow it to be serialized. At which point, of course, Paramount stepped in and offered 100,000 dollars for the film rights. Which belonged to Korda.

'Quite all right, darling,' says Nancy Mitford. 'Don't grieve for me. *Do* admit, there isn't so much money in the world, anyway.'

When I last saw Nancy it was on a terribly snowy day in Northumberland, Mother and I, Lord Redesdale, Jack Mitford and lots of other people whom I never identified in heavy boots and tweeds, crouched round a little log-fire and ate home-made cakes in Redesdale Cottage. It was a terrible day, snow muffled in great blasts against the window and we drove madly back through to Newcastle before the drifts swallowed us for ever. That was tea in a cold climate with a vengeance.

But Nancy really lives in Paris; a place where she has now put down her roots for ever.

Was it on this weekend in Paris, or some other, that jonnie and I were introduced to Jean Cocteau, the fascinating poet to whom Diaghilev had said, 'Astonish me,' whose films of *Orpheus* and *Beauty and the Beast* had certainly astonished *me*. Cocteau was marvellous. We met him in Le Grand Vefours, that famous restaurant in the Palais Royal where every seat is named after a French writer, and where little brass plaques proclaim that genius sat here, ate here. Cocteau wore a very loose and becoming ski-ing sweater. His shoulders showed through it bony as a skeleton. He wore fascinating grey suede après-ski boots, too. Both given him, he said, by Jean Marais, the actor, his friend, for his birthday. He pounced in conversation like a bird. Like a thin pigeon he circled; one could almost hear the beating of his wings. He complained about language. He couldn't speak English. He said there was a wall of blood between us. (I can't say I noticed it. I found him a most sympathetic man.) He warned me about New York. He said it was an electrifying city, where the pavements could give me a shock if I didn't wear rubber-soled shoes. And he flew away after a while to lunch with the Editor of *Paris-Soir*, M. Lazareff, on the other side of the room. Everybody called him 'Master' and kissed his hand. I found this very strange, for he had seemed so young. Younger, far, than the Editor.

And then on this magic Easter in Paris there was Colette: Colette, the greatest woman writer who has ever lived. Caged, alas, with arthritis when I met her, mauve-haired, mauve-eyed, warm in personality, she seemed to take each second of life as a child would take it, considering it with wonder. 'Me!' she cried. 'Me! Imagine *me* eighty years old . . .' She growled like a lion or a panther, she glared out at the Palais Royal where children played and a nursemaid would sometimes throw a gay, bright ball, that flashed for a minute in the sun. Colette made everything significant because it was all reflected in her marvellous eyes.

Although my spoken French is almost non-existent, for some reason we were able to understand each other perfectly. We sat hand-in-hand and looked at her photographs . . . we saw her in other lives than this. Colette has had as many lives as a cat. We even saw other husbands. For Maurice Goudeket, her last and dearest husband, had crept out, softly shutting the door and saying, 'You will get along all right. You will amuse her, you'll see.'

There was Monsieur Willy . . . naughty M. Willy who had locked Colette in her room and made her write naughty books about her schooldays and had then pretended to have written them himself . . . Maurice Goudeket in swimming-trunks, 'Maurice is well-made, isn't he?' . . . M. de Juvenal, the father of her daughter. 'Oh . . . you must meet my daughter. She is so lovely . . . lovely, and she has an antique shop in the Rue Napoleon. She is away now though, what a pity, staying with a Sugar King. What on earth is a Sugar King? I ask you . . .' I found a picture of a wedding-group and asked, cautiously, was this her daughter? 'Oh, my God, no . . . My daughter's much better looking than *that*.' And then there were the photographs of the animals she had loved, lions, tigers, cats, pumas, even a little wet cat swimming in the river with her master. *'La chatte qui nage.'*

And all around Colette, life glowed and twinkled in objects rare and remarkable because *she* had collected them. There were glass paper-weights with brightness caught in them, butterflies transfixed for ever, red and blue and gold and green, an Indian blanket of mad, marvellous crimson, a yellow sofa cushion where her head rested. And there was an open fire with flames that whispered among the logs. I almost put out my hand to stroke the cats that should have lain there. But there were no longer any cats . . . there were only ghosts of cats . . .

Colette gave Jonnie and me a letter of introduction to Dior, saying, 'If you want to write about Paris, you must write about Dior. He *is* Paris.'

He was in the midst of his collection, of course, but the name Colette opened the doors in the Avenue Montaigne like a latchkey. The flunkeys looked a little bit sideways at us, in our jeans, as we stood dwarfed in the enormous *salon*. Dior had hopsack figures that year, I remember, with diamonds for eyes.

But 'a letter from Colette', they said, and we were swept on and up: and as we reached the innermost rooms, of course they became progressively less grand until we were talking to Dior himself in a little grey room no grander than 8 South Mall, Cork, where my sister had made less famous clothes.

And Dior himself was quite serene and simple too. He folded his pink hands in his lap and smiled all over his pink and well-scrubbed face as he talked of Princess Margaret (so intelligent), his new country house (so peaceful), and Colette.

'Ah . . . that dear, *dear* woman,' he said. 'How is she? Does she suffer much? That horrible arthritis. If only there were something we could *do*. She *is* Paris, Colette . . .'

It is strange, the effect that an encounter can have. Colette had a miraculous effect on me. Long after I left Paris, left Dior, left Colette, I saw things through her eyes, intensified as though a prism had been held up to the world. No, possibly not a prism. It was as though a glass film had been taken *away*. I went back again, of course, and so did Jonnie: and we had a happy time hearing what she had for lunch (pig's trotters) and she was delighted that *we* had had venison cooked in red wine.

There are people whom one loves immediately and for ever. Even to know they are alive in the world with one is quite enough. And Colette was like that.

She died in 1954 and of course she was honoured. Everyone wrote of her and there were yards and yards of words in her praise in the newspapers, of her significance, her splendour, her importance.

I was in New York when I heard the news and I wept, not because she was dead (that was good for *her*) but because I would never hear her roar again, never hear her growl. I wept a little out of sheer self-pity because I should miss her so.

Darling Colette. She wrote in her books for me. She wrote in her favourite *Chéri*: 'A souvenir of my 80th birthday.' But in *La Fin de Chéri* she wrote under the words 'The End of Chéri – and without doubt jolly near to mine, too (?) Colette.'

I know the things that people write in books seldom mean anything, but when Colette marked in that triumphant question mark, I felt the sudden pang of loneliness I was to feel again, years later, in Central Park, when I heard that she had been set free from her cage.

'But you have nothing to do with death,' I cried, as I watched her mark that question mark, and felt the tears start behind my eyes.

'Oh, no,' she said, comfortably. 'It bores me.'

Chapter Fifteen

On our return from Paris I resigned from *Books of Today,* and so lost a very important thing, a rent-free office with a lovely little gas-fire, where I could work all day long and people could call me up. Moreover, T. Werner Laurie Ltd. moved from Piccadilly to Doughty Street, Gray's Inn Road. So I was faced with blank desolation in the day time. I had to keep office *hours* to get my work done, but I had no office to do this in.

First of all Jonnie and I would drop Nicky off at school. By now he was a big, handsome leggy boy of six with fine sticking-out ears, going to the Lycée in Queensberry Place and speaking French with a remarkably good accent. Then we would sweep on to Doughty Street, where Jonnie would disappear into her mysterious world of book jackets, paper, typefaces, and printers. And I would be left outside the little side door. Jealously, let's face it. For I no longer had a proud title like Editor or Production Manager. I had no office and no desk. Jonnie lent me her red M.G. because she was a darling. But awful things happened to me in it. (It once caught fire outside Nicky's school.) And it took me hours to get back to 35 Carlyle Square where I sat at the table in

Nicky's nursery. And it seemed increasingly obvious that I wasted forty minutes getting back there, whereas if I stayed in the vicinity I might only waste about five . . .

So I found a bed-sitting-room in the Doughty Street area. It had a gas-fire and it was in the house of a lady novelist. All went well, and I worked like a Trojan until I caught chicken-pox from Nicky. Neither Nicky nor I had it badly, but I had it *spectacularly*: big pink spots like flowers rose boiling on my nose, forehead, and back. They were, alas, painfully obvious to anyone who met me face to face. So the lady novelist, meeting me one day, picked me up, neck and crop and flung me out into the snow. 'Family life,' said darling Jonnie, with a naughty grin, 'you see how good for you it is.'

There was a slope outside the house, I remember, where I used to start the car when the battery had flattened itself (which it very frequently did) by pushing from behind, running alongside and leaping in and then putting the car violently into gear. I can't think why the gear-box didn't fall out. A complete saga could be written about Jonnie's little red M.G. and its gallantry. I feel disloyal every time I suggest it wasn't quite like other cars.

So I found myself another bed-sitter, this time in the elegant house of chums in Upper Cheyne Row. Instead of driving through London with Jonnie, I walked round the corner, feeling desolate and lonely.

Nevertheless, I finished another detective story.

Moreover, I had had another lunch in the Caprice

with Oliver Robinson, who said, as soon as ever we were sitting down, that he wanted me to be Literary Editor of *Good Housekeeping*. He agreed to guarantee me £40 a month and pay me extra for any additional features I had to work on. But as he was 'pushed for space' he could give me no desk and no telephone. But, he said, I would have to attend Conference.

Conference. I looked blank.

'From time to time,' said Oliver nervously.

Conferences are no doubt very valuable indeed to some people. I only know, dating from the good old days when Terence Horsley used to turn up with his trousers held up with parachute cords, that they have never been any good to *me*. However, for the sake of the extra twenty quid a month, I said O.K., I would come to Conference if that was what Oliver wanted.

Conference, strangely enough, only happened to me once. It happened one morning, in Oliver's big office at 46 Grosvenor Gardens . . . and I can remember very clearly that I was introduced around and learnt from everybody what jobs they were doing. Jane Stockwood, Ethne Davis, Nora Aris, Gladys Williams, Michael Griffiths, they sat there, in heaps, big-eyed. So did I.

Jane Stockwood was on the Editorial Staff of *Harper's Bazaar*. I had met her before, with Angus Wilson, when she had written a piece about him: 'Everyone is talking about – Angus Wilson.' Ethne Davis was a good hard-working girl, who knew all about what lipstick went with what occasion. She was Fashion and Beauty Editor.

Nora Aris was the child psychologist. Gladys Williams was the Assistant Editor, a perfect pet, whose business it was to filter the proofs slowly backwards and forwards to the printer, with corrections on them. Gladys was always on my tail because I was so naughty and wilful about correcting them.

Gladys spoke very slowly and deliberately: because she was so used to keeping a grip on her proofs. Then there was Michael Griffiths.

I am devoted to Michael. He is a big man, with big black bushy whiskers and a wildish streak of unfulfilled fantasy. Hidden away in this lies a genuine sales flair. (So if I went to Michael and said, 'See here, what price Humphrey Bogart writing about Glamour?' he would reply, 'Yes, that's all right, they've heard of Humphrey Bogart in Wales.') Michael tells me that my presence at this Conference killed it stone dead. I can't see why. I don't even believe it. But it *is* a fact that that was the last Conference I attended.

Some of the effects I had on the magazine were all right, however. There was the bright idea I had, for example, about the Duke of Windsor.

The Duke of Windsor had a book coming out that year entitled *A King's Story*. It was to be published by Cassell and serialized by the *Sunday Express*. I got on to Desmond Flower of Cassell and said how about 'A Post-script to *A King's Story*' . . . how about the life he lives now, compared with the life he lived then and all that sort of thing? Desmond Flower was very kind and said yes, of course, the Duke was very co-operative about anything that would help the sale of his book. So I rang the Duke's Private Secretary, Mr. Waddilove, and asked if I might send His Highness a list of questions? 'But *do*,' said Mr. Waddilove.

Oliver and I then prepared a list of questions so exhaustive that it took twenty strong young women twenty days to type them. We then posted them off to Mr. Waddilove. Then, very casually indeed, I rang Mr. Waddilove and said that as I happened to be in Paris anyway next Wednesday, perhaps the Duke would sooner answer them in person?

Mr. Waddilove sounded surprised. 'Well, why not?' he said. 'You can come and see the house, anyway. He may be in the South. How would you feel about going to Antibes?'

Well, I always like going to the South of France, I said. And that was that. I set off to get this World Scoop (for the Duke of Windsor had received no English journalist for a formal interview since his abdication) with a return ticket by air to Paris and about £20-worth of Travellers' Cheques in my pocket. It was no use appealing to the Paris Office of *Good Housekeeping* if I ran out of money, either . . . for it was holiday time. The 14th July was just around the corner. I was on my own, and well I knew it.

As soon as I arrived I rang Mr. Waddilove. He was very kind. 'Come on round and see the house,' he said. 'I have some news for you.' So I went round. All I can remember was the vast emptiness of the *salon*, a wonderful picture of the Duchess and an enormous case of Scotch whisky in the entrance hall. 'For the Duke's guests,' said Mr. Waddilove. 'Well, I do hope he drinks *some* of it,' I said.

'The Duke,' said Mr. Waddilove, firmly, 'will receive you on the yacht *Sister Anne* in Antibes on Friday.'

It was then Wednesday. I had to get down to the South and back and keep alive until Saturday. I bought a return ticket to Antibes and a sleeping-berth . . . that took about £15 of the money. I had to pay hotel accommodation for Thursday. That took another £5 leaving, as you will see, nothing at all for the sort of incidental expenses that are always cropping up in France. Tips, for example.

To make matters worse, I went out to dinner that night and got off with a wild Persian gentleman who sprang on me with a low growl in the taxi coming back and gave me a black eye.

Never mind. I caught my *rapide* from the station next morning and thundered South, only very occasionally fingering my bruises.

I arrived at about 10 that night . . . a warm, soupy July night, pinging with mosquitoes, and I couldn't wait to plunge into the warm, soupy Mediterranean. My date was for 3 Friday afternoon, but even so I couldn't resist wandering along the romantic coast road, down to the glittering, smelly little sea village: to see what the fabulous *Sister Anne* looked like. I hadn't been in the South since 1939.

Antibes was all that I could wish. There were the

strange little alley-ways, the sudden pools of sunlight with cats curled in them. There were the lascars, the Maltese seamen, the little bars with strings of beads clattering in the doorways. And there ahead of me was the big archway that leads into the little port, where the millionaires' yachts lie slopping, slipping, softly side by side in the green and tideless Mediterranean.

But there was no *Sister Anne*. And I couldn't even see her coming.

Bitterly disappointed, red hot, with tiny aching blistered feet, I went back to the hotel, where I bought a swim-suit for about 4s. 9½d. Foolish, you will say: or alternatively, 'Where did you get the money from?' Well, I found it . . . in little dirty notes in my note-case. Oh, the joy as I rushed into the water. And oh, the horror as my little bathing costume burst with a crash along all the seams. Oh, the humiliation as I lay there in the warm water and asked passers-by for safety-pins to pin me together again. Eventually, I came out of the sea pinned all over. I was turning out a cupboard the other day and I came on this frightful object – rusty marks where the pins had been – and that glorious blue day swam up before my eyes again, dazed in the heat haze of the early morning. And I even felt worried again because the *Sister Anne* wasn't there in harbour.

From time to time, I remember, I reassured myself. The chap is Royal, I said. After all, he was once the King of England, I said. *He* will be there. He said he would be. Don't worry. (But still I *did* worry.)

And when I walked down to the harbour again that afternoon, now in a summer dress and bare legs and sandals: and under the arch and *once again* the *Sister Anne* wasn't there, I still didn't lose faith.

An enormous green Buick materialized from nowhere, with a very nice chauffeur from Letchworth. On the door, in chromium letters, was emblazoned H.R.H. The Duke of Windsor.

'His Highness is at the Carlton Hotel in Cannes,' the chauffeur said, 'and asked me to take you there. The Duchess had to have her hair done.'

We were held up for a moment or two while he collected a little tissue paper parcel from one of the other yachts, explained away as, 'The Duchess's belt. Never misses anything does the Duchess, he's more vague like.' And then we were off swirling along the glamorous coast by Juan les Pins, Golfe Juan. I only half-listened to the monologue of the chauffeur. Mostly it was about how awful the ladies and gentlemen of the Press had been, quoting him when he had never said any such thing. 'Fancy,' I murmured. 'Fancy.'

'My mum,' he said, finally, 'is of the old-fashioned sort. That's why I never told her who I was working for.'

Eventually, in heat so grand that the pavements seemed to ache, we drew up in front of the Carlton Hotel, Cannes. I had never been there before and was truly horrified by the number of old ladies like skeletons or pink piggy porkers with hardly any clothes on at all.

Then I was handed from one *maître d'hôtel* to another, until I arrived in a suite filled to the brim with roses, with the blinds half down against the glare. And there in pale blue trousers and a blue and white checked shirt, his hair fair and fine as a child's, was the man who used to be the King of England.

He was completely charming to me; but had it not been for this build-up I don't know that I should have recognized him, so little did he resemble the news photographs of him that were always appearing at this time. I thought him excessively handsome, and almost exactly like all the pictures that used to appear on chocolate boxes and biscuit tins, when he was Prince of Wales and half the women in the world were in love with him.

I still cannot believe that when I met him he was in his fifties. Anyway, I was utterly charmed – and from the moment he opened his mouth, utterly on his side. To begin with, he paid very, very great attention (like a little boy, almost) to the questions that Oliver and I had concocted for him. But as the afternoon wore on and I sat there completely fascinated, and quite disregarding any of the things I had been told about saying 'Sir' or 'Your Highness' or waiting for him to speak first, he quite relaxed and chatted to me in a perfectly ordinary way.

Sorry I'd missed the Duchess . . . yes, she was having her hair done. *She* read detective stories. She had probably heard of me (twinkle there, as if I might mind that *he* hadn't) . . . Yes, that was the yacht he had chartered from a friend, Mrs. Fellowes. He waved a hand vaguely at the hot horizon. That was the white ensign he was flying 'on the authority of a warrant issued to members of the Royal Yacht Squadron'. We quibbled for a second about this, while I said surely he was still an Admiral of the Fleet, so he could probably fly it, anyway? And what about his personal standard, too?

He looked dubious, but he pushed his glasses up on the top of his head and I think he began to enjoy himself. I know that I found him the greatest fun. At all events I really made him laugh, about twice. Once about his clothes and how silly King George V had been about the turn-ups to his trousers. ('I don't think I'd mind what a son of mine wore as long as it wasn't shorts.') And once about my behaviour at an interview.

'But you don't take any *notes*,' he said, suddenly, accusingly.

'No, I know,' I said. 'I never do. Must I? It usually puts people off . . .'

I got a real roar of laughter for that, and he seemed quite touchingly delighted that I wasn't afraid of him. I know I thought him terribly over-sensitive, terribly over-scrupulous and certainly over-anxious to do his best. Now that some years have elapsed, two things I do remember with brilliance – the extraordinary quality of his skin, so fine and supple, clear as a child's. And his kindness and courtesy to me (an unknown reporter) who had turned up in the middle of a hot summer's afternoon when he should have been having a *siesta*.

He came downstairs with me afterwards and crossed the busy road that runs by the sea in Cannes and handed me into the Buick. No one has ever done this for me before or since from an hotel. Lord Beaverbrook showed me to the door at *his* home, Gilbert Harding has pretty manners, too. But the Duke of Windsor crossed right across the street, among the honking cars, the palm trees, the crowds and opened the door of the car for me. One of those Candid Snappy Cameramen appeared from nowhere saying, 'Souvenir of your holiday, please?' as if he were, indeed, indistinguishable from the other men in gay shirts and trousers all around us. The Duke fled, dodging among the traffic until he was safely in the Carlton Hotel again. 'Pity that photographer didn't get it,' said the chauffeur. 'That would be something you'd remember all your born days, eh?'

To tell the truth I don't need any photograph to remind me of the man who was once King of England.

We drove back to Antibes, where later that night I clambered into a hot, grimy, gritty *couchette*. I was now faced with the awful prospect of staying alive until Saturday evening, when my plane left Le Bourget. I got to Les Invalides with exactly 400 francs in the world, having crossed Paris by metro and sent Jonnie a triumphant cable saying, 'Got him stony broke please meet.' I bought nougat, I remember, and sucked it, trying to keep enough francs to pay for the bus out to the airport, and for fifteen long hours I wandered round and round the park by Les Invalides, thinking about the Duke of Windsor.

There was a sort of fair to attract the Youth of France to join the Army, I remember. Over and over again I did the Intelligence Tests Necessary to Join the Foreign Legion. But even as I pushed trees into holes shaped like them and picked out the one Un-citrus Fruit amongst five citrus, I thought about the 'Dook' (as he calls himself).

What a nice man. And what good manners. I was quite right about this, for years afterwards he sent me an autographed copy of his book and one Christmas, quite suddenly, a Christmas card. Funny thing. As with Colette, I felt I knew him so well. And yet I suppose I shall never see him again.

I duly wrote my piece for *Good Housekeeping* and it duly appeared. And (equally duly) I had letters saying what a disgraceful thing and they would never read the magazine again. But as they always forgot to put their name and address there was no way of replying to them.

I did a lot of funny things for *Good Housekeeping,* come to think of it. Such as 'ghosting' the article about Glamour by Humphrey Bogart. I crept down to the set where they were making that famous movie *African Queen* because, if you remember, Michael Griffiths said it was O.K., they had heard of Katie Hepburn and Humphrey Bogart in Wales.

Mr. Bogart was up to his neck in a tank of water when I arrived: the *African Queen* was foundering. He eagerly climbed out and dried off, taking the only dressing-room on the set (a square wooden box somewhat like The

Specialist's little house) to do so. To my amazement, Miss Hepburn didn't even bother to dry off. With her freckles standing out on her face like gold dust and her red hair sopping wet, she seized me by the shoulder and pinned me against the scenery. For about a quarter of an hour she told me what Glamour was. It was very interesting.

'We had a word for it in that movie *The Philadelphia Story*,' she said. She snapped her fingers with excitement. 'Like a ship,' she said. 'Every woman has individuality. And that is her personal glamour. If only women would really be *themselves* people would find them exciting . . . magical.'

By this time Mr. Bogart was dry and waiting for me, so I reluctantly left Miss Hepburn, thinking that really it was rather unfair: she had definitely written the piece. A pity, I thought, that she didn't sign it. Mr. Bogart thought so, too. 'She's a great gal, Katie,' he said. 'Shy, though. Genuinely shy.'

To seize a total stranger by the shoulder and thrust her up against some scenery is the strangest form of shyness I have ever encountered. And it struck me at the time that if Miss Hepburn was shy of strangers she definitely wasn't shy of ideas.

Since this first astonishing encounter Katie Hepburn and I have become, if not intimate, at least 'confidential'. I met her for the second time on the set of *The Iron Petticoat*, when my dear friends Betty Box and Ralph Thomas were making this film with Hepburn and Hope.

On the first of these occasions Katie was making a mild scene because Bob Hope's dressing-room was a little bit bigger than hers. 'Just because I've got styes in both eyes,' she said, 'you think you can keep me in a pig sty, huh?' (I *did* not endear myself to the great star on this occasion by murmuring 'Hey, there, you with the styes in your eyes . . .')

However Katie laughed about this later on when she became more used to me. By and by we had a wonderful time. Once, I was making an advertising film at Pinewood Studios (yes, I was selling Lifebuoy Soap, but I don't think the sponsors liked me) and I got there at about 7.30 a.m. A little red-headed figure (something like Chataway clocking up a mile in a pixie hat) went by me like a bomb and I asked, 'What's that?' 'It's Miss Hepburn, ma'am,' they told me. 'She always arrives like that.'

Then we started to talk to one another in real earnest, paging up and down the dim, shadowy depths of the studios (so like aircraft hangars) between takes. Katie, dressed to the teeth as a young Russian pilot in 'crackerjack' boots by Huntsman, invited me to sit in a chair without a seat and really *roared* with laughter, flinging back her head as she did so, like a naughty little boy of 10. I was charmed by her. I think she has the most beautiful teeth I've ever seen. I had ample opportunity to look at them, and each one was white and crisp and even, right to the last back double molar.

Katie became downright expansive about her clothes and why she, too, wears slacks.

'I can't bear suspender belts,' she said. 'And stockings. Anything cramping round the waist. Valentina makes all my dresses with expanding waistlines. And then of course I can't bear to be dirty, so I do all my own laundry. I always wear the same. White socks, white T-shirt, oatmeal-coloured slack suit. And I wash my hair every single night in Ogilvy's Oil Shampoo.'

I gasped.

'Bottles and bottles and bottles of it travel all over the world with me,' she said.

'Is it really true that you stand on your head while you eat lunch?' I asked.

'Of course not,' she said. 'I always eat lunch lying flat on my back. In fact I won't go to a restaurant to eat with friends, always join them afterwards for coffee. In company I always get over enthusiastic, and this leads to indigestion. Also, I hate to waste time on things that bore me. So I always eat the same lunch every day. *That* saves time in ordering. Steak, salad, and a butter scotch sundae, I would eat chocolate, but chocolate makes my face break out. So I carry a bottle of Butterscotch around the world with me, just like the Ogilvy's Oil Shampoo. No, they haven't got mixed up yet.'

I asked if *she* ever got dressed up, and if so, why?

'Of course I do,' she said, sharply. 'I would always dress up for someone I was fond of, and if he wanted me to. But I wouldn't dress up just for Joe Doaks.'

I liked Katharine Hepburn enormously. She struck me as a girl who has devoted 100 per cent of her time and energy to being herself: and not someone else's idea of her. A deeply refreshing girl, who left me determined to be more myself in future, too. And yet one of the things she told me was by sophisticated standards perhaps a little bit corny? Above her fireplace in the house where she was born in Hartford, Connecticut, in 1909, was a remark in wrought iron, left by a poet who had once owned the house: 'Listen to the Song of Life'.

'There now,' said Katie Hepburn, her head on one side. 'Fancy being born with *that* above one's fireplace. One couldn't go far wrong with that, would you say?'

I said nothing. Simply nodded nervously for I didn't want to disagree. Afterwards I wrote a piece about Katie and showed it to her. In it I had said she was probably 'the greatest movie actress in the world'.

'No I'm not,' said Katie Hepburn, briskly. 'Anna Magnani is. You must go and see her in *The Rose Tattoo*.'

I did so, I may say, and have never been so bored in my life. But these are the only two things upon which I would disagree with Katie Hepburn.

That year, too, I went to New York, and I met Noël Coward. To go to New York I had to mortgage several months' money from *Good Housekeeping*. But it was well worth it. Noël Coward was well worth it, too.

Pat Wallace, Edgar Wallace's daughter, rang up and said why don't you come over for a drink and I said thank you and why not: and I walked into Albany and there in a chair sat Noël Coward. Just like a real person, I thought. Just as though he weren't a legend at all, and known to half the English-speaking world as 'The Master'. He was taller than I had imagined, not so Chinese looking and much, *much* kinder. 'I am curiously untouched by my great success,' he said, elegantly giving an imitation of himself speaking like a typewriter. Because he is a genuine Cockney, and not a Cockney by adoption like me, he always has the quickest, most spontaneous wit in the room.

He called me 'Molly, dear' on this occasion, so that I thought he had me mixed with a famous dancer of the 20's called Molly Spain. But not at all. For since then he has, with some elaboration, called me Nancy Price, Wimbledonia, and the Cricket First Eleven. But then, what else can you expect of a man who once named a Rolls-Royce 'Fluff'?

'You're going to New York?' he said. 'That's wonderful. What will you do, I wonder? What will you think of it?'

Now that I still think is mighty civil. What did it matter (to anyone but me, that is) what I thought of New York? But here was Noël Coward who implied that he (anyway) would be interested in what I thought. Lor' . . . He said lots of other things: some brilliant, some touching, some wise. He was excellent on bullfighting, which he said was a horrible bore. He was quite first class about television. 'I have to have television,' he said, again giving an imitation of himself, 'to keep in touch.'

'In God's name,' cried Pat Wallace, 'in touch with what?'

'Wonderful, beautiful, vital things. I was looking in the other day and saw a swimming gala. It was in Manchester. I should never even have known it was on . . . But there on the side of the bath I saw a perfectly *splendid* woman hopping up and down. She must have weighed fifteen stone at least . . . and three of her children were swimming champions . . . and when one of them won she put on a tartan woollen hat and danced a dance of victory. She was called Mrs. Bottom. Wonderful, vital, beautiful things,' he turned to me and wagged his finger under my nose. 'I should never have seen that,' he repeated, 'but for television. You will find a lot of that,' he concluded, 'going on in New York.'

I sat at his feet for a bit: and so impressed was I by his description of Mrs. Bottom that Jonnie and I bought a television set on the Never Never. Most of my visit to New York I was glued to the television set in the hotel bedroom, too . . .

Flying to America was like flying into the sun.

When we stopped, just before dawn, in Newfoundland, the sun was just sliding up beyond the rim of the world. And we flew down the great Atlantic coastline and the plane caught the light on its wings until it looked as though it were made of purest gold. And then, alas, we flew into a thick woolly fog and the lady who met me at the airport had to keep apologizing for the way that New York looked.

'That should be the Empire State over there,' she said, pointing, 'if only you could see it. There's Macy's and Saks on 5th, very famous stores . . . what a pity you can't see them . . . Oh dear, you should have been here yesterday, the City really did look swell yesterday.'

It was a most wonderfully Ruther Draperish business. When I got to the hotel and that was shrouded in mist, too, I became slightly hysterical. I lay flat on my bed and I called up all the numbers I had been given to 'contact'. And everyone explained that tomorrow was Columbus Day (which meant a stoppage of everything, rather like Whit Monday or August Bank Holiday in England) and everyone was leaving town for the weekend.

By the afternoon I felt I had done my duty. And the most extraordinary meal I have ever set eyes on had been wheeled into my room. A television set was already there – and a young man called Marlon Brando had appeared on the screen . . . and I couldn't get out of the room. As I ate I sat and stared at the television . . . I saw first nights, parades, commercials, plays, musicals, cowboy films, interviews, fights: the whole teeming world splurged itself before me in eight flickering channels. For three days I sat with my eyes out on stalks, occasionally eating the food on the trolley. Then I thought Mr. Coward would be ashamed of me. So I put the set out of order and went out to see what I thought of New York. Instantly, I got lost.

I have never been really steady in my counting over ten. And when some helpful character (say) tried to direct me to 854 E. 29th Street, I had the gravest difficulty in figuring out which was East and which was West and which side of the Avenue I should be. Over and over again some enthusiastic stranger took me in hand. 'See here,' they said. 'It's easy. This is the Hudson River and this is the East River and all the Avenues run that way. And Broadway goes across the whole thing diagonally. See? And all those Avenues are numbered except Madison and Park. And all the streets go up and down and they are numbered, too.'

How I wished, foot-sore and weary, as I struggled up one street and down the next and counting all the way, that I had paid more attention to arithmetic at school.

All the time I was in New York I never discovered which was the Hudson and which the East River.

The food appalled me, too. Devil's Foodmix and crayfish and crawfish . . . and clams . . . and soft shell crabs that somehow looked like spiders . . . and chiffon cakes and French fried potatoes and steak hideously overdone . . . and lemon meringue pie so huge that you could only just tuck it into a hat box.

Better, I thought as indigestion hit me a whack in the solar plexus, if I don't eat anything at all. So I stuck to bacon (always very thin streaky overdone and crisped beyond recognition) and so-called scrambled eggs, which meant they were beaten up in a bowl and poured loosely over a hot plate on the grill. (If I wanted what I called scrambled eggs I found I had to call them buttered. But by then it was too late.) I drank orange juice in the mornings and milk in the afternoons and on the whole I got along very well when I was by myself . . .

But then, one evening, I met a very handsome man called Alan, with huge dark eyes and a kind heart. And he determined to show me a hospitable time. And he took me up to his apartment to meet his wife. And in the apartment was a man called Alfred Katz, who knew where Hermione Gingold was staying. (I remember Alan well because he was a film executive and he said about a book called *Desirée,* which we had just bought for a *Good Housekeeping* serial, that no one gave a damn about Napoleon in America. Napoleon was just a man in a funny hat to the Americans.)

Alfred Katz took me to an old brown-stone house in the East Fifties. He dropped me outside the front door and gave me a push.

The door was open and I crept upstairs. Right up to the top floor I went, peering into room after room. On one floor I remember there was a woman playing the cello. She had turned all the chairs around so they faced her. She was giving herself a concert, I suppose. This seemed to me very sad. But I still hadn't found Hermione Gingold.

So I went down to the front door, which was by now closed, and tried again. I pressed a bell marked Gingold and there was a buzzing note. And the door swung slowly open, like something in a Dracula film. But I heard Miss G.'s well-known tones croaking, 'Right across the entry, de-ah.' And there she was in a flat which she had somehow contrived to make an exact replica of her little house in Kinnerton Street. She was like a breath of fresh air, lilacs, stocks, herbaceous border and all. I never thought to see the day when I should say that about Hermione Gingold.

After I met up with Hermione I really had a lovely time in New York. Her friends were lovely to me, particularly a young man called Jerry Kilty who was prepared to talk all night long if necessary about Life and Love and Literature and could one ever write the twentieth century King Lear story?

For every now and then when there is a pause in the conversation, remembering Thayer Hobson my conscience strikes me and I ask people what they think of this as an idea for a book. Usually they are appalled. But Jerry was mad about it. He even worked out a play outline with me, scene by scene and bullied me into typing it, coming round to my hotel to do so. (I found this the other day and was particularly surprised by the scene where Mrs. Lear goes mad on Hampstead Heath and gets a job as a lavatory attendant.) Instantly my bedroom filled with engineers trying to mend the television, chambermaids changing the bed linen and towels, and other chambermaids wanting to talk to the *first* lot of chambermaids. Jerry continued to dictate, lying on his back on the floor throughout.

In the end, when the television was put right, they went away . . . and then, alas, Jerry and I had no wish to write any more but sat enthralled by a programme presented by Glorious Swansdown Cake Mix.

After four or five days of such happiness, Jerry said I had better bustle about and make friends and influence people. So he made me ring up Maria Riva, Marlene Dietrich's daughter. She was astonished: but she agreed to have lunch with the English journalist at Sardi's.

'Sardi's is very *grand*,' said Jerry, pushing me out towards it in my best bib and tucker. 'Sardi's is just like the Ivy used to be. Only the very *greatest* theatrical names go there.'

I presented myself at the appointed time and Mr. Sardi *(was* it Mr. Sardi? He stood there in the entrance, this man, with a little black moustache on his upper lip) said that No, ma'am, Mrs. Riva hadn't booked a table, but yes, ma'am, Miss Dietrich *had*.

This remark had a terrible effect on me. It took me ten minutes heavy work before I told myself that it was just a kind mother making a reservation for her little daughter and I wouldn't be expected to meet Another Legend so quickly. (Noël Coward was quite enough, I felt, plus the Duke of Windsor, for one year.) In time I tottered downstairs to the restaurant where Mrs. Riva presently arrived.

'It is you I am interested in,' I said sternly. 'Don't give me all that stuff about your mother. Let me hear how *you* became a television star.'

No use. No matter how we tried the talk always came back to Mother. Mummy did this. Mummy did that. Mummy did the make-up. Mummy helped with her rehearsals. She, Maria, helped Mummy with her songs. Now she did for *her* children just what Mummy did for *her* when she was little; she made gramophone records and posted them off like letters every day. Mind you, I was all for this. I cannot imagine anything nicer than a long, cool chat about Marlene Dietrich with someone who really knows her.

How would I know what I ate in that fabulous restaurant, with that fabulous child? She seemed to want to eat the most extraordinary things, I remember. A raw steak hamburger, a piece of chiffon pie (this was terribly nasty, I thought), but I ate exactly what she did. It was easier.

She was surrounded by high-ranking theatrical friends and she talked to them, introducing me politely, incessantly. She was very composed. Eventually I left. But I shall always have an impression of a charming girl: intelligent, friendly, who had evidently suffered at some time or another and was not again lightly going to let her barriers down. Strangely enough, she seemed to me a counterpart to the Duke of Windsor.

After this Jerry made me go and see a lot of Editresses.

Editresses are amazing, particularly in New York. In New York they sit couched in splendour behind their desks, wearing *hats* all the day long.

I have never been able to wear a hat. My hair is peculiar in that it grows so fast that any hat I put on instantly leaps from my head. (I had terrible trouble in this way in the war, in the W.R.N.S.) So I looked at these ladies in awe. I met Marie Louise Aswell of *Harper's Bazaar* (known as 'The Bazaar' in New York) and I met Maggie Cousins of *Good Housekeeping* (and she had a silver spur on her desk given her by Ethel Merman). I rang up a number of other editors of magazines with titles like *Town and Country*, *House Beautiful*, *Woman's Day,* and *Reader's Digest*. They were fascinatingly uninterested in England and what went on over there. (Except for Princess Margaret and the Royal Family. They are the exception to every rule.) So in the end I told this to Jerry and he stopped nagging me and we just had fun . . .

We went to Chinese restaurants and we met a friend of his called Herma Briffault who had ghosted many, many books. We walked in Central Park where the trees were gold like bonfires and in the morning the mists rolled up from them as though they were indeed, alight. We walked down the Avenues and looked in the shop windows and once I saw a live eel for sale. We went to Woolworth's on 5th Avenue and I was dazed by the toys. And then, with great care, we spent my dollars on space guns and space helmets for Nicky and tiny lighters and nylon underwear for Jonnie.

Once, too, I went to a party where I was to meet a lot of Television Packagers. To this day I do not really know what a television packager *does*. I imagine them packing the sets into great big cartons, something like cornflake boxes, but this cannot be so. Anyway, this television packager was a smart young man with curly black hair, who wore a suede shooting jacket with a zipper down the front, who said from time to time, 'Oh, what a lousy host am I.' Brian Michie was there, I remember, lying on the floor in his shirt-sleeves. Brian is a big man and he felt that the chairs wouldn't hold him and he was hot so he took off his coat. For some reason we were talking about the war. A lady came up and stared at us.

'You English,' she said. It was more of a threat than a statement.

'Yes,' said Brian.

'Hm,' she said. And went away.

By and by she came back with a lot of her friends and they looked at us gravely, as though we were some kind of wild beast. 'They were talking about the war just now,' she said. And then they went away again.

'Look,' said Brian to me, 'I am hungry. You must get off, dear, with someone and take me out to dinner.'

'Well, none of those people are any good,' I said. 'They don't think we're human, anyway.'

'They ought to *feed* animals,' said Brian, gloomily.

Then a little man in brown detached himself from the throng.

'Do I hear English voices?' he said. 'You do,' said Brian.

'Then which of you,' he said, 'is the writer?'

Brian pointed at me and he sat down on the chair that Brian felt wouldn't hold him. 'I am interested,' he said, 'in a project whereby the better American authors, such as William Faulkner, will be sold in Manchester, England.'

I opened my mouth to say that I didn't like the works

of William Faulkner and that I didn't think that it would be easy to sell them in Manchester, England, but Brian kicked me and told me to shut up. 'This is it,' said Brian, under his breath. 'This is where you get off and we all go out to dinner.'

'What's that?' said the little brown man.

'I was saying,' said Brian, magnificently, 'that William Faulkner is one of my favourite authors, in fact a *winner*.'

'Yes,' said the little brown man.

'Look,' said Brian, rising from the floor in sections. 'Suppose we go and continue this fascinating conversation over dinner. I never can talk about literature when I'm hungry.'

'I don't think I've got any food at home,' said the little brown man.

'Then let's go to a restaurant,' said Brian.

'I have no money,' said the little brown man.

'Then you must borrow some from your host,' said Brian. And he led him gently up to the young man in the suede zipper jacket, who said he only had twenty dollars.

'That is quite a good sum,' said Brian. 'We can have a good dinner on twenty dollars.' And he folded the bill and stuck it in the jacket of the little brown man and made him drive us in his enormous Cadillac to the Chinese Restaurant on 4th Avenue, where I had been first taken by Jerry Kilty.

'How very American and wonderful,' said Brian, 'to have an enormous Cadillac and no money.'

When I wrote this story later I didn't use Brian's name, but called him 'A Lord'. Brian was rather hurt, although he enjoyed his elevation to the peerage. He asked me to restore his name, so everyone would know that it was he. I sent it to the *New Yorker,* they said it was 'thoroughly Anti-American' and they wouldn't dream of printing it. But I liked New York so *much*.

Even now if I shut my eyes I can see the view from the top of the Empire State Building, the sky-scrapers reaching up, growing towards me, like flowers from the garden of Manhattan. The frozen lily of the Chrysler building, the great cathedral of the Rockefeller Centre – the flashing absurdities of advertisement in Times Square, *so* vulgar, on such a grand scale that they surpass vulgarity.

And then when the sun goes down and dark falls and the whole of New York is made of black velvet and the windows appear, one by one, golden blanks in the night . . . Oh, then New York is so beautiful that it stops my heart.

For everyone had told me such a lot about New York, you know. But they never warned me how beautiful it was.

Chapter Sixteen

It was on the flight back from New York that I learnt for the first time what tremendous roots of love and dependence I had now put down into London. Much of the way I sat in the pilot's cabin and I can remember my homesickness as clearly as the moisture that dripped all the time from the cabin roof. Could it have been open to the fierce sun? Surely not. I suppose that heavy frost had formed outside the cabin in the night. I had never been in the cockpit of an aeroplane before and it made a terrific impression on me. It is so much easier to *see* in front. The grey Atlantic looked like shining silk below me: every now and then it was dotted with ships, small as insects. Even a great liner (one of the Queens?) made no more ruffle on the surface of that great lake than a baby duck might make in St. James's Park.

Ireland seemed small, too. It was a green and semi-precious stone, curiously carved, here one second, gone the next. We did not set down at Shannon. White breakers appeared on the coast of Wales, hummocking brown and green moorland swelled below us and then we were suddenly spiralling up the Thames valley – no wider than a silver thread, bless it, but then growing and growing until hedges spanned it, dirt stained it and it became the Thames I love. Then we circled, to save the buzzing in our ears, and we swerved in glory while the great field of London Airport spread miraculously below. The pilot, explaining how such things were strictly forbidden, allowed me to rest my hands on the dual control. So I felt as though I and I alone brought that great bird down out of the sky.

There was another miracle. I saw the little red M.G. waiting among all the other cars in the car-park and I even picked out Jonnie, faithfully dancing there with impatience to know what Woolworth's was like in New York. Can you wonder I was glad to be home with such a welcome?

And it has always been like that whenever I go away.

As I get older and I go away it is increasingly dear to come home to London. Those maddening suburbs, those endless streets, that dear Covent Garden, the terrible traffic, the absurd tube, the strikes: all this is home. I could not change it for any other city on earth.

Although Jonnie was so nice about it, we both felt that this had been a meaningless (and very expensive) trip to New York. But we were wrong. For after I had welded the crazier of my experiences into a piece for the *New Yorker* and the *New Yorker* had turned it down – I sent it to the *New Statesman* who printed it. And the piece was apparently read by George Malcolm Thomson who showed it to Arthur Christiansen, the Editor of the *Daily Express*.

I have been told that Chris read this piece of mine and asked Harold Keeble to go and get me. Anyway, some months must have elapsed, for Hermione Gingold came home from New York, too, and made a big success on the Home Service with her Charles Addams Family: Mrs. Doom's Diary, which appeared under the title *Home at Eight*. I was sitting in Hermione's house when I first became aware of Harold Keeble, a faint voice on the end of a telephone, wanting to know where *I* might be found.

At that time I was much plagued with the suggestion that I should write Hermione's life story (perhaps, for once, Harold wanted Hermione to write *mine*? No, it wasn't likely) and I was convinced that this was all that poor Harold wanted. I ignored the little voice on the telephone and the request that I should go and see him at once.

'Oh, *do* ring him up,' said Hermione. 'Please. I want to know what it's all about.'

But I didn't. I went back to *Good Housekeeping,* in spite of the fact that I had never persuaded anyone there to let me have a desk or an extension or even to acknowledge my existence in any way. At *Good Housekeeping* I found the Art Editor, Michael Griffiths (of the black whiskers and the fantastic mind), with a message from Harold Keeble of the *Daily Express*. 'I should ring him, Spainy,' said Michael. 'You never know.' But I didn't.

When I got back to Carlyle Square that evening, I found that Margaret Shaw, our treasure, had a message for me. 'Would I please ring Mr. Keeble of the *Daily Express*?' It was some days before I began to wonder if in fact it had anything to do with Hermione at all. Then, of course, I rang up and said to Harold, somewhat rudely, 'What do you want? If it's anything to do with writing Hermione Gingold's life story, I won't.'

'But no,' said Harold, as though humouring a lunatic (which, of course, by now he was convinced he would have to do for ever and ever amen), 'the Editor wants you to come and write some book reviews for us.'

It was in this way, at the age of thirty-five, that I came to Fleet Street. Strangely enough, I had fulfilled my childish boast when I was sacked from the *Empire News*. I came when 'they sent for me'.

A lot of false glamour surrounds 'The Street', for this is what journalists insist on calling it. They would greatly like to provide it with a parallel mystique to 'The Brigade' (of Guards). There are pubs there: The Cheshire Cheese, El Vino's, and the King and Keys, where little nests of happy hacks meet and delude themselves of their happiness. There are eating places: The Wellington or Shortland's, whose names strike joy into the heart of the provincial newly arrived. These places are more than pleasant. They contain the breath of life, life breathed by the sort of people with whom it is a joy to talk, educated, tough, unafraid, the salt of the earth. But journalists who never leave the Street are a terrible thing; as bad as writers who consume other writers at literary parties. Eventually they know nothing about anything except other journalists: and though this is very enjoyable for them, eventually they wither and die. They lose their fresh innocence of vision. They become cynical, tired, young-old men, with hair whitened by catching perpetual deadlines with stories that aren't quite good enough. The stories are usually not good enough because they haven't left the Street 'to go and see'. They have remained in the Street and used the telephone. But there *are* journalists who aren't like this, who in the face of twenty years or more of the battering of their daily life, come up honest and gay and as enthusiastic as a child of two and a half. Most of these men, it seems to me, work for the *Daily Express*. But there, I suppose I am prejudiced.

Fleet Street is a magic street for me, whether I stand at the top of it under the great black bubble of St. Paul's, or whether I stand at the ignoble legal end of it by the Law Courts, menaced by the mad black dragon at Temple Bar. I love to see the vans flash by, trying to beat each other with the afternoon editions of the evening papers. Green for the *Standard,* red for the *Star,* yellow for the *News,* which they say has the greatest front page in journalism. *(Not* as great, I tell you, as the *Daily Express* . . .) These vans are noble things, ungoverned by the laws that hem lesser creatures. Because they carry the sacred news they jump the lights, they swerve in and out of traffic: their rubber wings protect them from catastrophe, their flashing signs and honking horns are regarded with grave benevolence by the policeman who directs the traffic at the bottom of Chancery Lane.

I once knew a man who drove such a van and he was immortal. He had need to be. His name was Douglas Gray and he had a violent red beard and he collected Victorian musical instruments.

Fleet Street is quite different from the way it was in Johnson's day. There are too many women there now; and these spoil the much-protected masculine mystique. But it is still a good place, almost the best in London,

When I drove down Fleet Street to confer with Harold Keeble, I had great difficulty in parking the car. There is, I believe, a car-park that goes with the great black glass building that Lord Beaverbrook ordered from Sweden; it is somewhere around, hidden in fallen masonry and bomb damage; but I have never found it. The entrance to the *Express* was, and still is, marvellous. On my left there was a glass-covered counter – something like the departure platform in an Airways, where patient men cope with callers. On the right there was a massive great sculpting in bas-relief – a sort of Benares brassware job – showing the Mother of Empire surrounded by her children. Right ahead there was a short flight of rubber-covered stairs and two lifts. At the bottom of the stairs, his generous mouth tightened as though he wanted to stop himself bursting out laughing, was the Epstein bust of Lord Beaverbrook. Why shouldn't he laugh, if he wants to? This was the house that Beaverbrook built.

Symbolically, as I approached these portals for the first time, the little red M.G. (now fast approaching its climacteric) burst into flames. It burnt merrily for some time outside the Press Association building until I put out the fire with my duffle coat. Nobody noticed, but one young reporter from P.A. came and asked me who I was.

Harold Keeble eventually came down and saw me in the hall. He was a square, short, bustling young man with thick, straight, fair hair cut short in the nape of his neck. He looked a little like a bull. Indeed, many of the men who work for the *Express* do so. I mean no disrespect by this. I am devoted to bulls and never waste an opportunity of attacking bullfighting. Chris, the Editor, looks like a bull. So does John Gordon, the Editor in Chief of the *Sunday Express*. So does the greatest of them all, Lord Beaverbrook.

Editors in the *Express* are constantly charging about from pillar to post within the organization, but for that first mad month Harold endured me and I endured Harold. Only once did he take my copy out to dinner with him and leave it under a table in the Grill Room at the Savoy Hotel. Only once did I try to get the phrase 'Nothing Succeeds like Incest' past him and into a respectable family newspaper. Sometimes he would lose his temper with me, shrieking and raising his hands high above his head. Once he made me rewrite the whole column at nine o'clock at night, saying as I typed, 'This piece is being very carefully read, I tell you, very carefully read.' This meant, of course, that Lord Beaverbrook was lying in the sun somewhere, scowling slightly, waiting to sack yet another book critic. But I simply didn't understand what Harold meant. *I* thought he meant (poor innocent booby) that the *public* were probably reading it . . . bless their four and a half million hearts.

At the end of this madcap month Harold went away to be Editor of the *Sunday Express* and I worked with Colin Valdar, a mild young man more like a pussycat than a bull, who wore a long-sleeved button-up-the-front crochet-work sports jacket. Then Colin left to be Editor of the *Sunday Pictorial* and I worked with Tony Hern, a nice man with uneven teeth, usually clenched on a pipe, no nasty habits and fortunately for both of us, a wonderful sense of humour. Those early days with the *Express* were marked by terrible duelling (known as Crossing Typewriters) over the body of N. Spain. This upset my mother, far away in Newcastle, who said that she and Mr. Currie, the milkman, couldn't see why the *Express* kept me on when everybody hated me so . . .

For example, I said that authors were lazy and *Denise Robins* attacked me. I said Colonel Pinto, the famous spy, was beastly to suggest that women spies were only harlots and *Colonel Pinto* attacked me. I said an author called Max Catto was wrong to assume that our dock-yards were run by a lot of commies and *Max Catto* said, 'Minds like yours leave me Petrified!'

I became Book Critic of the *Daily Express* in the spring of 1952 and the first words I ever wrote for the paper were, 'Can you read?' My dear friend Tony Hern has since taken me to task over this arrogant, impertinent little phrase. Unworthy of me, he says it is. By June of that year, by the time that Lord Beaverbrook 'sent for me' I made a collection of letters from angry authors. The best ones we now stick on a board in the hall.

By June, Chris had kindly told me that I was entrenched. But I still used to creep into the church of St. Mary le Strand to ask God to make me a good reviewer and to thank Heaven that I still *was* one. It was just before he left for the *Sunday Pictorial,* I remember, that Colin Valdar told me about Louisa M. Alcott. 'You must write something about her,' he said.

'Oh?' I said. 'Why?'

'Well, Chris is always on about her. Says that the paper has no heart. That he wishes Louisa M. was writing for us.'

That very week Louisa M. Alcott's life story was published. It wasn't very good, but it made a talking point. Eagerly I wrote that 'No child need be lonely while Meg, Beth, Jo and Amy were in the house'. And Lord Beaverbrook sent for me in the afternoon.

Lord Beaverbrook has since sent for me many, many times: and I have gone with my heart beating in pleasurably terrified anticipation. As soon as I am inside that great penthouse that occupies the whole of the top two floors of Arlington House, my heart resumes its normal pulse. Only once has The Old Man sent for me to give me a cursing. And though this was a tremendous experience, rather like being out in a thunderstorm without an umbrella or an overcoat, I know it was probably the most *valuable* experience of my life.

'I was reading your column about Louisa M. Alcott,' he said. 'You say she is a great writer?'

'Yes,' I said.

'You mention her book, *Little Women*: would you say this was a saleable book?'

'I *know* it is,' I said. 'I was checking and there are about five editions of it still in print.'

'But do the public *buy* it?'

'Oh . . .' I said, exasperated, for what a waste of a conversation with the most powerful man in the world. 'You *know* they do . . . Ask anyone.'

What followed next may well have been a dream.

It seemed to my bemused eye that Lord Beaverbrook picked up the telephone and said, 'Give me Mr. R. A. Butler.' As I protested feebly that I had been tipped off about Louisa M. Alcott and the whole thing was a waste of time, he was connected up with somebody who appeared, indeed, to be the Chancellor of the Exchequer. 'That you?' he said in that marvellous Canadian voice which has so often snarled in my dreams and nightmares. 'Have you heard of Louisa M. Alcott? You have? Would y'say that she is a good writer? Y'would. Do y'daughters read her? They do . . .' And he put the telephone down. 'You were right,' he said. 'Would you like a drink?' I said yes, thank you very much, and accepted a very large whisky and soda. Then Lord Beaverbrook put on a coat and a rather shapeless hat and led the way out on to the balcony overlooking the Green Park. Far, far away through the tufted tops of trees one could see the top of

Buckingham Palace and the Royal Standard. We sat in an icy blast. I was quite enthralled by him.

'I thought at first you would be no good as a book critic,' he said. 'Too literary. But I see now I was wrong.' He looked at me keenly for a long moment with eyes that I thought were yellow, but now checking and rechecking down the years I see are blue. 'I think you may be very good indeed,' he said. 'As good as James Agate.'

Now the awful thing about this is that James Agate (whom I deeply admired as a theatre critic) was a wonderful theatre critic because he knew and loved the theatre. But he did not know and love books. Indeed, I think he seldom opened one if he could help it. His impact as a book reviewer revolved entirely around the sale of review copies, which he swelled to gigantic proportions, sometimes ringing publishers for another copy of a book while the taxi vibrated at the door, waiting to take it to Foyles, where he would sell it at one-third of the published price. So my heart didn't react very happily to this praise.

'I don't know that it's right to keep you on books,' he said next.

Oh, God, I thought, with sudden horror of the unknown.

'Tell me about yourself,' came next. 'And where were you born?'

I cannot really believe that Lord Beaverbrook really wanted to listen to the story that has occupied the last 261 pages. Fortunately when I said 'Newcastle-on-Tyne,' he riposted, 'And I was reared in Newcastle, New Brunswick, so that is quite a thing. My mother at the age of eighty had a great fancy to see the other Newcastle, your Newcastle. And once, when her train was travelling to Scotland she learnt that it would stop in Newcastle-on-Tyne at five o'clock in the morning. So she rose and dressed herself and descended from the carriage. And so she was able to say that she stood in Newcastle-on-Tyne. It was too much for her. She died shortly after.'

I adored Lord Beaverbrook on sight. His quickness, his humour, his generosity (particularly in praise) are so much greater than any other human being's that for days after one has left the charmed atmosphere around him everyone else seems exhausted and dull. Five minutes with the Lord and adrenalin courses through the veins. Fifteen and I can move mountains. Four hours, the length of a happy dinner-party, and I long somehow to mark the hours with a white stone or a little crock of gold. So does he, it seems, for once after a particularly happy meeting he suddenly sent Jonnie and myself a present of £50. More important, though, is the vitality and enthusiasm he gives away.

I met him once on a grey day in June, walking with John Gordon in St. James's Park. They were crossing the road together and suddenly he saw me and he waved and I couldn't help but leap out of the car and run to shake his hand. We both nearly got run over, cars hooted right down the length of the Mall: but it was such a happy thing, and I was so pleased to see him, that it set me up for days to come.

It isn't easy to write about him. I have never been to the morgue and looked up his cuttings, never wondered where his first £10,000 came from, I once asked him if the first £100 were important to a millionaire. 'No,' he said; '£10,000. If a boy has managed to make that quickly and stick to *that* much he is well on his way to the first million.' So what I know of him I have only seen with my eyes.

Often, however, bits of The Legend come my way. Then I wait eagerly until I see him again to find out if it is true. When I met him first he was seventy-three. His round, amazing head was like a bronze head . . . of a faun, a Greek faun, or the Lincoln Imp. He is brown because he perpetually, methodically, soaks up sun from the South of France or the Bahamas. He once told me that the only room in the world where he had never had asthma was in an hotel (was it the York Hotel?) in Canada . . . and it is apparent that when he is bored, or fed up, or disapproving of something and unable immediately to speak his mind and clear his soul of his disapproval, a red spot will come in his cheek and burn there. If these conflicts within him are unresolved, he *does* become breathless.

His head is marvellous. So are his hands. Huge, very sensitive, usually relaxed. He loves to stretch them suddenly above his head when he is pleased. Often when he does this he roars, abruptly, with laughter. Round his throat (against the occasional breathlessness, I suppose) his collar is always loose and his tie is loose, too. His suits are not spectacular: usually they are dark blue. But his trousers are perfectly wonderful. I cannot imagine where there is a tailor in London who can achieve the perfection of cut that the Old Man's trousers show. He also has very beautiful feet, very elegantly shod, usually in brown calf. His feet, like his hands, like his head, are large. All these things are wonderful about him. But above everything else is his youth: his youth and joy in everything down to the smallest and most easily forgotten detail.

Oh yes, I love Lord Beaverbrook. It is impossible to work for him and *not* love him. He is, I would say, the only genius I have ever met. He has his enemies, usually small men, mosquitoes in the world of finance or literature who buzz about saying that he only wants to do harm. This is untrue. But sometimes these stinging flies have hatched out in his benevolence; and he has found them wanting in some respect. So then they never waste an opportunity to bite and do *him* harm. But Lord Beaverbrook is used to the tropical insects of the Bahamas and Jamaica. He doesn't even seem to trouble to scratch.

'Is it true,' I once asked him, 'that you receive your editors stark naked and sitting on the lavatory?'

He gave the matter grave consideration.

'Naked, yes,' he said. 'On the lavatory, no.'

And someone once told me that Beaverbrook went to a performance of Wagner: to *The Ring* in its entirety, or some such interminable thing, and emerged into the daylight, blinking, after three days of it, saying, 'This Wagner, now. Was he a clean-living man?' 'Is *that* true?' I asked him, at two o'clock in the morning, after a prolonged (and glorious) dinner session.

'If it *is* true,' he said, 'and it might be, I suppose, I said it as a joke, do you understand? A *joke*.'

This is the great thing about Beaverbrook that no one ever seems to grasp. He has a colossal, all-embracing, stupendous sense of humour. It gives him, of course, infinitely more sense of power than all his £40 million or his fabulous chain of newspapers.

Dinner with the Lord is a tremendous thing. Sometimes he has guests. Then you might easily find Lord Margesson, Sir Beverley Baxter, Gilbert Harding, René MacColl or some other brilliant charmer. Sometimes you are alone with him: and this is best of all, because less confusing. I once heard him tick off a man who was hogging the conversation. 'There was,' he said, 'a man called Horatio Bottomley, who liked to hog the conversation. And one fine day he found himself at a dinner where a tremendous French courtesan was telling about another French courtesan and her legendary attractions. Finally Bottomley could stand it no longer. "She was my aunt!" he cried, in tones of thunder. And that, dear, is you.' The wretched man who had been so brilliantly reprimanded didn't turn a hair. He continued to bob unperturbed, like a cork on the conversation.

If I dine alone with the Lord I usually find him sitting,

dictating into one of his little machines or standing with his back turned, working at a sort of wooden lectern. As he finishes with anything he throws it on the floor. So any room that he leaves is littered with pieces of paper, magazines, newspapers, all demurely picked up and replaced by the valet or the houseboy. Albert is the house-boy, a charming Cockney with glasses and a deep, worried smile.

'Where did Albert come from?' I once asked, fascinated as Albert fetched a zinc bucket full of ice to cool a bottle of Rhine wine. It was quite an ordinary zinc kitchen bucket, which annoyed Lord Beaverbrook. 'Good God,' he said, looking at it. 'Haven't we any better bucket than that? Albert used to bring the bread up to the house. He was the bread boy.'

As the door swings slowly shut behind me Lord Beaverbrook will advance through the littered magazines and shake me by the hand. His handshake is quite unmasterful. It is not at all what you would expect. It is gentle, pliant almost. 'Will you have a cocktail?' he says. This is always a tricky moment, for I really do loathe cocktails and sometimes Lord Beaverbrook has a lovely new shaking machine that he wants to show off and then *he* is disappointed. If he senses this reluctance on the part of his guests he is kind about it. 'Well, you can have a glass of champagne then,' he says. Jonnie, Lord Beaverbrook and I once drank three bottles of champagne between us . . .

The dining-room is curiously bleak. The table goes

undecorated, except for the marvellously clean food (usually roast chicken and large quantities of fruit) and a centre piece of cherubs bursting out of what looks like an Easter Egg. I have often wondered about this ornament. (Is it Dresden?) I long to pick it up and look at the mark on the base, but I have never quite had the nerve.

I am worried, too, by the absence of flowers in the flat: and on his seventy-sixth birthday I rang the valet, Charles, to find out was the Lord perhaps allergic to them?

'By no means,' said Charles. 'I think he loves them.'

So I sent round a very silly, highly feminine affair of pale pink sweet peas and pink roses all tied up with a massive great bow of pink ribbon. 'So very many thanks,' he wrote by return, 'for the beautiful flowers which I have set in the centre of the table. Visitors come and ask me "Where from?" I answer, "A woman."'

Soup comes. It is usually thin, clear life-giving *consommé* in broad low plates for the guests. But Lord Beaverbrook gets his in a sort of tea-set and he spends about ten minutes pouring it backwards and forwards from the milk jug to the cup and saucer.

'Whatever are you doing there with your soup?' Jonnie once asked him. 'Sunburnt lips,' replied the Lord. This still means nothing to me, as obviously the milk jug keeps the soup much hotter than a broad low soup plate. Perhaps china gets less hot than a metal soup spoon.

Dinner is usually served by Albert and Charles, who betray very little emotion at the astonishing conversation.

I suppose they have watched history being made, these two, so long that they would be moved by nothing less than the arrival in the lift of Greta Garbo *and* Marlene Dietrich, riding pillion on a white horse.

At one time we always had roast chicken for dinner, but since the publication of a very witty book by Daphne Fielding (former Marchioness of Bath) complaining about this, there are occasional variations in diet. For example, a week or two ago we had cutlets, about twenty-four of them. There was no question of Family Hold Back. Pudding is usually tapioca or semolina (both favourites of mine anyway) with large quantities of fresh peaches, pears and grapes. Lord Beaverbrook obviously adores fruit and once wasted a good ten minutes extolling its virtues – how it grows in such profusion in Jamaica and all that.

'To tell the honest truth,' I replied, 'I'm afraid I rather hate fruit.'

For some reason he loved this: and simply *roared* with laughter.

Then there is coffee (very good coffee) in very small cups, and he is usually eager to show the treasures that he has collected from the world of art. On one occasion there were about fifteen canvases (of varying degrees of excellence) by Graham Sutherland scattered about the penthouse. Some of them were very tricky indeed, and there was one of Lord Beaverbrook himself that looked as if it had been worked up from photographs. I remember a magnificent Matthew Smith with a nude girl, very brown, in the midst of it. And I remember best of all a very exciting woman's head by, of all people, Fragonard. The woman was proud and contemptuous. Her head was half-turned, her neck muscle brought into superb relief. She said, plain and arrogant as anything, 'I don't give a toss for any of you.'

'I love that picture,' said Lord Beaverbrook. 'I have carried it across half the world with me.' As he said this his eyes burnt quite, quite blue like little flames.

To me Lord Beaverbrook has always been kindness itself: gentle, inspiring, and generous. And when I have annoyed him, he has, with rare patience, told me so and forgiven me.

Nineteen-fifty-two was indeed a vintage year for me. Not only did I meet Lord Beaverbrook, I met three other remarkable people. 'Teach' Tennant, Joyce Cary, and Thomas Bartholomew Laurie Seyler.

'Teach', now sixty years old, has a shock of white curly hair and a face that looks as if it were made of soft brown leather. She has the manners and disposition of a Buddhist monk and she has the vocabulary of a wise-cracking San Franciscan teenager. She is the tennis coach who made world champions of Alice Marble and Maureen Connolly. She has also made good 'club-standard' players out of a number of American film stars. She invented the 'tennis clinic' method of teaching fifty or sixty school kids at a time and can (if the right temperament comes along) make 'killer' champions out of individuals.

This extreme talent has at last sickened Teach. She has

(or so Teddy Tinling tells me) retired at the very peak of her success. She says she refuses, ever again, to give individual tuition. Teddy called on her last year in her little house at La Jolla, California, and found her happy and well, but serenely withdrawn from worldly desires and ambitions, reading great tomes of comparative religion. It is easy to say 'What a pity' and to complain that we shall see no more Teach-manufactured champions at Wimbledon. For in order to achieve this peace Teach must have had to scrap at least one-half of her philosophy.

In 1952, Teach was still saying cheerfully, 'All champions have some killer in them. You have to be mean to be a champion. How can you lick someone if you feel kindly disposed toward them? Why, your adrenalin ducts wouldn't let you do it . . .' And this message she handed on to her pupils to such good effect that they licked the world. But the basic badness of it eventually became apparent to her. It distressed her to the point where she, too, became sick. And I think this completely explains her disappearance, for all time, from Big Time tennis.

The other points in Teach's philosophy are less destructive.

'If I had my way I'd shut every pastrycook shop in the country. Howdya expect ya pancreas to deal with that amount of fat and sugar, anyway?' she'd say, knocking ice-cream cornets and cream puffs out of her pupils' rigid grip.

And what a life Teach has already lived through. She

was a child when the great San Francisco earthquake hit her and her family. She was about seven when she played hookey from school in order to learn how to play tennis, stole a tennis racket from a house-guest and hid it behind the wood pile . . . She was nineteen when she was selling two rival newspapers door to door and taking commission on them both. She was twenty when she became a saleswoman for Standard Oil and the highest paid lady commercial traveller in California. It was at this point that she started to teach tennis. 'My oil deal helped my tennis . . . my tennis helped my oil sales,' and found to her horror that she was a professional. So she bought her way back into the world of amateur sport and was soon ranking third in the U.S.A.

Teach's unsuccessful marriage, divorce, and subsequent emotional confusion were followed by a beat back to health and strength by way of restaurant management and tennis coaching at The Bishop School, La Jolla, which was interrupted by two violent experiences. She rescued Alice Marble from a T.B. sanatorium and coached her back to health, strength, and the Championship of the World. She encountered the twelve-year-old Maureen Connolly and made her, at seventeen, the greatest player the world has seen since Suzanne Lenglen.

Her relationship with these two gifted girls brought her to despair and heartbreak. So she left the world of competitive sport for ever. Alice Marble served with distinction in the American W.A.V.E.S. during the war and recently saw herself portrayed in *This Is Your Life* on

American T.V. . . . Maureen Connolly broke her leg when her horse reared by a lorry on a main arterial road in California. Maureen, at least, has married the man of her choice.

Teach's goodness of heart and zest for life is something I seldom encounter. I remember many splendid evenings of overeating and drinking in her company, of wildish conversation about Buddhism, Confucianism, and Roman Catholicism: and one hot July evening driving out to Marlow to hear the sound of the Thames falling over the weir and the ludicrous bubbling of some highly overrated nightingale. Dear Teach. I can see that no juvenile threat to the world championships will ever bring you from your Californian Karma. There is nothing for it but for me to go and see you.

Joyce Cary, the novelist, is another creature who loves life, and is unashamed to say so. I met Cary in Oxford. He lives there in a small red-brick house in Park Road, surrounded by portraits of his late wife and his children, all done by him, which explains his understanding of the only 'believable' painter in fiction, 'Gully' Jimpson, of *The Horse's Mouth*. His wife had been dead about eighteen months when I met Cary and he said he missed her dreadfully. She used to type his manuscripts for him, but most of all he misses her 'lovely, passionate, inquiring mind'. I asked him about his Christian name 'Joyce' and he was vexed at the suggestion that it had anything at all to do with the author of *Finnegan's Wake*. 'It was my mother's maiden name,' he said, 'that's all . . .'

He stalked beside me all the way from Park Road to the Mitre. He wore greenish tweeds and a brown cap. He reminded me of a long-legged water bird, walking beside me; a bird that you might find in the green valleys of County Antrim or Down, a crane or a heron, perhaps. He was in his sixties when I met him, and already acknowledged a very considerable novelist indeed, a man likely to win the Nobel Prize.

His working methods are quite unique. He collects the notes for his books together in great cardboard folders: here a scene, there a personality, here a figure banging up psychologically against another. And then when he has the whole body collected together within the folders, so to speak, he takes it out from his bookcase and *talks* it, dictating to a secretary. For this reason his novels are nearly always in the first person.

Joyce Cary has a marvellous and most incendiary mind, ready to catch alight immediately over things so diverse as the tides off the coast of Cornwall, the art of Flagstadt, the importance of Graham Greene. But he didn't tire me. Far from it. So vast was his enjoyment that he gave me a renewed strength of outlook and a renewed passion for my job of reviewing books. I only wish, after this, that I had *enjoyed* the two books that followed my meeting with him, that went to make up his trilogy about Nina, Chester Nimmo, and Jim. For it was my wild enthusiasm over the first of these three, *A Prisoner of Grace,* that had sent me all the way to Oxford to meet him, by appointment.

This encounter with Cary and the new light that it shed on his work taught me humility. Reading and writing is not a simple business. It is a complex relationship between reader and writer, as difficult and exasperating as a love-affair, each participant bringing to the page all the knowledge and experience in his command. So now, when I find myself lacking in some quality necessary for the understanding of a book, I remember this trilogy of Joyce Cary's and only wonder how I can learn faster.

Lord Beaverbrook, Teach Tennant, Joyce Cary were important people whom I met in 1952. But Thomas Bartholomew Laurie Seyler was probably the most important of all. For on my fondness for Tommy, the baby whom I have seen grow up to become a prospering boy now four years old, depends the remainder of the revolution in my heart that makes me fond of children, and therefore, being fond of children, fond of people, too.

Tommy is the youngest of Jonnie's responsibilities. I admit I didn't like him much to begin with; but there were many corners of selfishness and self-protection in my make-up that needed rubbing off by Family Life. When I first saw him he had damp black spikes of hair and hot, angry blue eyes. When he was good he simply lay and slept and was rather boring. But when he was angry he went scarlet all over (chest and stomach particularly) and bellowed the place down. To begin with I decided I would have as little to do with him as possible . . .

But I hadn't a hope. One day everyone went down with flu and I was the only one in the house without infection. I had to bath him, feed him, tuck him up in bed. He *smiled* at me. And he has dominated my life ever since.

Whether he flies into a rage and kicks me in the stomach (and this he very frequently does) or whether he falls over and blacks his eye, screaming like a steam whistle, or whether he coos like an angel and clambers all over me, I have to admit that I love him, desperately, hopelessly, devotedly . . . Like sweet Alice (Ben Bolt) I tremble in fear at his frown.

Goodness knows what it *is* about children. Like dogs or kittens we give them our hearts to tear, along with all our best coloured picture books and balls of pretty wool. And we glory in the battered fragments they leave behind them. 'The *clever*' I hear myself drooling as Tommy fetches me a sharp kick on the ankle, '*Wonder* boy,' I croon as he cries, shrilly, 'Ba-Ba-Back-sit' or (a terrible swear word this) 'Baa-*lamb*'. 'What miracles of self-expression,' as he looks coldly at a rather famous actress on the television, saying to her, 'Bye-bye *bus*.'

Who the hell cares that he can't say, 'Baa baa black sheep,' when he obviously has all the charm in the world?

Chapter Seventeen

By 1953 Jonnie and Nicky and Tommy and I had moved from poor old dry-rotting Carlyle Square to a very pretty but hideously uncomfortable mews cottage, tucked away behind Lowndes Square. Geraniums hung from its windows in baskets, there was a little bit of bomb damage opposite where Jonnie could keep the car: and there was a courtyard where the sun frequently shone. We had a very complicated arrangement now about cars. Jonnie had a new second-hand M.G. Magnette and I still continued to use the little red M.G., known as babycar. Nicky built himself space ships in the mews and Tommy could loll there in his Moses basket. But for Jonnie and me, the two adult members of the community, who were by now feeling old and grey and full of sleep, it was not luxurious.

I slept in the study, I remember: a dank three-cornered room with windows that opened smartly into the studio. A studio, I may say, that was the envy of all our friends, so tall and airy and 'longing to have parties given in it' did it seem. Also, alas, a soil pipe ran down the back of the study, and one night a bit of broken tile got caught over the lip of the pipe. Immediately there was a heavy

(Coronation Summer) downpour and the room slowly filled with water. I was working at the time, trying hard and giving with the prose, and I didn't notice that my chair was slowly rising, that I was by now two feet deep in water and books and things were floating all round me. Jonnie found me splashing sadly about. To this day she says that I never noticed. But I couldn't help noticing when it all drained away that it left a terrible smell. So then I slept surrounded by a little battery of Air-Wicks.

Then the kitchen ceiling fell on Nicky while he was eating his tea. And we all got rather cross and decided to move again. But it took a very long time before we found our present house.

I acquired a small office for £3 a month in Chancery Lane that year. It was the size of the average brushes cupboard (indeed, that is what I think it was) ventilated by three round holes in the door and a won't open window that showed the shadows of people passing in the street above me. A complication of pipes ran round this window, which let the damp in terribly. But it positively never let in any air. Almost everyone who ever saw it got claustrophobia just by looking at it. It was curiously comforting and womb-like in there, with my typewriter and desk, my teeny-weeny typing chair and my telephone. After an hour or two I always got a splitting headache but I loyally put it down to the basic wear and tear of working for the *Express*. My only problem was the neighbours. Nice men who sold insurance on either side of me used to come and chat if I left the door open. So quite often I would shut the door and cower there in semi-darkness, pretending that I wasn't at home. It is a strange fact that none of the other tenants in Chancery Lane seemed to come to their offices to *work*.

I wasn't always at home or in that office, however. *That* was the year the Queen was crowned, the year I went to Rome and saw the Pope and Mrs. Clare Luce; the year I flew to Corsica to try and interview the Sultan of Morocco and covered the last Test Match when England got back the Ashes from Australia, I also went in the circus and the ice show and generally made a poppy show of myself. It was all most enjoyable.

It was my idea to interview Mrs. Luce. When she was appointed American Ambassador to Italy I got very excited: I even rang up Mr. Christiansen about it and asked if I could do it. 'All right,' said Chris. 'But I'm not going to send you to New York. There's no point in that. The *story* is what happens to her in Rome.'

Tony Hern and I discussed it all ends up. The only way (Tony explained to me) that I could justify the expense of such a trip was by writing brilliantly in all directions. Making a sort of Travel-Note Book of it. Yes, indeed. 'You must go by train,' said Tony. '*Nobody* travels by train nowadays. It should be very interesting.'

So I one day found myself in Victoria on a dirty May morning, with the rain pouring down the windows of the carriage. Such a very, very elegant carriage, too. For this was the Rome Express.

The Rome Express. Think of it. That meant Romance

all right, I thought. That meant Dame May Whitty appearing suddenly through a cloud of steam . . . and as suddenly vanishing . . . corpses falling sideways in the corridors . . . the sun and all that. Or so I had always thought.

Instead, I found no beautiful spies among the passengers. There was an American matron with a jewel-case and bright blue hair. There were two very, very First Class business men with piggy skin cases. And all of them had obviously been on the Rome Express before. They were *bored*. I was shocked to death. I wrote a poem about them:

> See him labelled as First
> Class Holder of a railway pass
> Shows him happier, serener
> Smoother, brighter, neater, cleaner . . .
> Better (God forgive the word)
> Than his brother in the Third.

I decided that I was thoroughly third class at heart and went along the train to have a look at the third-class passengers. Of course I loved them immediately. There were American G.I.s, tots belonging to two French ladies travelling to Paris. (The French ladies were handing round garlic sausage.) There were two dear English girls called Jo-an and Elsie who were (they told me) on a tour with the Poly. They were counting their lire because, like me, they had never been to Rome before. They told me that the only Italian they could speak they had learnt off the music of The Pixies Patrol when they were kiddies. 'Pizzicato,' said Jo-an reminiscently. 'Well, I don't suppose *that's* going to get you very far in Capri,' said Elsie, savagely. And we all ate some garlic sausage.

But they were dear girls and I loved them. If I had asked I expect they would have given me some of their lire, too, for in the Third, you see, everybody shares everything with everybody else:

> In the Third they sing and smoke
> Share the fags and share a joke
> Speak of love . . . and times of sailings
> Drink – and Uncle Arthur's failings
> Dream and eat, or sleep and write
> Underneath one central light.

But at Dover I had to go back to my beastly First Class carriage and First Class Preferential Treatment. So I finished off the poem.

> In the First each one apart
> From his neighbour hides his heart
> Lest in some unheard of way
> By word or look he should betray
> (He dare not think which would be worst)
> He is not used to going First

So the train rocked on, down France, through warm muggy French rain. (This rain wasn't half as depressing as the stuff that had fallen in Victoria, because of course it was rain falling Abroad.) Everybody thought I was mad because I kept changing backwards and forwards from the third to the first class, looking for something to write about. And one French ticket collector, who was delighted with the whole thing and said I was as crazy as an American, bought me a bottle of Pouilly Fuissée and a paper bag of cherries. The cherries were dark and glossy, like his eyes. And as the train rocked and clattered along between stations and over endless exciting level-crossings, he became very, very friendly indeed.

And so night fell in a series of heavy crashes all the way down to the South of France.

But at seven o'clock in the morning there, suddenly, was Italy: a great blazing blue slice of sky.

Italy swam by my window all day. Blue-green sea with little pebbly beaches . . . and not a soul swimming in it for miles. I couldn't understand this, as I longed above all things to plunge happily into the Mediterranean and wash the accumulated dust of Victoria, Dover, and Paris out of my hair. Blue sky with pink villas dotted about on tufty hills, wearing strange red roofs like funny hats . . . Endless meadows where oxen, smooth and white or beige mushroom-coloured, clanked bringing in the hay. Genoa, where the tenement houses are festooned with washing and scarlet hibiscus that hang from the same strings. Rapallo, where a line of shouting porters meet the train and each one is labelled for a different hotel: and the train snores off through a tunnel where every now and then the sun blinds through a chink in the rocks and the cliff falls sheer to the blue . . . the eternal sea. Pisa, where Elsie and Jo-an, maddened by inactivity, leapt from the train and bought themselves pink plastic reproductions of the Leaning Tower.

Then we ran into Rome . . . just as the clock was coming round to four o'clock tea-time. Gasometers, power-houses, railway lines, railway bridges unromantic and very utilitarian. Just the same, I knew that I had reached civilization. For on the walls everywhere the hoardings announced 'The Personal Appearance of the One and Only Frank Sinatra' – at the time the bobby soxer's joy. I pointed this out to the elderly porter in the peaked hat and blue blouse who was pushing my luggage on a barrow. He shrugged his shoulders. I told him how in my country, wherever he went, Mr. Sinatra was mobbed by the bobby soxers.

'Bobby soxers?' he said, with the magnificent and scornful roll of Dante's *Inferno*. 'Here is one city where Sinatra will go unmobbed. We have no bobby soxers here.'

This was a curious but indisputable fact. Wherever I went, up and down the length and breadth of Italy (and I went to a lot of places, Capri, Naples, Rome, Rapallo), there were children or there were adults. There was nothing in between: no awkward gangling boys with spots and red wrists, no anxious, lumpy girls with the wrong shade of lipstick. Crises of psychological inadequacy may strike the Italians late in life: but they do not do so in puberty. Or if they do, they do not affect the looks. Italians, particularly lower-class Italians, are very beautiful.

I settled into my hotel, where I was surprised to find a small, dark, half-Glaswegian–Italian receptionist, who reminded me that he had once typed letters for Hermione Gingold. He was called Jacanelli and I did, vaguely, remember him. I put my typewriter and my briefcase on a little square table under the window and then I set to work, mostly by telephone, to assail the formidable fortress of protocol and international whispering that contains the beautiful Ambassador, Mrs. Luce.

I tried all the usual channels. I encountered an amiable young American P.R.O. sitting nerve-racked behind an enormous desk in the American Embassy. To begin with he was just a voice on the telephone, saying that it was useless for me to bother even to come and see him. He was having a terrible time, he said, wearily. He had had to veto all possibility of Mrs. Luce interviewing anyone until after the elections.

'Jenny Nicholson is livid with me,' he said.

That was the end of the poor young man. If he had said anything else at all I should probably have let him off lightly and gone sadly home, with my tail between my legs. But my mind flew back to those strange days in the radio programme, *Women at War*, when Jenny Nicholson had seemed so terribly sophisticated and obviously knew *everyone*.

'Ah . . .' I said. 'I'm going to write the feature about Mrs. Luce settling in whatever you say. So I'm coming round to see you to discuss background material.'

Poor young man. I put on my best dress and I sallied

forth, down the baked, orangey-red street, under the broad blue shade of the plane trees to the massive palace of burnt umber and burnt sienna where Mrs. Luce was then top girl.

Mr. John P. MacKnight was a serious, sincere young American with a crew cut and a nylon shirt. He started right in about how 'Your *Picture Post* and your *Illustrated* have been here . . . and it isn't a bit of good . . .'

Then by a series of extraordinary events, chief of which was I am sure the fact that Clare Luce knows and is very fond of Lord Beaverbrook, Mr. MacKnight softened up and decided to let me meet The Ambassador.

As a matter of fact that week I discovered that Mr. MacKnight had written a very good book about The Papacy, and I eagerly reviewed it in the *Daily Express*, hoping that Mr. MacKnight might see it and be softened up still further.

I well remember reading that book late at night in my red hot hotel, with all the blinds drawn. I remember reading that book on little tables on the pavement. I remember reading that book all day and all night, in fact, while I waited to hear whether Mrs. Luce was going to see me or not. I nevertheless found it a most enjoyable book: it contained fascinating details about how the Pope kept fit by pedalling on a fixed bicycle.

But he was gasping and gulping a bit as I carried on with the conversation.

'Now I can quite see,' I said, 'that Mrs. Luce can't receive me officially. That would cause too much trouble, and we mustn't upset Jenny Nicholson, must we, so I think I had better go out and have a look at the villa where she lives and hear from one of her secretaries how hard she works and how nice she is and all that. And if you have any handout material about the marvellous work the Americans are doing on Lend–Lease in Italy, I shall be glad to have that, too . . .'

Mr. John P. MacKnight was now swallowing hard as he handed over the material.

'You had better ring Laetitia Balldridge, the social secretary, at this number,' he said, weakly. 'I will tell her about you. Then you can go and talk to her.' And he gave me the address of the villa. He stood up suddenly and shook hands and grinned. And he looked very young and extremely gay and good-looking. Hitherto he had just been a rather pompous worried young man. I suddenly liked him very much.

'Good luck,' he said.

And I went away down marble corridors hung with immense paintings of glorious dead ladies and gentlemen. As I went, tinkling laughter echoed somewhere from a great high-ceilinged room on my right. Madame Ambassador, perhaps, giving an audience?

All the way back to the hotel I was dancing with impatience. I bought a copy of the *Express* at the kiosk and I saw it was only one day old. So I must get that book review off as fast as I could. So I read *The Papacy* in double quick time, lying on my bed in the still, Italian afternoon. And then I wrote 750 words about it (and I think a book by Evelyn Waugh) and something else and airmailed them. Then I rang the number of the villa and asked for Miss Laetitia Balldridge.

To my amazement I got her, first go off.

'Oh yes,' she said. 'Mr. John P. MacKnight has been on about you. Come on out. You know the way?'

So I leapt into a taxi and rushed out to this enormous cool villa in the heart of residential Rome. We passed all sorts of terribly fascinating ruins on the way. But it is no use complaining that I didn't stop and look at them. This is not a book about archaeology. And Mrs. Luce seemed to me (after the Pope) the most important person in Rome that day. After all, she was the first female to be appointed Ambassador to any considerable European country.

The villa was silent, apparently smoothly and harmoniously running itself from within like a great quiet humming-top. A butler in a little white coat let me into an enormous empty, shady room. There were solid silver cigarette-boxes littered all around. I opened one. It was crammed full of cigarettes. What a pity that I don't smoke. There were no book-cases and nothing to read.

To keep myself occupied I made various little sorties in all directions from this room. Tiptoeing I once got as far as the hall where I saw a massive great Visitor's Book, heavily embossed. And then a sudden noise that sounded, once again, as if the Ambassador was actually roystering with her guests. It sent me terrified back to my base.

Then I crept through the half-open french windows into a very formal bone-dry garden, where hydrangeas were blooming their heads off. My feet crunched the gravel. And two minute pale grey balls of fluff came bouncing round the corner as small and silly and endearing as a couple of pom-poms on a court presentation dress. They yapped shrilly and someone admonished them. They were *Scusi* and *Prego,* Mrs. Luce's poodles. (These are the two terms most constantly in use among the Italians; and they mean 'Excuse me?' and 'Please!')

So I crept back once again to the awfully correct drawing-room, before I was actually arrested and thrown out. I sat with my ankles crossed and my heart beating until the butler came back to fetch me.

He led me up more marble staircases and more incredible grandeur. We traversed long corridors where the carpets seemed to be blue. Then I arrived in a much less formal, much more untidy room: that reminded me of a sewing-room in a country house in Ireland. There were a couple of office typewriters and a telephone that rang more or less incessantly. And there were two charming ladies: Laetitia Balldridge, who seemed to me six feet high and instantly said, 'Call me Tishy,' and a Roman Countess or Duchess who was slowly typing out the menus for the Ambassador's formal dinner-party that night. Tishy was ringing up the Secretary of another Ambassador while I sat there, saying, 'What is the Italian for *loup de mer*?'

There was also a big round table littered with little

pieces of paper and cellophane and coloured ribbon and little dainty boxes.

'Those are the Ambassador's presents,' said Tishy, observing my curious eye. 'Whenever she has a lunch date with anyone she always sends them a present afterwards.' Madame Ambassador's personal maid was employed on very little else (and the Ambassador's *clothes,* of course) because she was such a wonderfully good packager. 'Almost as good as the packagers in Macy's on Fifth,' said Tishy cheerfully. 'Considerably better,' said the maid, with a sniff. Hundreds of little packages seemed to go off daily with a dainty gift in them with Madame Ambassador's Best Wishes inside. Every now and then, too, the Roman Duchess or Countess would push back her long black hair with a little groan.

'It's not a bit of good,' she said. 'We'll have to go and collect a woman who is a real expert at calligraphy. A real Roman. And she will know how to spell and everything. And she will be very glad of the job.'

'Oooh,' I said. 'What fun. Can I come, too?'

'Why yes,' said the Roman Duchess. Almost, I offered to lend my handwriting to the cause. But I was highly delighted that this little expedition across Rome in one of the Ambassador's motor-cars did not instantly take place. For suddenly through the door there pranced the two delightful bundles of fluff that I had seen bouncing in the garden. Scusi and Prego, towing Madame Ambassador behind them.

She was framed in the doorway like some cool, pale

gold flower. She was wearing a pink and grey taffeta dress with two enormous patch pockets and there was a marvellous pink rose at her belt. She had pale blue rimmed glasses that matched the warm blue of her eyes and when she put them on her nose she took them out of a warm blue spectacle case.

Yes, Madame Ambassador was beautiful. Madame Ambassador was jolly polite. And Madame Ambassador said with a smile so like an *un*-fallen angel that it almost broke my heart, 'Let's see now . . . Lord Beaverbrook is your boss, isn't he? Will you remember to give him my love,' and then she took me on a quick brisk tour of the presents that kept pouring in to her since she had arrived. Madame Ambassador had handed me a world scoop feature, bless her kind heart.

There was a wooden gondola inscribed *Come to Venice Sometime*. There was the first dictionary ever printed in Italian. There was a little bronze Roman soldier and some gift that I didn't see, which was inscribed hopefully, *Amor est Luce* . . . The entire Embassy was trying to trace this quotation.

'Have you managed to find that saying, Tishy?' Madame Ambassador asked, with her hands in her pockets and her head slightly on one side and her two hopeless little dogs, bounding and barking here and there. 'Is it a Youth Movement motto, or what?'

She showed me with touching pride the Cardinal Newman plaque that she had been awarded for Distinction and Religion, for 'doing good for her country'.

Right alongside it was her other most cherished posses-sion, a signed photograph of Churchill. She giggled a little bit about Italian plumbing ('When you press the knobs nothing comes out') and she pooh-poohed my sympathetic murmuring about her sinus trouble.

'Hmmm,' she said, looking me up and down, 'there's nothing wrong with me except that I have eight hun-dred letters of congratulation to answer. Pity you can't write Italian. You might be able to help.'

Almost I offered to learn.

And then Madame Ambassador and the two little bouncing dogs went away. (I picked up both dogs and they were very soft and enchanting, almost like kittens, so soft.) And the Roman Duchess and Tishy and I packed ourselves into an enormous Cadillac and went swirling away across Rome to find the lady who would write the dinner menus.

All the way Tishy and the Roman Duchess kept point-ing out ruins. Yes, I said, yes. By and by we entered the Rome of *Bicycle Thieves*: heaps of terrifying sun-baked rubble and piles of blind modern flats rising above them . . . The slick shops, the carefully studied calm of the American Embassy, the cafés where everyone sat and stared at the world, the chattering crowds slid behind us. The Colosseum, said the Duchess . . . the Appian Way . . . But I kept on thinking about Madame Ambassador and the feature I would telephone through that night. *Speed,* that was the thing. Before Jenny Nicholson had the same idea as me. The Cadillac pulled up outside the block of flats. We all got out and climbed tenement stairs. The concrete under our shoes was gritty, worrying. The people who opened the doors to us, stared, hostile. I hung back, realizing how far removed from understanding of Roman problems we all were. Except the Roman Duchess. She knew all about it. She swept into that flat, calling out, 'I have a job for you!' fully expecting everyone's face to light up at the thought of the good honest American dollars that would presently pour into the household. But Mummy, the lady handwriting-expert, was out. And only two very small, spotless, highly suspicious babies (aged about five and two) were there to look after the house and each other. Tishy adored them both, of course. The Roman Duchess wasn't so keen on children, and she had to deliver a highly complex message: so she was a little vexed. I was simply fascinated. The hot sun beat outside, and the warm and stuffy flats were so different from the cool and studied grandeur of the American Embassy – no wonder the Italians resented the almighty American dollar that was going to restore their equilibrium as a country. How would the exquisite, fascinating, cool, collected, *charming* Mrs. Luce make out with these people? (Very well, I thought, in the long run. Because tact was obviously her middle name. How tactfully, how gently, how casually she had given me my scoop, knowing so well what she was doing.) And out of this confusion of material I had to make a feature article and telephone it through . . .

Obviously Clare Luce was ambitious. Something had

driven her successfully, successively through *three* worlds to arrive at her lonely peak . . .

Clare Boothe was born in 1904 of 'Good New England stock'. She has married twice: once to Mr. Brokaw, from whom she obtained a divorce and who later died, second to Mr. Henry Luce the publisher of *Life, Time,* and all those. Before she became a politician and President Eisenhower's blue-eyed girl, she had already succeeded with some violence *(a)* as a journalist, *(b)* as a dramatist. Her play, *The Women*, has never been equalled for sheer brilliant cattiness. It is, as you might say, a *gossip columnist's* play, built up on the weaknesses of humanity (and smart cracks about these weaknesses), and therefore very shocking. It was hard to reconcile that play with the creature of gentle strength and certainty I glimpsed that afternoon.

I thought about the rest of the story.

They said that her only child, her daughter by Mr. Brokaw, was killed in a car smash. Distraught with grief and guilt (because, 'they said', she thought she had neglected her child while she was being a success as a playwright and journalist and publisher's wife) she sought sanctuary in the Church of Rome. And the wise-cracking journalist and catty playwright disappeared. Mrs. Luce, the fighting propagandist, the biographer of saints, emerged to become the so-nearly saintly Ambassador who was just about to be accused of meddling in Italian politics. Behind that lily-maid-like exterior obviously flamed all the chaos and burning contradictions of a creative artist.

Why, on the eve of her appointment to Rome, she had even sent for King Zukor, the film director, and handed him a new script of a new play. What was the theme? It was set at the time of the Crucifixion. It was called *Pilate's Wife*. When I met King Zukor he remembered this. 'She got paid a lot,' he said vaguely.

Whatever next? I thought. Whatever can a woman with her looks, her power, her imagination *want* to do next? Obviously she is going to be a huge success in Italy. But what will she do after that? Is it possible that the United States of America (itself a gigantic experiment in government) may try one more experiment and vote the Girl Clare for President? After all, the U.S.A. is a woman-ridden world. It's not all that impossible. When I suggested this to Rebecca West she said musingly that *The Girl Clare* was obviously the name of a latter-day ship, like the *Marie Celeste*, which, found floating empty by the Arctic circle, would be suddenly found to contain 300 strangers . . .

I got back to my hotel, nervously avoiding a suggestion that Tishy and the Roman Duchess should drop me at the Colosseum: and wrote my 750-word piece about the girl Clare. Then I got on the telephone to London and dictated it to the dear boys on the typewriters in the news-room. My call came through just short of midnight, when the temperature was still about 90 degrees. I remember the sweat dripping off into the mouthpiece of the telephone . . .

In the middle of all this Charles Foley, the then Foreign

Editor, came through with the surprising suggestion that I should fly to Athens to interview Somerset Maugham. 'One thing at a time,' I said to Mr. Foley. 'I'm not at all sure that Mr. Maugham would welcome me . . . and besides I have arranged to go to a public audience with His Holiness the Pope on Thursday.' Mr. Foley sounded rather annoyed when I pointed out that it would cost money to go to Athens. 'Drachmas,' I said. 'Have you got any drachmas?' I felt so light-headed about the Girl Clare scoop that I fear I was rather cheeky to Mr. Foley. 'Yes, yes,' said Mr. Foley. 'How many do you want?' 'Lots and lots,' I said. 'If they don't come, I warn you, I shall go to Capri instead.'

I had worked out, you see, that if I went to Capri next day I should be back in Rome in time to interview a Monsignor in the Vatican about the Index of Banned Books and to attend my public audience of the Pope.

So next day I went by train to Naples which is one of the most unattractive cities I have ever seen. I did indeed see Naples and nearly die. I ate an octopus, I remember. It was bright pink and tasted a little like tripe and it clung to the plate as it was served to me in an awful naked way, with big reproachful eyes. I went by boat from Naples to Capri, in a violent thunder storm, and very strange it was. We sat about under cover in a little air-tight cabin, full of good Italian fug (garlic and so on) and we drank very, very fiery brandy. And everyone sang songs. 'Santa Lucia' and 'O Sole Mio' were two that I can remember with no difficulty.

By Sorrento the sun was shining again and everyone was singing about it. The Mediterranean (which had been a sullen gun-metal colour) became blue again . . . and the lightning and thunder died away, muttering somewhere behind the clouds on the silky horizon. So my first view of Capri was enchanted: perfection, a great lump of glorious rock rising from the still waters. They say that this was the isle where the sirens sang to Ulysses and he blocked his ears and tied his crew to the mast so that they should not jump overboard. Curious, isn't it, that Gracie Fields should so constantly be discovered there singing 'Sally' and 'The Isle of Capri' by her own swimming-pool? I expect people still lash themselves to the mast.

Porters met the boat again, just as they had at Rapallo. I remember one enormous American matron calling out, 'Caesar-Tiberius! Caesar-Tiberius!' and I was alarmed that she might be seeing visions, until I realized that this was the name of an hotel . . .

Lord, what a beautiful place. I had read all about it of course, in at least three books (*San Michele, Extraordinary Women, South Wind*), and I have listened to Monty Mackenzie muttering about the Good Old Days there, so I thought I would find it ruined by people, by tourists . . . But it just isn't so. Capri (like Great Britain) has swallowed up her invaders without trace and the strange rock with its endless steps to the summit of Anacapri, its eternal winding roads, remains one of the loveliest places in the world.

I can't remember the name of the hotel where I stayed. But it was in Anacapri, just below the famous villa of San Michele, built by Axel Munthe, and now given over to the education of Swedish students who want a vacation with a difference. I got up very early next morning to go over San Michele and also to meet Clark Gable who was staying at the Caesar-Tiberius. I escaped into San Michele because a handsome Italian wanted to show me the Blue Grotto. And as soon as I was inside I was pursued by a satyr in the shape of an elderly Swedish poet in a velvet coat. I had to climb 783 steps to the summit of the rock to elude him . . . and came down panting to find him hidden behind an olive tree. Bounding here and there on the marble steps I was afraid I might sprain an ankle and *not* keep (as I was keeping) three jumps ahead. There were tortoises moving about under the trees that the poet said were 200 years old. I must say I envied them their calm.

I escaped from San Michele hideously out of breath and bought a musical box that played 'Santa Lucia' and a silk scarf that showed all the show places of the island. It was a big relief to meet Mr. Clark Gable who, like the tortoises, didn't want to move about at all. He sat gravely in a deck-chair and stared across the water to the Bay of Naples, saying that he was a tired old man who had gone there for a rest and a little sunshine.

He talked about 'Teach' Tennant and Frank Sinatra. 'Poor Frankie forgot one of the basic facts of life,' he said, smiling gently. 'That tenors actually originated in

Naples.' For poor Mr. Sinatra was having a sticky time with his tour of the Italian cities. In those days he was married to Ava Gardner and the Italian people would not let him finish his act until he had brought her on the stage with him. Which may, of course, have been less of a reflection on his voice than a compliment to her beauty.

We talked about lots of things . . . and I liked Clark Gable enormously. He really *was* a big craggy man with mighty thews, as he appears in the movies. I have met so many movie stars who appear to be men on the screen, who at close quarters turn out to have tiny little features like girls and hardly any thews at all . . . I could see that behind Mr. Gable's politeness he was just dying to go back and have a nice bit of kip, so I excused myself and walked back to my hotel refusing on the way three more eager invitations to visit the Blue Grotto. Then I took the bus down to Capri from Anacapri.

I have to admit that Monty Mackenzie is partly right. It *is* a little bit crowded in Capri. It is a little bit hot there, too. But it was nice to meet people again and hear happy cries of, 'Look, Doreen! Come and look at this . . . a shopping bag exactly like the one I paid 250 lire for in Rome. And it's marked 1,250 lire here,' and, 'Charlie! Leave the gentleman's mule *alone*.'

Much as I love people I was glad when my boat nosed back to Naples. Much as I love people I was glad when my slow, slow political train drew away from Naples Station, (I shared a carriage with four representatives of each party concerned in the Italian elections and they all tried to teach me their points of view.) For the pedlars who sell silk scarves and musical boxes and mother-of pearl mandolines even swarm on to the trains in Naples. And they are not contented until they have parted you from every single lire you have in the world . . .

If they can't take anything else from you in Naples they will take cigarettes. Obviously there is some deep basic human reason for this unattractive behaviour; and it probably has something to do with emotional dissatisfaction and economic instability. But the fact remains that if ever I go again to Naples I shall lock myself in one of the carapaces from the 200-year-old tortoises in Anacapri.

In Rome the tremendous experience now awaited me of sharing in a public audience of the Pope. 'Properly *accolado*', I had to be, like it said in my invitation. So wearing a newly bought Italian skirt and white blouse, and a very chic black veil borrowed from the wife of the *Daily Express* 'leg man' I presented myself at St. Peter's and marched through lines of marvellously dressed guards into the white marble aisles of the great church itself.

They do say that Michael Angelo designed these uniforms and helmets, the strange clashes of colour that glow amongst the Papal guards. Michael Angelo himself could possibly have painted that great whispering, worldly, innocent crowd that jostled and pushed like a theatre audience in their efforts to get the blessing of His Holiness.

299

It was a supreme experience. That good little old man in his white robes, his white skull cap, mounted in a palanquin, high on the shoulders of his guards, tossing here and there above the roars of applause, of welcome and joyous pleasure. No, Presbyterians could not have been shocked at such a demonstration in God's House. Nobody is more Presbyterian than I, and I adored every minute of it. People cried, people laughed, little boys were handed up for the blessing. Men in the crowd detached themselves, carrying white tonsure caps . . . and the Holy Father knew their intention and blessed them. Sometimes he even changed caps, tossing down his old one, and putting the new one on his head with a smile of sheer glory. And the happy pilgrims from Sienna, or Normandy, or Galway *roared* their approval. Yes, the Irish were there. Thrilled through and through they were with the joy of it all. An Irish priest behind me . . . a monk in a brown habit with beautiful bare feet in sandals cried out, 'Ah now, isn't he great, the Holy Father?' And the very, very richly dressed scented crowd beside him, in minks and morning suits, clapped and cheered as though they were peasants.

My word. How I loved it. I even cried a little, richness itself. For how few things there are, when you think of it, at which you may have the little luxury of a weep for joy.

When I came out . . . into the broad and sunny square of St. Peter's and the people were scattering, making for their own homes and hotels, I saw two tall, American

nurses, Army girls. Had they enjoyed it? I asked them.
'Oh, yes,' they both sighed, like trees in the wind. 'And
wasn't it wonderful to have managed to get in?' 'Ah me,'
said one of them, who came, she said, from North Caro-
lina. 'How anyone could come to Rome and *not* try to
see the Pope I just don't understand . . .' I felt she should
have explained this to Charles Foley for me.

After this I went by train back to Rapallo. I had booked
a seat in an express that would take me right through to
London, but I wanted to see Sir Max Beerbohm, if I
could. (I greatly admired him.) A foreign female voice
answered his telephone, quite horrified that an English
pilgrim should want to give The Master news of his
native land.

So, thanks to whoever guarded Sir Max (so much
more determined than those who guard Mrs. Luce, the
Duke of Windsor, Noël Coward, Marlene Dietrich,
Joyce Cary, Lord Beaverbrook, and the other people
whom you have met and are still to meet in this book),
I was able to take the day off.

I simply lay in the Mediterranean all day. I played with
an Italian baby aged about three and a half. I watched sea
anemones open and close as the water touched them . . .
I saw the sun set and fire-flies come out in little brilliant
spots all along the urban length of the Italian Riviera,
and I only wished that Jonnie and Nicky and Tommy
could have been there. For what use is a peaceful day
unless you can say, 'Look, darling,' to your family round
about you?

Then it was time to go and my train came panting and swearing into the station, an enchanted, romantic train, stuffed from end to end with the people who wanted to get back to England in time to see the Queen. For that was Coronation year, remember . . .

It was a very crowded train. But there was one carriage smartly labelled Calais-Dover, and I got into this carriage. Unfortunately about 40,000 other people got into the carriage with me. There were certainly twelve elderly Boy Scouts who played the mouth organ – selections from *Tosca* mostly – they came from Malta G.C. and they talked of nothing but the Queen. There were at least three completely Italian families, with bulging cardboard suitcases, who were seizing the opportunity to visit their daughter and granddaughters in Soho. There was an American commercial traveller, who said that queens were baloney. But I think he was trampled to death, for I never saw him again . . .

And there was a thoughtful young lady from the Windmill Theatre, who told me that she had once slapped the face of a policeman in Ostend, because he was trying to stop her mother from getting on a boat. (She had ran out of money and she borrowed 30s., which was later returned, with a note of thanks from Vivien Van Damm, which just goes to show what a wonderful institution the Windmill *is* . . .)

And so we thudded North, crammed elbow to elbow, climbing upon one another in our efforts to stretch our arms, eventually lying in heaps in the corridor, our heads in one another's laps.

What did it matter to us? We were going to see the Queen.

The crickets and fire-flies fell into place behind us, as we climbed steadily into the cold Alpes Maritimes. The Boy Scouts began to sneeze, for they had forgotten that May was not yet out. And so we climbed through the long, long night, while the girl from the Windmill Theatre told me her life story and gave me an orange and the sun came up, and seemed to stay a long time on the horizon by the River Loire, like a golden Coronation Souvenir.

Then the over-loaded carriage was shunted, grunting like a bullock cart, across Paris, round the suburbs, from the Gare de Lyon to the Gare de Nord. And here it suddenly became very, very chic indeed, and part of the Golden Arrow, the *Flèche d'Or*.

Here we picked up the princes, the potentates, the ambassadors. There was His Excellency the Ambassador to Brazil. His Excellency the President of Chile. There were a half-dozen sky-blue Brazilian nuts in uniform, blazing with gold braid and good will, who were met at Dover by a black-hatted worker from the Foreign Office. I know who all these people were because they were paged repeatedly: 'Will His Excellency the Ambassador to Brazil kindly come to the purser's office for his passport?'

On the boat I met Sheilah Hennessy, insanely enough,

who had sprained her ankle somehow. And we sat in a chintzy little cabin and talked and talked, as girls do.

And then, miraculously, there were the fields of Kent in all their Coronation togs, the hops coming along nicely, the cherry trees, the lovely pale mists of a hot May evening unkempt above the dusty pub. 'Ah,' said one inaccurate toil-worn Italian traveller, 'Tunbridge Wells, *Qu'e bella!*'

But I saved my love for London, Queen Elizabeth's London: from the stern towers of the Abbey to the dreaming dome of St. Paul's where Fleet Street that week blossomed into a second spring of white Coronation favours. For I remembered London in un-holiday mood, with bombs falling, sirens calling the All Clear. And I have seen Rome and Capri and Naples. I have seen the sun rise over the Loire. But I can tell you this, London is still the one place in the world to come home to.

Chapter Eighteen

As I look backwards and see things happening so near to me in time it becomes increasingly difficult to pick out the most enjoyable. There is so *much* of everything and I have loved it all so. The year the Queen was crowned, for example, I became temporary film critic and T.V. critic of the *Evening Standard*, and I can remember with such pleasure arriving at various cinemas in the cool hush of an early May morning with Jonnie and sitting with her through various movies. When it was all over we climbed back into the little red M.G. and drove away, usually into the park, to discuss what we thought of the movie. Jonnie made all the best jokes in this series and provided all the best criticism. Indeed, I know it was impossible to make a success of this series without her. Looking back I know and worry about this. Did I ever give her credit, for example, for her appraisal of Greer Garson in that highly-coloured movie which I said was rather pretty? In fact, 'Some of the interiors reminded me of an old Dutch master,' I said.

'Hm,' snapped Jonnie. 'And some of the dialogue reminded me of an old Dutch cheese.'

The *Evening Standard* is a London paper, widely read

by all my acquaintances, so to write a series for the *Standard* carries with it a fascinatingly snobbish cachet. I danced around the studio at William Mews when Lord Beaverbrook rang me to ask whether I would pinch-hit until Sir Beverley Baxter returned from Canada: and I can remember throwing Tommy, the baby, in the air and both of us crowing with delight simply because I was so revoltingly impressed by the *Standard*. If London is a village, then the *Standard* is its local paper. (And this is so odd, you know, because I believe that the *News* and the *Star* have a wider circulation.)

Other things had happened that year with a touch of delirium in them. Jonnie grew a tumour of formidable size (it was 'innocent' though) and she went into the London Clinic to have it whipped out. So she resigned from her job as production manager to Werner Laurie Ltd. She was lying in bed one morning after her return from the Clinic telling me what was in the papers. For quite a long time now this had been her practice, thank goodness. Whenever, for example, Lord Beaverbrook sends for me, I ask Jonnie about the news, so that I don't appear too hopelessly stupid. (I remember one dinner-party when Lord Beaverbrook looked down the table at me and said, 'Should Evans have hanged?' As I hadn't even the foggiest idea who Evans *was,* I waved my hand grandly to Jonnie, sitting opposite me, and said, 'Miss Laurie's department.' And, of course, Jonnie knew all about Evans and answered up, very briskly indeed.)

However, one sunny morning Jonnie read out to

me a tale that sounded like something from the *Arabian Nights*. Tribesmen rising in the hills of Morocco, she said. Stirrups clashing, bright turbans flashing and the Sultan of Morocco had been deposed and had been removed in an airplane to Corsica with six wives and ten concubines. (Or ten wives and six concubines. No one was sure which.) It sounded very surprising to me, and I sat there with starting eyeballs. Whereupon, the telephone rang and a voice said, 'This is the *Daily Express* here,' and then presently, while I held the receiver, 'Would you like to go to Corsica and interview the Sultan of Morocco?'

'Eh?' I said. For that contract of mine, which I had so far exceeded as to suggest that I went to interview Clare Boothe Luce, said only that I must write about books for the *Express*. Books, it said, and nothing else. But it did sound awfully tempting, didn't it? I began to giggle and Jonnie asked me what I was laughing at. I covered up the receiver and told her, while the voice of Charles Foley continued to quack encouragement in my ear. 'You know the story, of course?' it concluded. 'Of course,' I said. Now it was Jonnie's turn to sit with starting eyeballs.

One way and another I found myself, that very evening, taking off from London Airport with a great wodge of travellers cheques in my hot little hand, my passport and a two-way ticket to Ajaccio, Corsica, via Nice. Jonnie stayed at home, more's the pity *(a)* because it was a passport to guaranteed sunshine and it would have done her a power of good and *(b)* because I was becoming increasingly aware that I was lost without Jonnie's judgment and common sense. But I didn't really grasp all this until this particular party was over. As I took off on that hot July morning I thought the whole thing was a high, gay old lark.

To begin with, there was a strike on in Air France. Even if I were able to get to Ajaccio it was more than doubtful that I would ever get home again . . . And what would have been highly amusing and enjoyable if I had been doing it in my own sweet time, expending my own hard-earned cash, started to be a little hysterical chore simply because the *Express* had initiated it. Those who go on rip-roaring romantic assignments to foreign parts are *not* to be envied, I discovered. Deadlines make dull, worried girls.

The plane came swerving down, in a great swoop over Nice. And there lay the Côte d'Azur in all its glory in the July heat. There lay Nice, and Cap Ferrat and Cap d'Ail (I imagined Lord Beaverbrook pacing up and down in Edward Molyneux's villa, La Capocina, wanting to read the very latest and hottest stuff about the Sultan, and my heart quailed) and there across the blue, blue Mediterranean, somewhere among the haze on the horizon, lay Corsica. And the Sultan . . .

I spent the night in an hotel whose name I have forgotten, nervously reading the French papers, for the latest about His Imperial Sultanship. It confused me to begin with, because my French is not very good and these papers kept on saying in the same breath that the Sultan was in his forties and also '*L'ancien*' Sultan. It took me hours before I discovered that '*L'ancien*' didn't mean 'ancient' but 'ex'.

Somehow, by bribery, corruption, and a very great deal of chattering I eventually managed to get myself on to a plane that was really going to Tangiers but promised to touch down fleetingly for me at Ajaccio. It was all highly dramatic and improbable and if I had been twenty-six instead of thirty-six I expect I would have enjoyed it all no end. As it was, as I waited in the airport again I suddenly felt very, very old and tired and lonely and I wished I was back in 20 William Mews with Jonnie and Nicky and Tommy, doing nothing worse than reviewing the new Evelyn Waugh.

As my plane darted in and touched down like a great lethal dragonfly, I rang Pat Wallace, from the airport, Pat (I dimly remembered) leased a villa called the Villa Revilia on Cap Ferrat for the summer. Pat was sweet to me. So were her three children, Mouse (whose real name is, I think, Elizabeth), Toby, and Harry. Pat, particularly, understood my mood of disenchantment. 'But of course ring when you get back,' she said, 'and you can have Mouse's room.' So *they* went on to swim at Eden Roc and I went hotly, stickily, on to Ajaccio, Corsica.

The plane came down in a tiny, windy air-field by a small tin hut with a galvanized iron roof. There was a wind sock flapping alongside, standing stiffly out at right-angles in the bright sunshine, and I remember thinking that the sun was probably four times as strong (even) as in Nice and it was only the wind that kept the temperature down. It wasn't unbearable, although the tar macadam was sticky under my sandals (newly bought in Nice) and my typewriter seemed to get heavier and heavier. So this was the island where Napoleon was born. I looked around curiously. There was a little bus waiting; and quite a lot of people besides me got off the plane and began to walk towards it. So perhaps it was a lie about the plane going on to Tangiers?

We got into the bus and drove inland for miles and miles, round sand dunes and various fascinating beaches where the sand lay white and crisp and even, and hot smooth waves slowly broke. And not a soul for miles and miles . . . There was a lot of green scrubland, known as Maquis. There were little green, wild olive trees and half-hearted attempts at vineyards, and the whole place smelt simply delicious; of traveller's-joy and mimosa and thyme and lavender bushes that have just been rained upon. My friend, Mr. Racca, the proprietor of the Hotel de l'Europe et de L'Univers in Ajaccio, told me that Napoleon had once said of Corsica, when he was on his way to Elba, 'Aha, my beautiful island . . . I can smell her in the sea, even when I am passing miles away.' This somewhat hammy piece of dialogue is no more than the simple truth. Corsica really does breathe sweetness under the near African sun.

But, to be honest, *Ajaccio* is a bit of a bore.

Heavy plane trees grow there and the drains are not so

good. Much wine is drunk there: but few people care if they make a living or not. So most of the day is spent in sitting around at little tables, talking politics; and most of the evening is spent sitting around at little tables; talking politics. But I *did* like M. Racca.

M. Racca was a heavy, dark-moustached, highly intelligent man, who wanted to talk about the novels of François Mauriac and the novels of Graham Greene. He had married an English girl called Evadne, from *Pinner*, if you please: and she was away staying with her mum in Pinner, so I wouldn't meet her, he said. Later on I *did* meet Evadne, on her way from Pinner to Corsica.

Thinking it over, I dare say if I had put my trust in M. Racca all would have been well. I might even have succeeded in reaching the Sultan.

As it was, I sat for hours outside the prefect's office in the thick-walled Prefecture, like a tremendous Moorish Castle, where the Sultan was cooped up, too. He was very civil to me, the prefect, showed me the drawing-room (with a little upright piano played by one of the concubines), and he wagged his hand towards the bed-room where the wives and concubines sat and sewed and chatted. But he couldn't let me in, he said. And he didn't know how many wives and how many concubines. (It was as much as his place was worth.)

Night fell while he explained to me that *(a)* I might be a Communist spy and *(b)* I might represent the All Islam League, both of which were sworn to snatch the Sultan at the drop of a hat. It was in vain that I pointed out that I hadn't a hat, represented one of the least left-wing newspapers in the world and thought that the All Islam League was probably a baseball game. The prefect could do nothing. Gendarmes all around us bristled with revolvers. They had orders, said the prefect, with a happy leer, to shoot at sight. The prefect left me alone for a minute in a little office, sparsely furnished with a very old-fashioned typewriter and a view of some very English huntsmen jumping slap over a brick wall on top of some black and white spotted hounds; so I ventured out. Instantly there was a clash of angry bayonets. *'Qui va la!'* cried a stalwart member of the Foreign Legion or the Spahis or something, thrusting at my stomach. At my time of life, I began to think, I would look peculiarly silly with a bayonet through my turn. So I crept back to my office and sat down and waited for the prefect.

Later, M. Racca explained *his* idea. I would dress up as one of his chambermaids and *wait on* the entire harem. 'Of course,' he explained, 'if you are caught you will probably go to jail and the chambermaid will obviously lose her job, so you must pay her a handsome compensation.'

I could actually feel the cold steel of the French bayonet running into me as he told me this.

'Yes . . .' I said. 'Yes. Any other ideas?'

'Well,' he said. 'I suppose you could deliver the laundry.'

So that was what I did in the end. I sadly ironed the burnous of the Sultan (a sort of white woolly dressing-gown with a hood and a high button at the throat) and then went down the hill to the prefecture to deliver them. I got quite a long way before I was recognized. Then I was thrown out. Next week *Punch* carried a comment, remarking that the Editor understood that there had been representations of Corsican laundrymaids to the *Express* suggesting that *they* should write my book column as a reprisal . . .

Then M. Racca set to work to get me back to the mainland in one of those planes. His strength of character, his power alone (I gathered), got the thing to leave the ground. I shall never forget the scenes as Racca threatened the young man in the office and he shrugged his shoulders. Eventually he said with a shrug that I could go out to the airfield and wait there. There *might* be a seat on the plane from Tangiers.

So I arrived back at Nice, very hot, very depressed and longing for a nice bathe before tea. The first person I saw in the airport was Elizabeth Jane Howard (one of my contributors to *Books of Today* in the good old days) as beautiful as ever, but with a brother and a wonderful tin home-made racing car in tow. Robin (the brother) was delightful about everything and gave me a lift to Pat Wallace at Cap Ferrat. So apart from the fact that I put my hand on an exhaust pipe by mistake, I was almost happy again. Poor Robin however later spent some hours in a French jail because another car hit *his*.

I even got my bathe before tea. We went out in a very small sailing-boat, right round the point of Cap Ferrat

. . . and then we dived and swam and fell about endlessly in the blue sea. But I couldn't help wondering what Lord Beaverbrook would say when he read my story next day. In the end I telephoned an account on the telephone in the Villa Revilia and Mouse and Toby were sweet about it and pretended that they thought it was a smashing story and jolly romantic to have it happen from *their* villa. But it would have been so much better if I could actually have seen the Sultan . . .

Toby and Mouse and Harry went in a yacht with the Earl of Warwick to see the firework display at Monte Carlo. And Pat and I sat on the end of the jetty at Saint Jean, Cap Ferrat, all the warm and enchanted night . . . and talked. We talked about everything in the world, I suppose. Jonnie and her operation and how we wished Nicky and Tommy and she were here too . . . Edgar Wallace, her father, and what a wonderful fellow he was. I well remember remarking that a song called 'Innocent, Lonesome Blue Baby' came out of a revue called *The Rainbow*, which I didn't suppose that Pat would remember.

'Remember?' she said, in tones of scorn. 'Krazy wrote the thing.'

Krazy is her name for Edgar Wallace.

Next day I was back in England with a fine, tickly sunburn, much unsettled by the failure of my mission and not at all sure that I was cut out to be a reporter after all. I was so tired, too, that I kept falling asleep on the bathroom floor while I was counting the washing.

Jonnie remarked (and rightly so) that I was getting too old for such goings-on.

We didn't have a holiday that year. Jonnie was so good and brave about her operation and pulled through it with such marvellous calm that one almost forgot that she had been under the surgeon's knife for a whole day. Her lack of emotion about this was very disturbing. She managed to find us another house, too, in Clareville Grove, South Kensington, and we removed ourselves there, mostly in a series of jerks by M.G. power. In the middle of the move one of our helpers ran out of cigarettes and Valerie Hobson gave us 200. I was able to thank her in a broadcast, saying, 'If anyone who hears this sees Valerie Hobson will they please say thank you for the cigarettes,' and Valerie, who was appearing in *The King and I* at the time, was much disturbed by people hammering on the dressing-room door to say, 'Nancy Spain says thank you for the cigarettes.'

All this time, too, Jonnie and Michael Griffiths's plan for *She* were materializing. It was decided that Editor Jonnie *must* have a holiday to put her on top of the world, ready for the great crises ahead.

So in March 1935 we sailed for Jamaica on the same boat as Gilbert Harding. We were in mid-Atlantic and I had only just recovered from my usual bout of sea-sickness when the first cables arrived asking, was I going to marry him? This newspaper intrusion certainly put paid to any possibility of a ship-board romance.

It is very, very expensive cabling to and fro in

mid-Atlantic, but for a while Gilbert enjoyed himself very much. He sent cables in verse to the *Mirror* and his own paper, the *People*. We are still (as it so happens) genuinely devoted to one another, although temperamentally so much alike. For one mad moment we even discussed the possibility of a full-dress, pure white wedding from the Governor's House, Jamaica, with Jonnie (by now radiantly pretty and in the best brown of health) as matron of honour.

I first met Gilbert in Leonard Russell's house at a dinner-party, Leonard is very happily married to Dilys Powell, the film critic of the *Sunday Times*. I am very fond of them both and they give wonderful dinner-parties. Indeed you may remember it was Leonard who launched me as a writer by sending a copy of *Thank You, Nelson* to A. A. Milne. At this party I sat opposite Gilbert and next door to the literary editor of the *Observer*, who kept asking me how I chose my books. (Strangely enough, he had married a girl who was the first person I ever saw in the *Daily Express* offices, because she used to be secretary to Harold Keeble. Stranger still, she afterwards, with Gilbert and myself, became a member of the T.V. panel of 'Who Said That?')

Spontaneously, I was mad about Gilbert. 'I would a tale unfold,' he said in the middle of dinner, 'as t'would make your face cream and mantle like a standing pond.'

He told story upon story, each one increasingly ribald, until I was his slave for life. After dinner, he continued until (overcome by emotion) I knocked over a whole marching procession of little china feet that Dilys keeps among the bookshelves in her drawing-room . . .

'Ignore it! Ignore it!' cried Leonard. But I couldn't ignore darling Gilbert. Our friendship continued through leaps and bounds, until he gave me a gramophone record called, significantly, *Mon Homme*. On went Gilbert, drawing my soul after him with the splendours of his over-crammed, chaotic, and splendiferous mind. People who call Gilbert the poor man's Doctor Johnson have never known Gilbert, never read Johnson. No, no. Gilbert is himself alone.

Oh, prodigious memory, oh, mind that can grasp a book in an hour, a page at a time; sunny nature, innocence of heart; oh, well-read, over-civilized man who enjoys all good things except exercise and wishes harm to no one. No wonder I love him.

Meanwhile, here was Gilbert, and how Jonnie and I enjoyed him. We went to his flat. We heard him roar out *Guys and Dolls* (he roars out *Kismet* now, but the principle is the same) and he generally became an indispensable part of our lives. More than that . . . he often listens very gracefully indeed to us and sometimes even asks our advice.

I shall not lightly forget that voyage out. To begin with, it was rough. (Wind force 11, which, Jonnie tells me, is very grand.) And Gilbert has for some years now lived in a world of his own, where fried eggs are done 'just so'. If the eggs didn't arrive at the table 'just so' Gilbert made a row and sent them back to the galley, where pots of boiling fat leapt terrifyingly about throughout the storm. After several of these scenes, when the stewards were hopelessly intimidated, Gilbert observed to Jonnie that she seemed displeased with him.

'I am,' said Jonnie, gravely. 'You give everybody at the table dreadful indigestion when you behave like that, Gilbert.'

Whereupon Gilbert disarmingly apologized to everybody at the table.

We all hated Jamaica, anyway. The people there seemed to dislike us so. The head-waiters in every single hotel required scenes to be made before we could even eat what we wanted. The factories (grinding out sugar cane into molasses into rum) sent me right round the bend and I was all the time expecting to be bitten to death by scorpions and puff-adders and sea-urchins. The beautiful blue Caribbean was alive with little fish that were not called 'Stingers' for nothing. Spiders were the size of tea plates and mosquitoes were downright poisonous. And to this day I shall never forget the hotel bedroom in which Jonnie and I found ourselves incarcerated in Montego Bay. It was, apparently, one half a Nissen hut, stuffy as only a Nissen hut can be, with angry taps that sighed when we pressed them. And in the bath crouched the usual outsize malignant spider.

I was in despair. Even though I had met and thoroughly enjoyed Ernest Hemingway's brother, Lester (who was running a day-trip in a big single-masted schooner to the mosquito swamps), I couldn't write a story about anything that didn't come out sour and disillusioned and sick at heart . . . Added to which the *Express* wanted to know if I was going to marry Gilbert.

I really behaved very badly. I collapsed, sobbing helplessly, in the bathroom, and darling Jonnie, gently, kindly, and efficiently, wrote and cabled the story that the paper wanted about my life with Gilbert Harding. It was the only story of that trip that the paper liked at all.

Mind you, there was a lot about Jamaica that was extremely beautiful. I loved the colours and the long Northern road where the waves came combing in and the palm trees looked as though their petticoats had been blown over their heads . . . and I loved the sudden glimpse of Noël Coward's house at Port Maria (perhaps everything would have been quite, quite different if The Master had been at home, but he had gone to Florida) . . . and I loved the cold mountain stream where we bathed as it met the warm and treacherous Caribbean. And I loved the night we spent in a wooden plantation house high up in the Blue Mountain, where the air was thick with the scent of orange blossom and the dew lay rough on everything in the early morning.

But basically it was the *people* I couldn't understand or like. It is literally the only place in the world I have ever been where the people never smiled. I suppose, like Ireland, there is a long history of oppression and riots and savage reprisals. And religion. Voodoo is so unsettling. And I suppose, too, that as Jamaica is such a small island (and hopelessly out of touch with the rest of the world) that it still lives in the century before last . . . the day before yesterday.

There was a mad little episode at Errol Flynn's island where a lady attached herself to us, telling us that the broker's men had just moved in and that we were to call her Stinker. It cost us about 25s. for a towel, I remember, there. No doubt the boy who mixed the Planter's Punches in the bar was making hay while the sun shone, too. Later, I heard from Patrice Wymore (Mrs. Errol Flynn) that a big American combine had bought the whole thing . . . and as our dear little ship slid away a shark, brown and lean as a wolf, slid under the keel. It seemed symbolic of our entire abortive voyage of discovery.

The voyage home was a real holiday and rest cure. The crew and officers were charming to us and apart from the fact that most of the cooking was done in coconut oil (if you have never eaten a fried egg that tastes lightly of coconut, you have never lived), we had a lovely time. Indeed, the whole of Fyffe's Line laid themselves out to be charming to us. The chairman, when he booked our passage, was kindness itself; and the eight days rolling out and the ten days rolling home in the good ship *Tetela* was exactly right for the new Editor of *She*. Jonnie disappeared into a flurry of conferences and late-night sessions that would have taxed the strength of twelve strong men. So I was delighted that she, anyway, had had that long sea voyage that the doctor ordered.

And I, insanely enough, went riding off with Jonty
Wilson, John Peel, and Philip Donellan down the Fosse
Way from Lincoln to Seaton in Devon. Anything less
like Jamaica it would be hard to find.

Chapter Nineteen

Philip Donellan was a tall, handsome BBC producer who turned up at Clarevllle Grove one evening before we went to Jamaica, introduced by Barbara Crowther of *Woman's Hour*. He had asked Barbara for a lunatic lady who could ride a horse and cared about Roman Roads, and Barbara had suggested me. Philip had a considerable mania about the Fosse Way, he said. The Fosse Way runs more or less as straight as a die from Lincoln through Newark, Leicester, Warwickshire, Gloucester, Somerset, to Devon. He had ridden up and down it on a motor-bicycle once or twice and now he dreamed of doing it on a horse. The BBC would pay for the horses and their food. Very romantic. Could I ride? Yes, I said firmly. But could I ride well enough to do twenty miles a day? After all, that would mean eight hours in the saddle. Laughingly I said, yes indeed.

Philip went back to Warwick, rubbing his head and saying very well then, I could come.

We didn't meet again until one Sunday evening in Lincoln when we went out to a riding-school and looked at the horses. They seemed amiable enough and the one that was assigned to me, the Lady Jane, was a little nervous. 'But pay no attention,' said her owner. 'Just give her her head and let her look around a bit and by and by she will trot on.'

Poor Lady Jane. She had been on the milk round. She had a nervous fear of practically everything on the Fosse Way. Ghosts of ancient Romans, telephone-boxes, aeroplanes, lorries, policemen: they all made her whinny and scream in terror, sometimes to the extent of standing on her hind-legs and waving her forepaws in the air. A typical milk-cart horse, apart from these neuroses she had a peculiarly bouncing, slapping trot. When her hooves struck the tarmac she was perfectly happy. Down would go her head, as though she were once more between the shafts and up would go her tail and she would trot, trot, trot to glory.

After I had met Lady Jane, and had decided I ought to have her psycho-analysed, I met Jonty Wilson. Jonty was a dear. I loved him at sight and I love him yet. He is a blacksmith from Kirby Lonsdale and seemed at first, second, and third glance to be made entirely from fine brown leather. He was loosely poured into an old Yeomanry tunic and wearing a very disreputable hat. Under the hat his face was bright-eyed. Had he darted into a thicket he would instantly have disappeared from human view, so perfect was his protective colouring.

Around dinner-time J. H. B. Peel, son of Gillie Potter, turned up. Sleepy looking, amiable, with a large brown and white spaniel called Simon at his heels, John admitted he was a poet. Certainly the mud of Hog's Norton had long been brushed from his heels. He had once been in the cavalry, he told me, and he didn't wear any underclothing. These things throughout our fortnight together were a source of wonderment to me. He and Jonty got on tremendously well and could often be heard quoting poetry to one another.

On Monday morning (after I had typed and posted off a book column to the *Express*) we gathered at the market cross, Lincoln. There was a group of cheering bystanders, a photographer. Time, tide, the traffic were forgotten. The Lady Jane waited for none of them. The moment she felt my weight in the saddle she set off at her usual slapping trot for the open country, with Jonty and John and Philip practically cantering behind, all of them shouting, 'Stop, Nancy! Not so fast, Nancy! If you go like that now there will be nothing left of your horse at the end of the day . . .'

They were wrong, of course. The Lady Jane thrived on this sort of exercise. *I* was the one who suffered.

And my borrowed Jodhpurs split from top to toe. So my first twenty miles were a splendid little nightmare. By the time I arrived at our first Outside Broadcast spot, two large blisters had risen on my buttocks, and I was longing for a dressing of some sort for them. I remember letting Lady J. out into a large pleasant meadow by a river with boats, and I remember being perturbed by a young woman from a local newspaper who wanted to interview me. I asked her to wait until I had had my bath. Indeed, I asked her to wait until we had done the broadcast. I then forgot all about her, because my mind was churning over and over, worrying exactly what *had* happened during that first extraordinary day. We were due on the air in about half an hour from that moment and I had to write a script for Philip.

We had jounced out of Lincoln, covertly eyeing one another in the plate-glass windows of various shops. Small boys had run beside us, whistling and huzza-ing and throwing their caps in the air and shouting, 'Where are the hounds?' And then the road had run straight before us, twenty miles of splendid, well-metalled road that ran complainingly past an air-field where lorries whizzed by our ears like maddened bees and aeroplanes took off like the roar of doom. Whenever this happened the Lady J. stood on her hind-legs and *yelled*. And there were several red telephone-boxes, past which the dear girl refused, sweating, to go.

However, we did the broadcast: and I had the usual instant complaint from ladies belonging to the Dumb Friends League. How dare I, they asked, ride a terrified horse in such a peculiarly brutal way? (How dare I? I, too, was wondering.) So I suggested that the ladies should come and see the performance for themselves. (It was by now quite *noticeable* which of us was the worst for wear and who was being cruel to whom. The Lady Jane was in the pink of condition, her coat glossy as a chestnut. *I* was the nervous, bleeding wreck.)

However, we did the broadcast and I even managed to remember the young woman from the local paper.

She afterwards printed an account of how I had cut her dead in the saloon bar. But I liked her very much and I admit that I was very glad to get to bed and I slept terribly well, beaten to the wide all through that extraordinary fortnight, waking in the morning with an appetite for breakfast that knew no bounds, what with trotting through the day with a liver behaving better than it ever has before.

My second day I had a wonderful encounter with a man who called himself Curling Myers in a broad-brimmed stetson hat. Curling Myers was the name of his farm. He *breeds bluebottles*: a profitable side-line to his knackers' business. He has sheds and sheds and sheds where pieces of raw meat hang and bluebottles breed.

'I hate waste,' said Curling Myers. 'So when I found I had rather a lot of bluebottles I thought I would sell the maggots for fisherman's bait.'

And so he does, sorting out the big, medium, and small maggots in a special home-made grading machine. I confided in him how terribly hungry I got at midday and he rang up an old friend and said I would be trotting by her door in half an hour's time.

Sure enough she rescued me and gave me two boiled eggs and mounds and mounds of bread and butter. She also attended to my poor, bleeding bottom, which didn't harden up until the end of the second week. This is, I swear, the last reference I shall make to it. After all, it was an awful bore even then: but I should like to put on record the kindness of every chambermaid along the length and breadth of the Fosse Way, every chamber-maid and every district nurse. Even Lady Barnett had a go, when I trotted nervelessly through Silesby. It was quite in her line, as before she married Sir Geoffrey she had been Dr. Marshall of Aberdeen.

Leicester I remember well because (quite apart from Lady Barnett, who was a darling and came along to be interviewed, to show what splendid people lived on the line of the Fosse), I found a little pottery medallion in the Leicester museum. It said, 'Marcellus the gladiator goes with Vera, the dancer', and it made the Romans seem almost human, for an instant. After Leicester the Fosse became a green road, entangled with briars and bushes, crossing meadows where the whickering friendly horses are so hideously well-bred that even the Lady Jane began to hold up her head and pick up her feet in imitation. On we went by Warwick and Gloucestershire, the Cotswolds, by Somerset into Bath. By now we were a National Institution. People really *waited* in to hear our adventures in the evening on the Home Service. As we passed by the bottom of their gardens, they rushed from their houses, carrying steaming cups of tea, asking for autographs, souvenirs, asking after the health and fitness of the Lady Jane. It was in this manner that a milk-cart horse from Lincoln became a National Pet.

Bath was great fun. I was sitting in the Hotel Francis, on the Dunlopillow cushion that was now my constant companion, when Joyce Grenfell walked up, roaring with laughter. The last time I had seen her was at another

Home Service broadcast with Ronald Searle and Arthur Marshall, when we had all described the invigorating and inspirational effect that our school-days had had upon us. (This was the occasion upon which we all sang the Roedean cricket song.)

Joyce Grenfell was kindness itself. We went back to her dressing-room (she was appearing in her own revue there prior, as they say, to London production) and she showed me her make-up and the switch of false hair she wore in certain roles and I bought a box for that evening's performance because Jonty had said he had never been in a theatre. (Devil's house?) To my dying day I shall cherish the look on Jonty's face when he crept round backstage to meet Miss Grenfell. 'My,' he kept saying afterwards. 'So yon's an *actress*. She seems a thoroughly respectable nice woman, mind?'

So, although my admiration for Miss Grenfell has no limits, I wished for one mad moment that she were a Really Actressy Actress. Like Gertrude Lawrence.

So up from Bath we rode to the great green hills of Somerset. Was it here, or was it earlier, that I encountered the Police University where Lady Jane went nuts and bolted whinnying through the flower-beds as if she had something very dreadful indeed on her conscience? That was a surprising interlude. I sat with the Commandant at the highest of high tables, rather meanly asking him pertinent questions about obscene literature, looking down on a wide echoing hall where 200 policemen from all parts of the Commonwealth ate bread and jam.

I can remember the O.B. point after that because it was a pub in which we ate superlatively good roast chicken. My mouth waters again as I remember it. I can also remember Lady Jane rushing down leafy lanes with her head up, whinnying, as if she feared she would never see her chums again.

What a fascinating cross-section of English life that ancient road showed me day by day. One moment I was pushing the Lady Jane through brambles and bluebells, sliding to glory over the highest point in Somerset on her tail . . . the next, I was walking round an enormous modern factory where they manufacture head-lamps and have an up-to-date nursery for babies. Then there was the antique shop where the two Mister Vaux, father and son, collected musical boxes. Some were by Fabergé, no bigger and no less fragile than a butterfly. Some were enormous, like the flaxen-haired doll that monotonously played waltzes by Chopin. Sometimes it rained, as it did on the day when we visited Sezincotes, and found a drawing-room full of débutantes resting after a Ball: it is a wonderful folly of a house, all cupolas and minarets built by a Regency nabob who had (so legend tells) six black wives whom he used to keep in a purdah room in the backyard. And then, sometimes, the sun blazed down and it was most uncomfortably hot. Like the day that I went spanking by Cricket St. John where Lord Beaverbrook owns a farm: where the grass grows long, and lush and rich, and the milk is obviously richer than any other milk in Somerset.

Eventually the Fosse disappeared for ever. John Peel and I went to investigate its disappearance in a meadow; and John said there was nothing, not even a Roman stone built into a house wall to suggest that the Legions halted here. So I think it is obvious that the main road, the remains of the Fosse, came up from Cornwall and we were on the wrong track trotting down to Seaton by the Sea in Devon.

However, I doubt whether the listeners would have stood for another week of our adventures in Cornwall. We all vowed eternal friendship; and Philip, whose dear wife Jill had borne him a son as we came down through England, said he would christen him Thomas Fosse Donellan. And then we all went home.

Chapter Twenty

In 1954, in July, I went to New York because I was writing a series of articles about Gertrude Lawrence for the *Evening Standard*. Lord Beaverbrook sent for me on the day when my sister was getting married to Sir Westrow Hulse; so with champagne coming out of my ears I reeled along to Arlington House, where Lord Beaverbrook lulled me into a false sense of pity by instantly rising to his feet and taking me with him to the dentist.

He wrote out a contract on a little pad while I sat in the back of the car too dazed, bewildered, and charmed by him to say that I was mistaken; that I didn't think I was adequate for the task and, anyway, what was wrong with his teeth? 'I have a rough bit here,' he said, pointing. 'Now you stay here and amuse yourself with the radio in the arm at the back,' and then he disappeared into a tall house in Harley Street. I afterwards discovered that this car was probably Lady Docker's, loaned to the Lord because his own big Daimler was elsewhere.

When he came back out of the dentist I was convinced in my folly. I see *now* that it was madness for me to attempt to write a biography of an actress at all, let alone a dead actress. But you try and figure that one out when you are sitting in Lord Beaverbrook's, or Lady Docker's, Daimler in Harley Street on a hot afternoon in July and you are full of champagne.

For, magnificent though it may sound, I did *not* enjoy that assignment. Pam, Gertie's daughter and I, delighted to meet after all these years, went up to Manchester and met Pam's father, Gertie's first husband. He was a thoroughly nice man, in looks somewhat like an intelligent and God-fearing mouse. And he was happily remarried to a handsome girl who had been a Tiller girl.

We had lunch with them in a perfectly respectable villa on the outskirts of Manchester with hydrangeas blooming madly in the garden; and hot boiled salmon on the table within. Pam, who no doubt was feeling the heat, suddenly went raving mad during lunch and in full and lugubrious detail gave us a physical description of the way that Gertie looked in the mortician's parlour. 'My,' said Frank Howley, pushing away his plate of salmon. 'How maca-bree.'

I ferreted around in London like a mad thing. I talked to Roy Royston (the original boy friend of *The Girl Friend*), whom I found running a dainty little laundry called The Debonaire in Walton Street, S.W.3. Roy had been an angel with Gertie in a children's play and had vaguely kept in touch with her in later years. I talked (in fact I laughed helplessly) with Noël Coward and Philip Astley, and by the time I set off for America I had a full-scale account (financial, moral, and philosophical) of Gertie's doings in England.

In order to appreciate just how thorny my path now became, you must realize that everyone in the whole world was trying to write a book about Gertie. Pam had written hers. Richard Aldrich, the second husband, had sold his for serialization to the American magazine *Women's Home Journal*. And to compete at all I had to complete mine in the space of six short weeks. What made it worse was that Gertie seemed to have become powerfully *respectable* in America . . . and not a bit like herself in England, where she was best known for having lots of lovers and not paying her laundry bill.

In New York I stayed with Hermione Gingold in an apartment that overlooked an iron bridge. Here lorries clanged and crashed all day long, as monotonously as the J. Arthur Rank gongster. We had five hours of holy hush in the twenty-four, from midnight to 5 a.m. And this shocked all of us so profoundly that we used to wake up sobbing. Chris Hewitt was living there too and from time to time I would look at him gloomily and wonder would I ever see dear old London again.

Hermione went away for the weekend and I flew up the north-east coast to Cape Cod, Massachusetts, where Gertie's respectability had set in. Gertie's second husband (known as Dick, but not to me) owned a lot of theatres there. He had a wooden one more like a church, really, it was so uncomfortable, where they did straight plays. He had an enormous circus marquee called The Melody Tent where they did things like *Oklahoma!* and

Rose Marie. I think he even owned some more theatres in other places . . .

The coastline fell away under me in a haze of cream and green froth, while I twitched uneasily at my round-trip ticket. We touched down at Nantucket Island first and I left the plane, thinking I was already in Hyannis, Cape Cod. How I discovered it was Nantucket, I can't think: as all those little airports look exactly alike. I might have been in Corsica again, to tell the truth. There was the same little galvanized iron shed, the same old wind sock. Only the people, in nylon shirts and smart fedoras, smoothly commuting from New York and telling one another how ghastly the city was at this time of year, were any different. I pelted back to the aircraft very out of breath and worried. But I *did* eventually arrive at Cape Cod.

I am sure it is a pretty place. I am sure everyone else in the world must love it. The houses are all clinker-built, something like Sussex. Some of them are of a silvery grey wood, like birch trees, some of them are painted white. There are dear little churches with turrets and bells calling the faithful to prayer every five minutes. There are cranberry bogs and pinewood and wind-swept sand-dunes, and jolly little houses where New Yorkers were getting away from it all. I found it very depressing indeed.

I still find it hard to believe that anyone *really* lives there with pleasure. Most of all, I could not understand why *Gertie* should have wanted to . . .

A nice madness was added to it all by the cables that now kept arriving for me. Among other people who assisted me in compiling a dossier about Gertie, was a Highland lass with 'the gift' who made a habit of attending séances and taking down trance material in shorthand. She had sent on a couple of scripts to me, saying that they had been 'taken down' at various times when Gertie was giving an afternoon performance on the astral plane: quite apart from everything else Gertie kept on giving messages for people to hand on to her husband. I even went to one or two of the séances and enjoyed them very much. And when I went to America progress reports were air-mailed (or in extreme cases cabled) after me.

These usually ran something like GERTIE SAYS TALLULAH MIGHT HELP GERTIE SAYS NO SEX IN HEAVEN STOP. When I told Lord Beaverbrook about this one he said, 'Bad luck. That's the worst news I've had in three weeks.' But when I told Hermione she said, 'Why do these people who have passed over waste their time sending us messages like *that?*'

However, hardly had I touched down in Cape Cod and clambered gloomily into bed in a little old New England four-poster, than further messages began to arrive saying, GERTIE SAYS TRY YUL BRYNNER.

This message was handed in at the hotel where I was stopping, and of course they had never heard of me. So then it was sent over to the theatre where they decided that I must be one of the new actresses, coming later that week. And finally it was given to Mr. Richard Aldrich, the boss. What his feelings were when he opened it and read it I cannot think.

He was probably reading it when I set out next morning to try and find him. I hate walking at the best of times, but walking ten miles before breakfast on Cape Cod surpassed everything I had ever done. To begin with I got hopelessly lost. There is nothing really to distinguish one sand-dune from another, or one clapperboard house from another; and wherever I went the world seemed full of great big hairy-chested New Yorkers in towelling dressing-gowns, doing exercises on their beautifully civilized lawns. I remembered a newspaper-cutting that Iris Ashley had written about Gertie on Cape Cod. There had been a little picture of a signpost saying, 'Old-Town Lane', and a quotation of Gertie remarking, 'Well, ducks, I started life in Old Town, Clapham, and here I am living in Old Town Lane. Haven't gone very far, have I? Back where I started.' So from time to time I asked one of the men if he knew where Old Town Lane was. In the end I threw caution to the winds and started to ask for Richard Aldrich. I did better that way: as the house, The Berries, is something of a notoriety around the Cape.

The Berries was hidden from the road by large clumps of bushes and trees. I banged on the door and Mr. Aldrich opened it. He was in the middle of shaving. He was very nice about it. 'Ah,' he said when I told him who I was. 'I have a cable for you. Perhaps you would care to come over to the theatre and get it at nine o'clock.' So I said, 'Yes,' and, 'Thanks very much,' and rushed away before I made a mistake and he set the bloodhounds on me.

Mr. Aldrich's office at nine o'clock was a riot of fun. There was a loose coating of sand drifting in on everything, because that good, clean, old Atlantic wind would keep a-blowing and a-breezing. There were two young men in the outer office. One of them sat at a typewriter, gloomily scratching his head. The other monotonously telephoned lists to a printer. There was a very nice, helpful female secretary and the walls were much decorated with playbills and things. Just the same, it wasn't anything like a theatrical office in England.

In the end Mr. Aldrich sent out for me and I went into the inner sanctum, a wooden room something like a cricket pavilion, loosely furnished with desks, telephones, and signed photographs of Gertrude Lawrence. Aldrich was a big, relaxed, attractive man, with a long nose with a sensitive tip to it. He sat in his shirt-sleeves and listened gravely as I told him what went on in the séances. Later, with great kindness, he drove me in a two-colour hard-top convertible, out to The Berries and showed me round. Apart from the unfortunate fact that he obviously knew a completely different Gertie from the one that we had all become used to in England, I liked him, and we got along quite well. And after all, I considered, Gertie *was* an actress, and the chances were that she gave every bit as good a performance as 'Mrs. A.' as she had as 'a Mother' at Roedean.

Good-humouredly, relaxedly, 'Mr. A.' played me smoothly back to New York, like a ping-pong ball, to his lawyer, Miss Fanny Holtzmann.

'She is a remarkable woman,' he said. 'You will find her most remarkable.'

He told me this as we went on our conducted tour of The Berries. It was like a set for a play manufactured from a Daphne du Maurier novel. There were piles of dolls and velvet animals and so forth in the bedroom, there were little old *objets d'art* collected by Gertie from all parts of the world. There was even a smart collection of garden hats, hanging inside the front door. It was beautiful, it was spotless, but it gave me the willies.

Mr. A. went on being carefully, conscientiously kind. He gave me tickets to his Melody Tent where I saw *Oklahoma!* He gave me Dorothy's (Gertie's maid) telephone number in Hyannis – the capital city of Cape Cod. But gentle and painstaking though he was, I couldn't help thinking that he was giving a rather good performance, too.

Well, I flew back to New York, to the warm embrace of that extraordinary city. I was glad to see it. In its beauty, its heat, its magnificent squalor, it was so much more my cup of tea than Cape Cod.

Almost directly I had a long telephone conversation with Fanny Holtzmann. For one weekend, from Saturday to Monday, when I said good-bye to her in her office, I walked and talked and ate ice-cream and drank milk with Fanny Holtzmann.

Fanny is a bustling, passionate woman in her late forties. She has eyes like prunes, she continually talks about Noël Coward, the King of Greece, and the Prime Minister of China.

She struck me as lonely. Indeed, although from time to time she painted a self-portrait in oils, or painted a portrait of Gertie in oils, or ran up a terra-cotta bust of Gertie, she seemed that weekend to have no other business to preoccupy her. Indeed it was very kind of her to take so much trouble over me. 'I will offer you rich, rich material,' she said, 'if you will only delay the publication of your story about Gertrude.'

'Well,' I said, 'where's the rich material?'

'In the office,' said she.

'Let's have a look,' said I.

'It's Sunday,' said she.

'Open the office up,' said I.

'I haven't got the key,' said she.

'In any case, it is for my Editor to say if and when he wants to print my story,' I said.

'Let's go for a walk in Central Park,' said she.

So, for hours on end, we walked backwards and forwards through Central Park, occasionally pausing at an ice-cream parlour, where Fanny Holtzmann insisted on buying me 'Real old, honest to goodness ice-cream'. I have never had what I should describe as a sweet tooth.

Eventually I said I had a red-hot date with a weight-lifter and ran away. But in the morning (7 a.m.) she was on the telephone, and at 9 a.m. in a torrential, warm downpour there was I at her office, waiting to see the rich, rich material. Her glass door was labelled Attorney-at-Law, there were ever such a lot of law books: and there were a lot more busts of Gertie. Surprisingly, too, there was a lady called Doctor Jellineck who said she had looked after the Lawrence throat in *The King and I.*

By now, as a result of the diet of milk and ice-cream I was thoroughly unnerved. So when Fanny Holtzmann produced two bound leather diaries of the 1930s and I found they were full of references to Lord Dudley and Douglas Fairbanks, I nearly fainted, I reeled away from Fanny Holtzmann's office, for ever, to the New York public library, which seemed to me more dull, but also more efficacious, as a source of material.

Yet I was impressed by Fanny Holtzmann.

As luck would have it I met Dorothy Parker directly after this. She couldn't have been kinder. She even gave me a great big Scotch on the rocks and, oh boy, did I need it after all that ice-cream . . . Meanwhile, Fanny Holtzmann was ringing up Hermione Gingold and telling her how nice I was, which Hermione Gingold found very surprising. 'You must have done something awful,' Hermione kept saying. So eventually we had a terrible row in the kitchen and when Hermione, later, gave a party in aid of a television panel game called *One Moment, Please!* and *Time* and *Life* magazine came to the party and took a lot of photographs and someone asked me who I was, so that they could correctly caption the photographs, I replied (without hesitation), 'Fanny Holtzmann.'

What is more, I almost believed it.

Chapter Twenty-One

In the end the Gertrude Lawrence story was finished, vetted by the lawyer and published in the *Evening Standard*, where my friends were very surprised by it. I was in the South of France when it came out, so I didn't see my name on the hoardings or on tops of buses or on the roofs of the little green *Standard* vans as they whizzed about their business. I lay in the sun and panted. I remember with particular joy the baby grapes outside the villa, ripening in the sun, a wonderful meal of river trout and Crêpes Suzette at a mountain village called Gourdon, and *all* the swimming, diving, and boating in the warm and caressing Mediterranean.

When I got back to London Noël Coward, Philip Astley, Joan Astley, and I had a celebration lunch in the Ivy, where we ate oysters and sang the 'Roedean cricketing song' and ate pheasants and drank burgundy and sang 'Wimbledonia'. Then, when we had drunk a fair amount of coffee, we reeled along to Russell Square, where Gertie Lawrence was still monotonously appearing at the séances. I giggled helplessly and was sharply chided by a lady who told me that other séances were going on all over the building. Eventually a medium appeared called Mrs. F. and she went smoothly into her trance.

'What do you see here?' she said, holding out her hands to Noël.

'A rather puffy Mount of Venus,' said Noël, obligingly.

'No! No!' cried the medium. 'What else?'

'I see no stigmata, if that is what you mean,' said Noël.

'No, no,' said the medium again. 'It's me dogbite.'

'Oh,' said Noël. 'Tell me some more about Noël. *He* interests me very much. Always did.'

'I shall come back, you know, I shall come back, as a nurse.'

'God forbid, dear,' said Noël, piously.

'Don't do that,' cried Philip.

'Please,' I added. Which sent the medium into a sideways spiritual spin.

'What about that little boy?' she said, dreamily. 'Where is he now?'

'Well . . .' said Noël, chattily. 'He had them out and then they dropped and then they sent him to a nursing home in Woking and now he's much better.'

And that was that. Lots more things were said, but they were chiefly of the 'Don't despair', 'It will all come right in the end' variety. Noël had a long conversation about the medium's great gifts and we came away. Afterwards, helplessly, driving round Russell Square in a tiny little Ford Eight, with The Master's knees just about on a level with his ears, he said, 'Did you notice that she quoted from *Blithe Spirit*? They always, always do, you know.'

'I didn't notice,' said Joan Astley. 'What did she say?'

'Well, I said when had she had her first trance,' said Noël, 'and she answered "when I was six". Well, she should have said "five", but the principle's still the same.'

And that, as far as I can truly remember, was the last sublime experience of 1954.

Many people who have been kind enough to take an interest in me, and in the sort of things I write, have expressed some astonishment that I manage to do 'such a lot'. I can't see it myself, for I am excessively lazy by nature, and whenever I get a chance I lie down flat, preferably in the sun and relax. I seldom go to literary parties, finding them exactly like all the literary parties I went to ten years ago. The same people are standing there, holding their glasses at the same angle, looking exactly the same as they did ten years ago. And I find that this depresses me. So I stay at home instead, where my life is a mixture of work and 'family life', in equal doses.

Fortunately I have *some* powers of concentration. I have worked hard at this, learning to think against all sorts of background noises and background silences, against other people's telephone conversations and so on. But even so, I can only really concentrate for one hour at a time. This is enough for most short jobs of work. It takes me roughly one hour to write in long hand and type out one thousand words of prose or read the average novel of 200 pages. And as there are twelve hours in the day I fill the remaining eleven with such preparations for work as talking, interviewing, making endless telephone calls, broadcasting and looking at television. But during that sacred hour of concentration I resent any sort of interruption, particularly incoming telephone calls, which send me right up the wall.

So, by simple arithmetic, you will see that one hour's concentration a day should produce, at the end of eighty days, a book of 80,000 words. Alas, this isn't so. The telephone, the demands of journalism, which always need the story written *now,* for tonight's paper, by four o'clock this afternoon, won't allow it . . .

So I have got into the habit of getting up at five a.m. to work. This is surprisingly enjoyable, particularly in the summer. It is a wonderfully hypnotic hour, five o'clock, when you get used to the shock of it.

I work until seven, when I am always so ragingly hungry that I go and get myself breakfast. This regime, carried out faithfully, morning after morning, produces the necessary tight string of continuity to finish a long piece of work like a book. So after breakfast I have a whole ordinary day left for broadcasting, journalism, answering the bloody telephone and meeting people.

This is the way that I managed to finish two detective novels, two books for children (and I illustrated them myself, too, which I deeply enjoyed) a short novel, various magazine stories and this book. In the daytime I was writing my stuff for the *Daily Express, She* and working on various programmes for the BBC.

I think I enjoyed writing this book most. Indeed, I have so much enjoyed writing this book, that when I was deep in it I used to look forward to five a.m. with real joy.

My next greatest pleasure, though, has always been meeting people.

By people I don't necessarily mean celebrities. Taxi drivers, bus conductors, booksellers (maybe these *are* celebrities) little boys of three and a half, women in shops, men in top hats outside Mayfair hotels, ships' stewards, pursers, waiters, a great crowd of such acquaintances trot through my mind: saying witty, endearing things as they go. Lovely people, all of them, who have taught me many things.

I have met a lot of people in my life, and I am likely to meet a lot more. I must say, I like it that way. I wish I could fill the eleven enchanting hours of the day with nothing else at all but meeting and talking to new people.

It was a young man called Tristram Humble who pointed this out to me. I remember sitting drinking light ale with Tristram in his house in Eslington Terrace, Newcastle-on-Tyne, many years ago. Tristram and his sister Sylvia were there (both of them people whom I have known and loved all my life) and young Watson of Pumphrey and Carrick Watson. There were others, too, but I don't remember them. And we were having the sort of conversation that young men and women normally have late at night in their rooms, drinking cocoa, at Universities. You know the sort of conversation. Full of impossible questions. Do you believe in God? What do you want most from life? Where are you going from here? What was the War *for* exactly?

I was at my silliest and most flippant that evening. I can even remember replying to one of Tristram's graver questions, about what I needed in life, with a sharp 'Paper, a fountain pen and *no* people.' 'Oh, no,' said Tristram kindly. 'You're wrong. More than anyone I know, you need people, Nancy.'

Tristram Humble was quite right. His common sense made me ashamed. Without people my life would have been meaningless. Just think how much poorer I should have been in spirit, for example, if I had never met Winnie Atwell, the famous pianist who has brought honour and glory to her native Trinidad.

Winnie first came into my life in the shape of a gramophone record called 'The Black and White Rag'. When it was new, this record dominated me. To tell the truth, it still does. So do many other Atwell recordings, notably 'The Poor People of Paris', but 'Black and White Rag' is still my favourite. Often when I am feeling old and tired and full of sleep (I have the decorators in at the moment, and there are few things more conducive to collapse) I put on this record. And like magic I feel some of Winifred Atwell's inexhaustible radiance and vitality recharging my batteries. I have never known it fail me.

Indeed, 'Black and White Rag' has the same rare, electric quality as Brighton or Bexhill air.

Around the time when I first began to depend on 'Black and White Rag' so much, I found out that Winnie was appearing twice nightly at The Chelsea Palace. So I used to make the pilgrimage twice an evening down the King's Road, Chelsea, from Carlyle Square. I never bothered about the rest of the bill (I mean no offence). I simply crept into my seat after the interval, caught Winnie's act and stumbled out again, feeling as though I had had some galvanic treatment. Dear Winnie. In those days when I was poor (and maybe you were, too?) and I hardly had the price of the seat in my pocket, that evening visit put me in shape to lick the world next day. Can you wonder I think 'Black and White Rag' is my signature tune, and when I was asked to come as a guest to *Woman's Hour* I had them play it for me, and on every occasion I could squeeze it in afterwards?

My experience isn't unusual. Winnie has 70,000 fans, all as loyal as I am. They aren't in a position to say such a public thank you, that's all.

Then I became fairly well known as a broadcaster. I was asked next summer, when *Woman's Hour* came off the air for the annual break, if I would do a full week, one hour per day, as a lady disc jockey. So I played a full hour of Atwell records.

Now, in spite of my violent admiration for Atwell the artist, I found myself rather at a loss for things to say while the records were being changed or turned over.

351

So I decided I must interview Winnie, get to know her. (This gave me another idea for a programme incidentally called *Getting to Know You.*) So I sought out Winnie in her palatial home in Barnet. I must say she took it very well.

I shall never forget her, sitting round that dining-room table. I kept looking furtively at those great massive shoulders, the forearms like a lady blacksmith, the pliant hands (each one worth £20,000) and thinking 'So that's what twenty years of piano practice does for you.' We kept drinking thick, strong cups of sweet tea. We kept listening to records sung by Frank Sinatra.

'I've got the world on a string . . .

The string round my fin . . . ger'

sang Frank Sinatra. And Winnie would roll her eyes right back, much to Lou's disgust. Lou is Winnie's very brilliant husband and he always punctuates the story of Winnie's life with stories.

Winnie was born in 1919 in Tunapuna, Trinidad, in Jubilee Street. It was in honour of this street she composed 'Jubilee Rag'. Her father, William Monroe Atwell, was a chemist and so was Winnie. 'I didn't care for it much,' says Winnie. 'Have you ever smelt castor oil in bulk?' The other day, in this disguise of a fully qualified chemist, Winnie beat the panel of *What's My Line?*

But even when she was a little girl of eight Winnie was giving Chopin Recitals, playing the 'Dead March in Saul' in error at her teacher's wedding, and generally doing her level best to equal and surpass a local Trinidad piano prodigy called Jessie Waddle.

This meeting with Winnie was the first of many. I have rocked with laughter in her dressing-room, where such characters as David Whitfield, Shani Wallis and eager music-publishers are to be found. I have been to fabulous parties in her house (why, I can even remember Norman Wisdom swinging lightly from a chandelier). I have corresponded, accepted free seats for shows, concerts: and all the while I have marvelled at the good humour and genuine sincerity that radiates from Winnie Atwell, the girl who has come such a long way from Trinidad.

Winnie is one of the most *genuine* people I know: even in music hall, where artists are mostly cosy and sincere. And I suppose the biggest occasion in her life was the evening when she played for Princess Margaret at the Café de Paris. Her reactions to this Royal Encounter were typically Winnie. With great good luck I turned up in Winnie's house the very next day, and so heard her spill out the whole story. Of how 'they' (by whom Winnie meant the exclusive upper crust of Princess Margaret's friends) had behaved just like other fans and clamoured for 'Poor People of Paris'. Of how when she played 'Clair de Lune' she expected a few wrong notes. But no. She was sensational. And then the Princess had sent for her. 'And oh, Nancy, you know the saying, what a *doll*? Well, that's how Princess Margaret is: a *doll*.'

As she stands, glittering, Winnie must be about the nearest thing to a millionaire in British Show Business. Those dresses, blazing in gold and silver, cost her around £500 per dress, in surprising contrast to the 'other' piano, which cost £4 10s. Winnie makes about £1,000 a performance, usually pulls in £3,000 a week, left £40,000 in tax to the Australian Government on her tour there. The hardest worker I know, Winnie does occasionally complain that she never gets a moment's peace. Before she sailed for Australia (while she was there I had a very funny letter from her entering Lou for a *She* handsome husbands competition) she left enough music on tape to be transferred to wax for a year's records.

Winnie came up the hard way: and she describes how much she owes to her mother and father. In fact, Winnie has a very keen business brain and once briskly turned down an offer to appear on the legendary *Ed Sullivan Show* in New York because 'the money wasn't right' and she 'didn't get enough time in the programme'. But she still maintains she owes everything to her mother and father. Mrs. Atwell bought her first piano (480 dollars) instead of buying the house they lived in in Trinidad (500 dollars). Mr. Atwell sent her an allowance of £45 every month, while Winnie was away in England. So now Winnie has built a separate flat for her mother and father inside her house.

Winnie's is a splendid establishment. She has a white piano, a white poodle, a white cat, a white Jaguar (registration number WA 2345), a vast collection of musical boxes (all play different tunes) and a kitchen with a gadget in the sink that grinds all the waste into pulp. Says Winnie of her piano, a Steinway, 'I hope you don't think I'm awful, but there are people I won't have in the house because I don't want them to play my piano.'

Had it not been for 'Black and White Rag', you see, composed all that time ago in 1908, I would never have met and made friends with Winifred Atwell. What an odd thing it is to be haunted by a tune, a memory from the past, a fragment of scratched celluloid. I suppose one of the most important things that has ever happened to me was to be taken (at far too tender an age) to see *The Blue Angel,* the film in which the world first became aware of Marlene Dietrich. To this day I still cannot believe that this fabulous creature, who has so often stopped all our hearts from beating once wrote to me: *Dearest Nancy, all my thanks again for your kindness, Marlene.* I am seriously considering having this one framed.

I wonder how old I was when I saw *The Blue Angel* for the first time? (One is *always* too young to see that terrible scene where Jannings is made to crow like a cock.) I am sure that our mother didn't know that I had gone to the movies. Our mother has always been dead nuts against cinemas, which she thinks are full of germs. But the impact of that figure in the top hat singing 'Blonde Women' with a sort of principal boy's strut was something that arrested my development for a good many years. Since then I have crept back to *The Blue Angel* a number of times, and also to other Dietrich revivals, notably *Destry Rides Again* (which I have seen eight times), *Seven Sinners* (they don't revive this one often enough) and *The Flame of New Orleans*. Dear me, how Marlene mops us all up, to be sure.

I remember complaining with some bitterness to a very important executive in Paramount, in New York, that Marlene hadn't *sung* in a film with James Stewart called *No Highway*. 'But Miss Spain,' said this man, 'where would you have had her sing? There was no cue for a song that I can remember . . .'

'I thought when Jimmy Stewart wrecked the plane in Newfoundland she might have climbed up on a wing tip, and said, "Are we down-hearted boys? No. Let's sing a little song,"' I replied. The Paramount Executive looked vexed. 'Well,' he said, slowly, 'she might've, at that. Pity we didn't think of it at the time.'

Marlene, bless her lovely pale face and her enormous blue eyes, thinks this extremely funny. Much funnier than the man from Paramount. For all I know, he is still biting his nails over it.

When I was first introduced to Marlene I was astounded, not so much by her looks (which I was expecting) but by her sense of humour, which no one had told me about. She is a creature of wit, and quickness and extraordinary tensions, and she seems to find her performance as the Fatal Lady of the 20th Century almost unbearably amusing. Ageless, genderless, so blazingly attractive that she snuffs out any woman in the room with her as effectively as a search-light would obliterate a candle flame, Marlene is at her very best when all her props have been thrown away and she stands there in slacks, or an admiral's overcoat, or a simple little well-tailored suit.

I met Marlene, after all these years, because I was asked, along with Lady Violet Bonham Carter, Dorothy Dickson, Lady Barnett, Barbara Kelly, Adrienne Allan, and various other stars of screen, television, theatre, and radio, 'to introduce Marlene Dietrich at the Cafe de Paris'. Gilbert Harding was a great help and told me what to say.

I deeply enjoyed doing this. Apart from the nervous terror of meeting Miss Dietrich face to face (she is, like Noël Coward, a legend who has turned out as good as her build-up), I got a free dinner at London's most glittering night-spot, free champagne, a little white cardboard star scattered on the tables to prove I'd done it, and a white carnation from the Dietrich buttonhole, which hung around the house for days, until Rita, our current treasure, not recognizing its value, threw it in the dustbin. I also had a lot of envy from my nearest and dearest and half an hour's cosy chat with Marlene, every word of which is engraved on my heart, like Queen Mary I and Calais. She talked a lot about spiritual healing. She was very funny about a famous critic who had praised her in 1953, saying the very things that she had always wanted someone to say of her, and then she met him, 'And he was a horrible little *boy* . . . a fan.' She showed me how she did her quick change, bundling out of the notorious diamond-studded gown 'that makes the evening sun go down', into her top hat, white tie, and tails. (The waistcoat, shirt, and collar are all stitched into one highly tricky unit.) Was it on this occasion, or some other, that she told me how she had gone to lunch with Mrs. Bessie Braddock at the House of Commons and there had been a young lady on her feet, breathlessly making a speech about the import duty on the 'P-r-rice of a-r-row-r-root'? Anyway, she was also very civil to Jonnie and Michael Griffiths who, as friends of the Intro-ducer, were standing, breathing heavily, just inside the dressing-room.

'Do you still like suet pudding?' said Jonnie, who had discovered this fascinating fact on Marlene's visit to London in 1954.

'Oh, yes I do,' said Marlene. 'But English chefs at English hotels are too snooty to make it for me.'

So next day the entire Good Housekeeping Institute was thrown into disorder while a spotted dick was baked for Marlene. Then it was wrapped in cellophane to keep it warm, a big blue bow was tied on it and it was taken to the Dorchester by 'Willy' Williams, the chief sub-editor of *She* magazine.

Alex Atkinson, a clever young man who used to be an actor and who now writes for *Punch,* was having lunch with Marlene when this pudding arrived. Willy stood in the door, rather red in the face.

'Miss Dietrich,' he said. 'There must be many men in London who would like to give you a pudding. But I am the lucky one who has been singled out for this errand.'

Marlene sprang to her feet and seized the pudding. Alex told me afterwards that she ate two enormous slices of it and made him eat one, too. It nearly killed him.

'That is what I like about the English,' she said, as the door of the Oliver Messel suite closed softly behind Willy. 'They are so *sincere*.'

Chapter Twenty-Two

I met Orson Welles that week, too, and did a short programme with him and his beautiful Italian wife for the BBC. I liked him enormously. He was as big as a barn door and very, very quick on the uptake indeed. He seemed able to talk on anything under the sun, but was particularly keen on King Lear, bullfighting, Ernest Hemingway, and English food. 'I was a bullfighter once,' he said and then, when I said it wasn't a sport, his actor's voice dropped three whole keys. 'Oh no . . .' he said, softly. 'It is an *art* – a tragic art.'

He also said (which was very surprising to me constantly told by one and all that I was a divided personality) that he thought I was very, very nice. This set me up for days.

All this time, too, my reserves of physical and nervous energy were being used up by various auditions for T.V. programmes. Mostly, these were panel games. The first audition I attended was in the Shepherd's Bush Empire, where actors and actresses queued up and pretended to be contestants in *What's My Line?*

I asked one actor afterwards how much he got paid for this and he said, 'Not enough.' I suppose it isn't much of a life pretending to be a Sagger Maker's Bottom Knocker.

But eventually I was chosen, along with Averil Angers, and Ian Carmichael and a nice, quiet, young sub-editor from Bradford called John Burns, not to play *What's My Line?*, but to play a game called *Something to Shout About*. We had a 'dry' run and lots and lots of rehearsals. Some of these were on the stage at the Shepherd's Bush Empire, some were in rehearsal rooms at the back of the British Prince, a cosy pub at the bottom of Lime Grove that has had greatness thrust upon it. Greatness in the shape of Gilbert Harding coming in for a quick one, Wilfred Pickles calling for a half-pint, Mabel asking for a gin, and Arthur Askey knocking on the door at five to seven on a Sunday saying that the Governor's watch was slow. The Governor is Mr. Edgar Payne, and a thoroughly nice man, usually wearing a short-sleeved silk shirt.

Macdonald Daly was chairman of this programme. T. Leslie Jackson (an adorable producer who was once a bantam- or flyweight champion, I'm not sure which, known to one and all as Jacko) was responsible for it. And there was a man called Peter Stewart who invented the game and who was very kind to us when we learnt to play it. He wasn't so kind afterwards when we had had our way with it.

The object of the game was to guess what challengers had done to get themselves a cup or a shield or a medal . . . a piano played a musical clue, invariably pounced on by Averil Angers. I can remember a blonde lady in a severe coat and skirt who had kept cacti on a farm in Cornwall and had also won the Yugoslavian V.C., and I can remember a lady in a cotton frock who had three years running caught the greasy pig at her local fête. There was also a man who had a 'conker' that had conquered thousands. But memory mercifully draws a veil over the rest of the programme.

It all took place every Tuesday for four weeks, in front of an audience. We wore full panchromatic make-up: bright yellow with white patches under the eyes and dead pink lips and I found it very, very exhausting to get tarted up after a heavy day's work interviewing, say, Gloria Swanson. (Mind you, I liked Gloria Swanson. She took me by the arm and said, 'Never mind me, dear, I'm just a mental vampire,' and I remember thinking how inaccurate and how I wished all stars were as honest.)

The T.V. Theatre was more fun to perform in than Lime Grove, partly because the audience was much larger and therefore made one relax more, and partly because there were some chaps who came and played the accordion outside the stage-door when we were being made up. They played tunes like 'California, Here I come' and 'Mobile', and I felt very sentimental about them. But the critics hated us and in the end the critics got their way. *Something to Shout About* was removed and made way for *Who Said That?*

Who Said That? was news right from the start, what

with the Unknown Chelsea Housewife, Joanna Kilmartin, being chosen for the panel without any sort of
audition at all, and the Return of Gilbert Harding to
Panel Games . . . Also, John Betjeman kept going away
for his holidays and Robert Henriques, who never let me
forget that he was a near neighbour of Evelyn Waugh,
took his place.

The 'dry' run was electric. Apart from the fact that
Joanna Kilmartin hardly got a word in edgeways as Alan
Melville, John Betjeman, Gilbert, and I all hogged the
mike and the camera as hard as we could, it was obvious
that this was Sound Radio of a very high order indeed.
Whether it is good T.V. I am still unable to judge. I
think perhaps it is.

For six weeks, anyway, I looked forward to Tuesday
nights with an odd mingling of apprehension and genuine pleasure. Pleasure was always uppermost by the time
I had drunk two glasses of my self-bought champagne.
One week Robert Henriques was a darling and took us
all out to dinner, but otherwise we all sadly starved to
death.

For one of the strangest things about this programme
was the fact that we were all expected to be as witty
as anything on empty stomachs. I am truly amazed by
this: for as a rule the BBC produce a dinner-party with
chicken Maryland and large bottles of wine for a T.V.
programme or a big Home Service feature. But not for
Who Said That? Oh, no. Whether we went on the air at
7.30, 8.30, 9.30 or 10 (always called one hour before for

make-up and rehearsal), all we had in our stomachs was a tiny sandwich.* Very odd. For wit waits upon good digestion and appetite, whereas only frayed nerves and bad humours can result from gin and Scotch whisky swilled and sluiced on an empty stomach.

I am sure, for example, that Gilbert Harding would never have attacked the Empire had he been full of New Zealand lamb or Australian beef.

Who Said That? seemed to give everyone innocent pleasure: I must say I adored every minute of it, even the people who came up to me afterwards in Lyons' Corner House and the Tudor Restaurant at Bentalls to tell me that I was a Faymous Fayce and that they felt they *knew* me and were friends of mine because I was on the Telly. The highlights of *Who Said That?* for me were Gilbert's attack on the Empire, and my proposal of marriage to Gilbert. After the panel had gone on quite a long time about how a wise woman would let her husband have her way I said that a wise woman wouldn't marry, anyway. This upset Gilbert, who started wagging his head like a sad old bear.

'My dear,' said Gilbert. 'I hope you don't mean that. A good marriage is a wonderful thing. I often wished that I had married . . .' and so on and so on, all in the same rather charming, maudlin vein.

---

* This, I may say, is not the fault of the excellent catering department of the BBC, but of the producer my dear friend Harry Carlisle who tells me I am the only person in the world who gets as hungry as that.

'You know quite well,' I said, 'that I'll marry you any time you like.'

'Ah . . .' said Gilbert. 'It's too late for that now.'

Forthwith the telephone began to ring. The *Daily Mirror*, the *Sketch*, the *Daily Mail*, six ladies from Eastbourne who had cherished an unwholesome passion for Gilbert for years, and thought I ought to be shot for my forwardness; one or two gentlemen who said that since Gilbert wouldn't have me *they* would: all these came on the line and upset the BBC duty officer. Oddly enough, the *People* and the *Daily Express*, to whom Gilbert and I were (respectively) under contract, didn't bother to ring. They knew better. They had been through it all before. Alan Melville summed it up very well when he said:

'Now, now you two . . . that's enough about *that* old affair.'

Who Said That? really taught me something. It taught me a proper humility and a deep, new respect for Show Business people. Once upon a time, for a week, I was Guest T.V. Critic of the *Evening Standard* and had been guilty of saying that Bernard Braden hit a new low in his chairmanship of *What's My Line?* When *Who Said That?* had been running for six weeks, I called up Bernard and Barbara Kelly, took them both out to lunch and apologized.

Also, I discovered that I wasn't such a rebel as I thought I was. Such opinions as I *do* hold are not as outrageous as I think them. However odd I might think I was being in saying, for example, how much I hate the country, there were always ten total strangers who would wring my hand in the street and say, 'God bless you for them words.' (And ten, for that matter, who would write to say I should be shot down like a mad dog.)

Who Said That? showed me up, to myself, once and for all as the same indiscreet, talkative, enthusiastic, apprehensive, Conservative, insular miss who left Roedean in 1935 labelled 'Speaks before she thinks'. Life, they have promised me, will begin at forty. So perhaps on my fortieth birthday there will be some damping down and I shall become, by some miracle, discreet, quiet, disillusioned, brave, Liberal, and cosmopolitan. But I doubt it. There will be nothing to show for it except some more white hairs and some more little brown gnarlings on my finger-joints.

One thing I may have learnt, but then I think I knew this when I was about four . . . it is best never to have a preconceived idea about anything. No sooner do I make some infantile sweeping statement than circumstances, or Fate, or whatever you choose to call it, neatly shuffles me so that I have to eat my words.

After a surfeit of literary parties, for example, I once said, 'Writers are selfish, lazy, and entirely wrapped up in their own sales figures.' And almost the next week I met Rebecca West, who is none of these things.

Lots of people have said she is the cleverest woman in the world. What most of them do not say anything about is her capacity for hard (and I mean *hard*) work, and her delighted interest in everything she sees.

I first met Rebecca at lunch at Mrs. Barbara Back's. Barbara had invited Beverley Nichols, too, and it was a rare pleasure to see these two nimble wits sharpen themselves upon one another, like two knives twinkling in a butcher's shop. Said Beverley, gibing at her, 'I have always thought of you, Rebecca, as the average English housewife.' Said Rebecca, 'In that case, Beverley, you shall always be my Housewife's Choice.'

And while they flashed and sparkled together I had plenty of opportunity to stare at Rebecca and wonder about her. She was *cosy,* for a start: and I had not imagined a cosy person writing such books as *A Train of Powder* and *The Meaning of Treason*. And she was small. And her eyes were like Black Velvet, that odd drink that is a mixture of champagne and Guinness. And her voice had an extraordinary quality, light, high, full, intensely feminine. And *young*. No one in their dreams could have guessed that she was sixty-two. Yet the other day Rebecca told me this, and said that she had had a strange dream that prophesied that she would die when she was sixty-three. 'It will be interesting,' she said, 'to see if that is right.'

Rebecca's life has been well worth living: it has spanned a half-century of changing manners, literary, social, and political. When Rebecca was a girl she decided she would have to take a *nom de guerre* because her mother might disapprove of the things she felt and said. Her real name was Cicily Isabel Fairfield ('A name that goes with golden curls, which *I* have not'), so when she wrote aggressive, anti-man letters and articles, Cicily Isabel signed herself 'Rebecca West', the name of an Ibsen heroine who died of love, plunging into a mill-race to do so. Once an early picture of Mary Pickford that went very well with the name Fairfield was sent by mistake as 'Rebecca West' to Canada. 'I didn't do a thing about it, but I took care not to visit Canada during this period,' says Rebecca. In the twenties Rebecca was very much the *enfant terrible* of criticism. 'All men dislike and despise women critics,' said Rebecca, looking at me sideways to see if I agreed. I did so, hastily. 'The Sitwells were always lovely to me,' she said, 'but Arnold Bennett hated me and so did all the Bloomsbury lot.'

When in 1927 Rebecca married Henry Maxwell Andrews and retired to her big, contented house in Ibstone in the fold of the hills around High Wycombe, we lost a critic of whom they said, 'She flays her victims with a happy laugh.' But we gained something else. A first-class reporter, of secure background and fanatical integrity. When Rebecca goes out to report some happening that has roused her anger or her interest, she doesn't rest until she has garnered the *whole* story. Quite often this takes her into considerable physical danger: for example, when she went to Greensville to report on the lynching of a black person by a gang of taxi-drivers, everyone told her that she was in danger of her life. This, I may say, hardly worried Rebecca at all. Rebecca remained, to tell the world exactly what the jury's verdict was, remarking plaintively: 'Of course, it was a bit of a bore not being able to take a taxi; as all the taxi-drivers were on trial, one had to walk everywhere.'

Watching Rebecca, the other day, strolling beside her gravelled drive where the border looks so like a rich Persian carpet, I reflected that had she been sent to Corsica she would somehow have contrived to interview the Sultan of Morocco *and* his concubines. Ah well. How fortunate I am to have met her, to have walked through her serene, untidy, lived-in house, enjoyed the possessions acquired by her restless, happy, perpetually enchanted mind: Aubusson carpets, worn and loved. Brilliant pictures bought just for the joy of them: a drawing that turned out to be a Rembrandt, a Bonnard that cost only £100.

The effect of Rebecca's personality is not cleverness, but richness. And it is richness used and shared, not shut away in banks or in glass cabinets. It is impossible to imagine Rebecca West pouncing from her house like a terrier to 'see off' an unwelcome journalist. Rather would she lure him into the library and hold him there, charmed, and send him forth after an hour or so infinitely better educated.

Henry Andrews is obviously responsible for much of this peace of mind. His enthusiasm and kindness and enormous happiness is an infectious thing. I have never been to Ibstone House to lunch without feeling better for it; even on the awful occasion when I was recording a conversation with Rebecca for the BBC, and the midget tape-recorder went wrong.

'I know how to mend these things,' said she. 'I shall treat it like my typewriter.'

And she picked it up and dropped it, three times, from the height of about a foot, into the lap of a large, comfortable arm-chair. Sure enough, it then worked perfectly. Yet, I have never heard tell that Rebecca, or Cicily or Isabel for that matter, are witch's names.

Chapter Twenty-Three

Obviously, I am not a millionaire because I have never saved. I have only invested, over and over again in selfishness, buying myself a holiday when I needed one, or a typewriter. Often I have avoided doing something I didn't want to do, in spite of the large sums involved. For example, there was one surprising day when an American newspaper syndicate rang up and offered an unheard-of sum (£47,000) for a series on Princess Margaret and Peter Townsend. Why, for that (I thought) I could pay some of my debts, buy a Daimler, rent a villa in the South of France . . . But then I stopped dreaming. There was the tax. After £3,000, I suppose, I would only be allowed 47,000 sixpences, which would only be £7,000 and only just enough for a Bentley.

And then there was the horror of climbing drainpipes in Brussels and spying on Peter Townsend. No, I thought, it just isn't worth it. 'Well, Miss Spain,' said the voice of the man in Chicago, 'will you do it?'

'No,' I said.

'Why not?' he said.

'Because I don't want to,' I said. Oddly enough as I turned down riches, I never felt better in my life.

However, when I feel low I sometimes point out to myself that £7,000 would have been a nice beginning to the £10,000 that Lord Beaverbrook says is the beginning of a million. But no matter how low I feel I am always sure that this isn't really true. Whenever I have tried to do anything For Money it has always led me astray.

Moreover, most of the months when the Chicago paper was expecting me to nip about gathering facts about Princess Margaret and Peter Townsend I was deeply concerned, I am proud to say, with Jonnie in the launching of *She* magazine. You may think it too early for me to assess future circulation of a magazine that only saw the light in March 1955. Yet, I love *She* dearly, and so do all the other people who have ever read a copy. I expect by the time this book comes out *She* will be selling a million copies a month.

Immediately, it seemed to me, we became preoccupied with millionaires, who are so dynamic. For part of *She*'s policy (and very exhilarating it turned out to be) was to present the Fabulous alongside the reasonable. To show, for example, a Fabulous number from Dior alongside a perfectly reasonably-priced one from Marks and Spencer. And along with this, of course, went fabulous facts about very rich people. How they lived. What they said. What they ate and drank. What they wore. And so on. For the very first number, Jonnie said, she wanted a piece by Lady Docker called 'How to Marry a Millionaire'.

This was afterwards modified to 'How I Manage My

Millionaire', but it was still basically the same article. Jonnie also acquired Gilbert Harding (by now a dear and well-loved chum) to criticize each issue as pungently as he pleased. And over a series of happy lunch- and dinner-parties she roped in Denise Robins to deal with adult heart-throb problems.

'Now,' Jonnie said to me, 'you go away and write some gossip.'

This gossip was somewhat confusedly known as News, for as I then had to write about things in October for December, there was every danger that weekly magazines or daily newspapers would beat me to it, or worse, as with poor Crawfie and Trooping the Colour, that something would happen to stop my news and it would never come to pass.

The year ground on: it was December. And there was only about a week to go to Press Day. And suddenly all the staff got flu. Everyone went to bed except Michael and Jonnie and I. We struggled on.

Each evening, on the stroke of five, the girl on the switchboard went home and I would arrive from the *Express*, or Broadcasting House, or Lime Grove. During one wonderful week I acted as temporary midnight office girl.

This was a surprising time. I have never worked all night and all day before. Yet no one became hysterical. No one even complained. Midnight would come and the radio (which we played to keep us working on) went off the air and we still went on. Sometimes I would rush out into Fleet Street into the snow (it snowed a lot that week and it was lying in deep drifts in Fleet Street) to fetch jugs of soup. As the morning came Fleet Street closed down, too. But we still worked on. Once I found myself curled on the office floor, fast asleep at 3.30 a.m. Jonnie sent me home. But then came the week when the magazine actually had to be passed for Press. And this was worse. For I wasn't allowed to help any more.

The battle-front removed itself to the Sun Printers, Watford, where Jonnie and Michael remained all of the last night, passing pages as they came up from the machines, working in a daze of temperature and flu aches and pains and Veganin and cups of tea.

All I could do was lie in bed and pray, quite unable to sleep. And the first issue of *She* came out. Now, whenever I read that first issue, I feel Jonnie's aching back, Michael's stomach ache, and my own red-hot eyeballs. Jonnie gave some of the people associated with the first issue of *She* a little china piggy bank with their name on. Never were three piggy banks called Michael and Jonnie and 'Tig' more hardly won.*

At the end of it all Michael quietly, and with great dignity, burst a gut. He was later taken away and operated on for hernia.

Jonnie remained serenely upright, only very occasionally losing her temper over her clothes. I don't

---

* 'Tig' is my nickname at home and is short for the only story of mine that Nicky likes: *The Tiger Who Couldn't Eat Meat*.

blame her. Editors have to be very, very elegant indeed, because they have to sit around and hob nob with Lady Docker while she is writing her piece, 'How I Manage My Millionaire'. And while it is not too bad working all night in jeans and a jersey, it really can be torture if one is dressed as a lady.

Most people know all about Lady Docker. She is a small, angelic-looking woman with honey-coloured hair and mauve eyes, who is loved most of all by those with whom she has had an argument.

Lady Docker is a very rich woman in her own right and thoroughly enjoys spending money. I once asked her how much she had. 'About a million?' I said. Lady Docker considered, with her head on one side. 'Well,' she said, in a funny little quiet voice, 'as a matter of fact, by the time they'd taken off the tax and the death duties and so on, all I had left was about £150,000.' We both looked at one another cautiously and then Lady Docker burst out laughing. 'Which is better than a slap in the face with a wet fish,' she said.

Lady Docker is a woman with a lot of sincere, warm charm. So whenever she invites me to dinner I am glad to accept and run the possible gauntlet as the midnight bell strikes and Norah, like Cinderella, starts to argue.

Once she took Jonnie and me to dinner at the Mirabelle and I had just found out that one could hire furs from Moss Bros. So I went along to Moss Bros, and got Jonnie a mink and me a sable at five guineas the piece. Mervyn Horder was with me, and he thought it was excessively comic. He read the pamphlets aloud and told me that 'Mayoresses were enthusiastic about the service.'

Duly minked up we presented ourselves at Claridge House and so heard Reed, Lady Docker's tactful maid, say, 'Your sables, Miss Nancy.' This is a remark that I should dearly love to have framed.

It was our acquaintance with the Dockers that made Jonnie think of the Millionaire of the Month feature for *She*. Quickly, she imposed rules upon me, as she sent me out to collect millionaires. They must be young, British (or Commonwealth), and they shouldn't do the same job two months running. For example, if I was fortunate enough to meet Leonard Lord in October, I shouldn't do Lord Nuffield in November.

'The only thing that is interesting about rich people is their money,' says Lady Astor. How wrong she is. *Everything* is interesting about millionaires; their motor-cars, houses, wives, children; and above all, their *business* ability. Moreover, they all seem to have a very great deal of charm.

I set out on this fascinating assignment with joy.

The first of the millionaires was Billy Butlin, to whom I was introduced by Godfrey Winn. Godfrey, incidentally, must be very nearly a millionaire himself by now.

Well, Godfrey invited Jonnie and me down to his country house in Falmer, Sussex. The Mill House stares serenely across two or three Sussex downs towards dear old Roedean and the Rottingdean cliffs. I love going to stay with Godfrey. It is always cosy, even in the depth of winter when six feet of snow lies in the dew ponds and no larks sing. Jonnie and I and Joan Gilbert and Joanna Kelley (the Governor of the Prison without Bars at Askham Grange, York) went down once for a Brains Trust with Godfrey in Lewes Town Hall. And Godfrey made me wear a skirt . . . my full pale blue satin evening dress with the pussycat bow, of which Noël Coward said, 'That baby blue satin wouldn't deceive a drunken child of two and a half.' So I nearly died of cold and Mr. Sponge, Godfrey's famous sealyham, tore off Joan Gilbert's dachshund's woolly undervest out of sheer passionate love at first sight. So Mitzi, the dachshund, nearly died of cold, too . . .

But when Godfrey invited us to meet fifty-six-year old, shortish Billy Butlin at his Ocean View Hotel, it was full summer. Bees hummed lazily by and in the great dining-hall (rather the same atmosphere as a very well-run NAAFI) clattered the knives and forks of satisfied Butlin customers. It was a Grand Gala Night at the Ocean View Hotel and the Association of Lady Water Rats (wives, mostly, of bill-topping music-hall artists) were out in force. Drink flowed like water. Billy Butlin moved through it all, inscrutable, gentle and inarticulate, monarch of the lot.

'But I wouldn't be a lord,' he said. 'I don't think the campers would like it.'

The Butlin way of life, with its *bonhomie* and neighbourliness, is well-known to one and all; so is Billy, with his beige and brown Rolls-Royce, his hushed offices above the efficient pandemonium of the halls in Oxford Street which, with recorded brass bands and violent moving pictures, exhort the passer-by to spend a Butlin Holiday and spend it Now. Billy is fascinating.

His office is furnished with relics of the Reichstag. Here stands Goering's inkwell, there Ribbentrop's desk. All the staircases are bright varnished blue and yellow. 'My favourite colours . . . meant to be sand and sea,' Billy explains. And he explains equally gently how he came to make his famous pile. He started off in the Canadian Army as a drummer-boy. Then he came back to England and set up as a fairground barker with a hoop-la stall.

'I made all my stands that the prizes stood on a bit too small,' he says. 'And so I gave away many more prizes. But I noticed that though I gave away more, I had bigger profits, too, because my turnover was bigger.'

He built his first holiday camp, as a result of a sad, wet weekend spent at the seaside years before. He had seen the people huddling under deck-chairs, because they were unable to go home to their landladies before supper-time. Indeed, he huddled himself. And he dreamed of a self-contained village of pleasure, with all its amusements under cover, with tennis courts and a swimming-pool and a mighty ball-room and a playground for children and lots and lots of amateur concert parties.

'Everybody has his party piece. And he just loves to get up and do it at one of my places,' says Billy, who has reduced the rough and tumble of the Family Holiday to a really manageable thing.

380

My next millionaire, strangely enough, was also under six feet: Cyril Lord, forty-two-year-old Lancashire textile genius. *He* walked up to me in Wheeler's one day, with his hand outstretched, saying that he had always wanted to meet me, and his wife, Bess, always bought the books I recommended and quite agreed with what I said about them.

Cyril and Bess are *dears*. Their weekend house, Wayside, at Donaghadee, stands on exactly the same strip of Northern Irish coastline as my Uncle Walter Smiles's. Uncle Walter's house, Portavoe, is still there, but Cousin Patsy lives in it now.

Cyril is miraculously fit. He plays tennis every morning at 6 a.m. in Hampstead, arrives at his office by nine, gets through more work than anyone I know: and is then ready to commute to Belfast and get through a weekend of hard, bouncing play. For Cyril really has a good time being a millionaire.

He owns a ChrisCraft that does thirty-eight knots (I don't know what that means exactly, but it seems awfully fast to me) and one of his passions is water ski-ing. He once set out for Scotland from Donaghadee and got there in 40 minutes. People come from near and far in coaches to Donaghadee to watch Cyril. I don't blame them.

In the weekend when we stayed with Bess and Cyril there was no one to drive the speed-boat. So Jonnie cheerfully said *she* would, and Cyril as cheerfully agreed that she might. I was amazed. So was Lord Glenavy, the other house-guest: an Irishman of seventy with all the wit and naughtiness of his son. His son is Paddy Campbell, a very funny fellow indeed.

Lord Glenavy and I worked out that there were five separate ways that Cyril could have been killed (or wounded) water ski-ing. He could have been cut to pieces by the propeller. He could have been strangled in his tow-rope. He could have broken his neck tumbling forward over his skis. He could have slashed a hole in his black frog suit, which could have filled with water and drowned him. Or he could have been strangled getting in and out of the frog suit.

This frog suit, which makes Cyril look like a handsome black Michelin man, bobbing along in the wake of the speedboat, is skin tight, made of highly elastic rubber. It is worn by Cyril to protect him from the terrifying cold of the water round Donaghadee. My Aunt Aileen Smiles, who has bathed in every major ocean in the world, including the Arctic, says that the Arctic has nothing on that bit of the Irish Sea. Frog suits were actually worn by intrepid frogmen during the war, those heroes who swam silently to clamp war-heads on battleships under water, I had always admired frogmen. But after seeing Cyril climbing in and out of his suit, helped by Bess and his handsome daughter Jacqueline, with little cries of, 'Quick now, Jacqueline, help your daddy before that bit of rubber gets across his mouth and strangles him,' I never realized quite what heroes they *are* . . .

Yes, Cyril and Bess are darlings and it is lovely to stay

with them. Their house, although one of the gayest bits of contemporary architecture and furnishing I have ever seen, is one of the most comfortable. Ages ago, Jonnie and I, greatly daring, bought some first quality apple green Wilton carpet to fit into the front hall at our new house in South Kensington. Cyril has the same fitted apple green carpet all *over* his house, right along the ground floor, the bedroom floor, even in the bottom of the *cupboards*. It is wonderful to stay in a house with the same fitted carpet all through. It gives such a sense of security.

It was, of course, this wonderfully cosy, luxurious weekend with Cyril and Bess Lord that made Jonnie look at me sideways and ask what I had done with all the money I had earned since I was seventeen.

I found it very much easier to explain about the money I hadn't made, the books that hadn't quite come up to expectations, the magazine that hadn't quite succeeded, the money from the American syndicate that I had turned down on account of my love for Princess Margaret.

'Nonsense,' said Jonnie. 'You are the most hopelessly disorganized person I know.'

It was all quite true. I had frittered away my money. But my goodness (I thought), I hadn't frittered away my life. I had had the most lovely time. I had been so busy having fun there had been no time to get organized.

And, alas, five feet six inches, forty-four-year-old motor dealer Raymond Way, the third of the millionaires who, like Cyril Lord, has become a chum, agreed with Jonnie. He was particularly annoyed about the way I wasted money on hiring motor-cars.

'Why, you silly—' said Ray. His language reminds me irresistibly of the twelve happy months I spent as a naval lorrydriver in North Shields. 'You could *own* that car by now.'

And since Ray was only six years older than me and was obviously doing all right at the time (he was wearing a very nice small-checked suit, real baby crocodile skin shoes, and an enormous pale green Cadillac whose roof wound up and down at the press of a button), I was inclined to listen to him. Ray, like Billy Butlin, started life as a fairground barker and has wonderful stories, jewelled in every hole, to tell about freaks and boxing booths and the strange behaviour of the idiotic, adorable, eternally gullible public. The first time I had lunch with Ray he had a little brain-storm because in the midst of a super-duper red-hot summer thunderstorm, when he had nothing to protect himself with but a big umbrella, I sold him Jonnie's aged, well-mannered M.G. Magnette. The second time we lunched we *were* going to the Colony, but Jonnie decided she wanted to see how fast the Cadillac could be driven. So we went out to London Airport instead and came back by helicopter. Next time he says he will take us by Viscount to see a bullfight in Spain.

The helicopter impressed me most. Lots of people had told me about them, and their vertical take-off. How they were going to revolutionize the traffic problem, revolutionize journalism, revolutionize generally. But nobody ever told me how beautiful the world looked seen from a helicopter.

When we rose gently into the air at London Airport, and the Great West Road to Bath became a small path, with tiny toy cars chasing along it, and the Thames became a smooth, blue trout stream and then a beautifully painted river on an animated map. And when I saw the mighty towers of Westminster Abbey and the box within box of Buckingham Palace; and the green and tufty parks lay spread all below us, idle as a bedspread, then, oh then, how I wished I had a helicopter of my own.

'If this is being a millionaire,' I shouted to Ray and Jonnie, above the noise of the engine, 'I think in the future I shall try harder.'

And so I shall. I shall really try to get myself organized. But whatever the next forty years turn out to be, I am sure of one thing. They couldn't possibly be more fun than the forty years that have gone before: whether I manage to become a millionaire or not.

Help us make the next generation of readers

We – both author and publisher – hope you enjoyed this book. We believe that you can become a reader at any time in your life, but we'd love your help to give the next generation a head start.

Did you know that 9 per cent of children don't have a book of their own in their home, rising to 13 per cent in disadvantaged families*? We'd like to try to change that by asking you to consider the role you could play in helping to build readers of the future.

We'd love you to think of sharing, borrowing, reading, buying or talking about a book with a child in your life and spreading the love of reading. We want to make sure the next generation continue to have access to books, wherever they come from.

And if you would like to consider donating to charities that help fund literacy projects, find out more at **www.literacytrust.org.uk** and **www.booktrust.org.uk**.

THANK YOU

*As reported by the National Literacy Trust